Jürgen Brauer

Human Pose Estimation with Implicit Shape Models

Schriftenreihe Automatische Sichtprüfung und Bildverarbeitung
Band 6

Herausgeber: Prof. Dr.-Ing. Jürgen Beyerer

Lehrstuhl für Interaktive Echtzeitsysteme
am Karlsruher Institut für Technologie

Fraunhofer-Institut für Optronik, Systemtechnik
und Bildauswertung IOSB

Human Pose Estimation with Implicit Shape Models

by
Jürgen Brauer

Dissertation, Karlsruher Institut für Technologie (KIT)
Fakultät für Informatik
Tag der mündlichen Prüfung: 10. Februar 2014

Impressum

 Scientific
Publishing

Karlsruher Institut für Technologie (KIT)
KIT Scientific Publishing
Straße am Forum 2
D-76131 Karlsruhe

KIT Scientific Publishing is a registered trademark of Karlsruhe
Institute of Technology. Reprint using the book cover is not allowed.

www.ksp.kit.edu

Print on Demand 2014

ISSN 1866-5934
ISBN 978-3-7315-0184-8
DOI: 10.5445/KSP/1000039083

Human Pose Estimation with Implicit Shape Models

zur Erlangung des akademischen Grades eines

Doktors der Ingenieurwissenschaften

von der Fakultät für Informatik
des Karlsruher Instituts für Technologie (KIT)

genehmigte
Dissertation

von

Jürgen Brauer (geb. Müller)

aus Trier

Tag der mündlichen Prüfung: 10.02.2014
Erster Gutachter: Prof. Dr.-Ing. Rainer Stiefelhagen
Zweiter Gutachter: Prof. Dr.-Ing. habil. Jürgen Beyerer

Abstract

Automatic scene understanding is a problem which is only partly solved. Two important subproblems in this context are the detection of persons and the analysis of their behavior. Many behavior and action understanding systems use sequences of estimated human poses as input. For this, human pose estimation is an important building block for automatic scene understanding. This thesis addresses the problem of estimating 3D human poses from monocular images.

The Implicit Shape Model (ISM) – a generic object model – has shown to be useful for detecting persons with the help of local features. Each local feature casts a vote for the object location and locations of high vote density are considered as detected instances of the object category. The main contribution of this thesis is to show how anatomical landmarks can be localized on persons using appropriate extensions of the ISM and how the resulting vote distributions generated by the landmark ISMs can be used for a subsequent 3D pose estimation.

The first step of the proposed approach is the localization of anatomical landmarks. Local image features, as, e.g., SURF features, are used to vote for possible locations of 15 different landmarks on a person. Since the original ISM voting strategy often generates unfocussed vote distributions for the task of landmark localization with many votes far away from the true landmark locations, we develop new voting strategies, that cast more of the overall vote mass near to the true landmark locations. The individual strategies can be combined into a new overall ISM voting strategy for the task of landmark localization which produces even more correct votes than the individual strategies.

The second step of the method presented here is to estimate a 3D pose based on the generated vote distributions for each of the landmarks. For this, we describe a new top-down method where the key idea is to project 3D pose hypotheses directly onto the vote distributions, i.e., compare pose hypotheses and the image evidence not in the image space but in the voting space, which allows for a fast evaluation of pose candidates. The pose estimation can then be formulated as an optimization process where we try to find a good pose and projection pair, such that the average vote density near to the projected landmarks is maximal. For the optimization we use the method of Particle Swarm Optimization (PSO) since it can deal with high-dimensional search spaces such as the search space here that results from the pose and projection parameters. Using pre-computed vote density maps and exploiting the integral image trick the objective function used within the optimization process can be evaluated quickly and allows to test several millions of 3D pose hypotheses per second on a standard desktop PC. For compensating errors in the landmark localization step we propose to restrict the pose search space by using pose priors. Two different pose prior representations are explored here: example poses and pose splines which can both be learned from motion capture databases. While both representations result in similar 3D landmark localization errors, pose splines have the advantage that the number of evaluations till the PSO based optimization procedure converges can be reduced significantly.

We also present an alternative approach to estimate a 3D pose based on a 2D pose estimate, which can be retrieved from the vote distributions, e.g., by taking the global maximum for each landmark. The method works bottom-up and exploits the idea of geometric reconstruction which makes use of 2D limb foreshortening information. While the geometric reconstruction was originally introduced only for a very restricted camera model – the scaled orthographic projection – we describe a new recursive algorithm that allows to reconstruct 3D poses even with a perspective camera model. We further show how to extend the original method which was only semi-automatic to a fully-automatic 3D pose estimator. Input parameters needed by the reconstruction algorithm as the person to camera distance and the focal length and are often hard to provide are estimated automatically by the method based on the average probability of reconstructed pose candidates for different parameter choices. While the geometric reconstruction method presented here needs to be extended in further work to deal with errors in the landmark localization process, it has the advantage that in principle any 3D pose can be reconstructed without the need to provide example poses.

The methods proposed in this thesis are evaluated on three benchmark datasets (UMPM, HumanEva, TUM kitchen) with a high level of difficulty regarding the designed experiments compared to related work. The quantitative and qualitative results show that anatomical landmark localization within the ISM object model is possible if the new voting strategies are used and that the 3D landmark localization errors are comparable with

state-of-the-art results for similar experiment settings. With this we introduce a new framework for monocular 3D human pose estimation on basis
of the Implicit Shape Model.

Zusammenfassung

Automatisches Szenenverstehen ist ein bisher nur teilweise gelöstes Problem. Zwei wichtige Teilprobleme hierbei sind die Erkennung von Personen und ihres Verhaltens. Da viele Verfahren zur Erkennung von Verhalten bzw. Aktionen von Personen auf Posenfolgen aufbauen, ist die Schätzung der Posen von Personen ein wichtiger Baustein für die automatische Analyse von Bildern. Diese Arbeit beschäftigt sich mit der Schätzung der 3D Posen von Personen aus monokularen Bildern.

Zur Detektion von Personen hat sich gezeigt, dass mit Hilfe des Implicit Shape Models (ISM) - ein generisches Objektmodell – Personen auf Basis von lokalen Bildmerkmalen im Bild erkannt werden können. Dazu gibt jedes detektierte Bildmerkmal für die mögliche Position eines Objektes eine Stimme (im ISM Kontext "Vote" genannt) ab und Orte hoher Vote-Dichte werden als detektierte Instanzen der Objektkategorie betrachtet. Der Hauptbeitrag dieser Arbeit liegt darin, zu zeigen, wie mittels geeigneter Erweiterungen des ISM Objekterkennungsmodells auch anatomische Landmarken auf Personen lokalisiert werden können und wie man die resultierenden Vote-Verteilungen, die durch die ISMs erzeugt werden, für eine anschließende 3D Posenschätzung nutzen kann.

Der erste Schritt der hier vorgestellten Methode besteht in der Lokalisierung von anatomischen Landmarken. Lokale Bildmerkmale, wie z.B. SURF Merkmale, stimmen hierbei für mögliche Orte von 15 verschiedenen Landmarken auf der Person ab. Da die ursprüngliche Vote-Generierungsstrategie des ISMs oft unfokussierte Vote-Verteilungen für die Landmarkenlokalisierung generiert, bei der viele der abgegebenen Votes weit weg von der eigentlichen Landmarke sind, werden hier neue Vote-Generierungsstrategien entwickelt, die einen deutlich größeren Teil der Votes nahe den eigentlichen Landmarkenpositionen platzieren. Die Einzelstrategien können hierbei in einer Gesamtstrategie für die Aufgabe der Landmarkenlokalisierung kombiniert werden, die eine noch größere Anzahl an korrekten Votes generieren kann als die jeweiligen Einzelstrategien.

Im zweiten Schritt des hier vorgeschlagenen Ansatzes wird eine 3D Pose auf Basis der generierten Landmarken-Voteverteilungen geschätzt. Hierzu wird ein neues top-down Schätzverfahren beschrieben, bei dem die Kernidee darin besteht, 3D Posenhypothesen direkt auf die Voteverteilungen zu projizieren, d.h. die Posenhypothesen werden mit der Bildevidenz nicht im Bildbereich, sondern im Votingraum verglichen, wodurch eine sehr schnelle Evaluierung der Posenkandidaten ermöglicht wird. Die Posenschätzung kann dann als ein Optimierungsprozess formuliert werden, bei dem versucht wird, eine möglichst gute Posenhypothese und Projektionsparameter zu finden, so dass die durchschnittliche Vote-Dichte nahe den projizierten Landmarken maximal ist. Für die Realisierung der Optimierung wird die Partikel-Schwarm-Optimierung (PSO) verwendet, da dieses Verfahren auch mit hochdimensionalen Optimierungsproblemen sehr gut umgehen kann. Durch die Verwendung von vorberechneten Votedichtekarten und der Ausnutzung des Integralbildtricks kann die Zielfunktion bei der Optimierung sehr schnell ausgewertet werden und erlaubt es damit mehrere Millionen von 3D Posenhypothesen pro Sekunde auf einem Standard Desktop PC zu testen. Um Fehler in der Landmarkenlokalisierung auszugleichen, wird vorgeschlagen, den Posensuchraum stark durch Posenvorwissen einzuschränken. Zwei verschiedene Repräsentationen von Posenvorwissen werden in dieser Arbeit untersucht, nämlich Beispielposen und Posensplines, die beide auf Basis von Motion-Capture-Datenbanken erlernt werden können. Während beide Repräsentationen ähnliche 3D Landmarkenlokalisierungsfehler liefern, besitzen Posensplines den Vorteil, dass die Anzahl der notwendigen Evaluierungen bis die PSO basierte Optimierung konvergiert, stark reduziert werden kann.

Desweiteren wird ein zum zweiten Schritt alternativer Ansatz vorgestellt, um eine 3D Pose auf Basis einer 2D Pose zu schätzen, die beispielsweise aus den Voteverteilungen durch Detektion des globalen Maximums in jeder Landmarkenvoteverteilung generiert werden kann. Die Methode arbeitet im Gegensatz zum vorher vorgestellten Verfahren bottom-up und nutzt die Idee der geometrischen Rekonstruktion, die sich der 2D Verkürzungsinformation von Körperteilen im Bild bedient. Die Idee der geometrischen Rekonstruktion für die 3D Posenschätzung wurde ursprünglich für ein stark vereinfachtes Kameramodell vorgeschlagen: die skalierte orthographische Projektion. Ein neues rekursives Verfahren wird hergeleitet, dass diese Basisidee für die 3D Posenschätzung aufgreift, dabei aber auch den Fall eines komplexeren, nämlich dem perspektivischen Kameraprojektionsmodell, berücksichtigt und es damit erlaubt, 3D Posen auch für Bilder zu rekonstruieren, die starke perspektivische Projektionsartefakte aufweisen. Wir zeigen weiter auf wie der ursprüngliche halbautomatische Ansatz zu einem vollautomatischen 3D Posenschätzungsansatz erweitert werden kann. Von dem Verfahren benötigte Eingabeparameter, wie die Schätzung der Distanz zwischen Person und Kamera als auch der Brennweite der verwendeten Kamera, werden hierbei automatisch auf Basis der durchschnittlichen Wahrscheinlichkeit der rekonstruierten Posenkandidaten für verschiedene Parameterwerte mitgeschätzt. Während die geometrische Rekonstruktionsmethode in der Zukunft noch erweitert werden muss, um mit Fehlern bei der Landmarkenlokalisierung besser umgehen zu können, besitzt sie den Vorteil, dass im Prinzip jede 3D Pose rekonstruiert werden kann, ohne dass Vorwissen über Beispielposen benötigt wird.

Die vorgeschlagenen Verfahren werden auf drei Benchmarkdatensätzen zur Posenschätzung evaluiert (UMPM, HumanEva, TUM kitchen), wobei die durchgeführten Experimente einen hohen Schwierigkeitsgrad im Vergleich zu verwandten Arbeiten besitzen. Die quantitativen und qualitativen Ergebnisse zeigen, dass die Landmarkenlokalisierung mittels der erweiterten Vote-Generierungsstrategien im Rahmen des ISM Objektmodells möglich ist und die auf den erzeugten Vote-Verteilungen aufbauende 3D Posenschätzung Posen mit Landmarkenlokalisierungsfehlern generiert, die vergleichbar mit Verfahren sind, die einen ähnlich hohen Schwierigkeitsgrad bezüglich der Experimente vorweisen. Damit wird in dieser Arbeit erstmals ein neuer Ansatz vorgestellt, der es erlaubt, im Rahmen des ISM Objekterkennungsmodells die 3D Pose von Personen auf Basis von monokularen Bildern zu schätzen.

Acknowledgments

This thesis is the result of my work in the department of object recognition at Fraunhofer Institute of Optronics, System Technologies and Image Exploitation IOSB over the last four years on monocular human pose estimation. Many other people have contributed to this work in different ways.

Without any doubt there are three persons to be mentioned first which accompanied this work over many years. These are my supervisors Dr. Wolfgang Hübner and Dr. Michael Arens at Fraunhofer IOSB and Prof. Dr. Rainer Stiefelhagen at the KIT. They spent many hours of their time for helpful discussions about technical details, decisions that had to be made in which direction to continue, or for giving me feedback.

I also would like to thank all the professors of the KIT which agreed to join the committee. At first I want to thank Prof. Dr. Jürgen Beyerer for his interest in my work, his time he spent for discussing the thesis with me, and for being in the committee as a second reviewer. Further I would like to thank Prof. Dr. Johann Marius Zöllner, Prof. Dr. Björn Hein, and Prof. Dr. Tanja Schultz for their interest in the topic and inviting me to discuss the thesis with them as part of the "Professoren-Runde" at the KIT. Thanks also to Prof. Dr. Hartmut Prautzsch and Prof. Dr. Björn Hein for agreeing to join the committee as well.

Many of my direct colleagues helped me to proof-read the thesis. For this, I am grateful to David Münch, Ann-Kristin Grosselfinger, and Hilke Kieritz. For a lot of fruitful technical discussions I want to thank my former colleague Dr. Kai Jüngling and my current colleagues Stefan Becker and Dr. Christoph Bodensteiner. Thanks also to all the other doctoral students I got to know during the PhD seminar of the group of Prof. Stiefelhagen in Bad Herrenalb and which gave me feedback concerning my work, especially Alexander Schick. With Dr. Wenjuan Gong from Computer Vision Center Barcelona I worked for several months during her stay as a doctoral visiting student at Fraunhofer IOSB which allowed to learn a lot from each other concerning different approaches to human pose estimation. Thank you as well to my students Alexander Dobler and

Sebastian Krah which I supervised during my doctoral studies and which decided to do their diploma and student thesis on human pose estimation related topics.

At the end of such acknowledgments it is common to say thank you also to the most important person of private life. I am pleased to continue this tradition. My wife Constance contributed to this thesis in many ways as well. She left Erlangen for me to move with me to Forst in order to make my doctoral studies possible and took care of our little son Julius such that I could concentrate on this thesis.

Ettlingen, November 2013 / March 2014

Nomenclature

Symbol	Meaning
$\mathbf{d}$	descriptor vector $\mathbf{d} \in \mathbb{R}^N$
$\mathbf{o}$	single observation vector $\mathbf{o} = (\Delta x, \Delta y, s, h_1, w_x, w_y, \eta)$ associated with a word and landmark, where the word was observed at scale s and location $(\Delta x, \Delta y)$ relative to the landmark, while the person height was h_1 and the reference point was at relative location (w_x, w_y). η represents a learned weight that encodes how reliable this observation vector can be used to predict the location of the landmark
$\mathbf{f}_i$	single local feature $\mathbf{f}_i = (f_x, f_y, f_s, \mathbf{d}, w)$, located at image location (f_x, f_y), scale f_s, while corresponding descriptor vector $\mathbf{d}$ matches best to word id w
$\mathbf{v}_3$	3D vote space location $\mathbf{v}_3 = (v_x, v_y, v_s)$
$\mathbf{v}_2$	2D image location of a vote $\mathbf{v}_2 = (v_x, v_y)$
$\mathbf{v}$	vote for a POI. $\mathbf{v} = (v_r, v_x, v_y, v_s)$ is a vote for the POI to be at image location (v_x, v_y), at scale v_s, and with vote strength v_r
$\mathbf{m}_i$	3D coordinate of landmark i: $\mathbf{m}_i = (x, y, z)$
$\mathbf{m}'_i$	projected 2D coordinate of landmark i: $\mathbf{m}'_i = (u, v)$
$\mathbf{q}$	a 3D pose represented by 3D landmark coordinates or joint angles
$\mathbf{q}'$	a 2D pose $\mathbf{q}' = \{\mathbf{m}'_i = (u_i, v_i) : 1 \leq i \leq J\}$ represented by J 2D landmark coordinates

$\mathcal{I}$ an ISM $\mathcal{I} = (\mathcal{C}, \mathcal{P})$ for an object class consists of a codebook $\mathcal{C}$ and a set of probability distributions $\mathcal{P} = (P_1, ..., P_{|\mathcal{C}|})$ that specify where and at which scale each word appears on the object

$\mathcal{C}$ a codebook $\mathcal{C} = \{\mathbf{d}_1, ..., \mathbf{d}_N\}$ is a set of word descriptor vectors $\mathbf{d} \in \mathbb{R}^N$

w word id, i.e., $1 \le w \le |\mathcal{C}|$

$\mathcal{P}$ a set of 3D probability distributions $\mathcal{P} = (P_1, ..., P_{|\mathcal{C}|})$ where each $P_i(x, y, s)$ represents the probability to find a word at some location (x, y) relative to a POI (e.g., anatomical landmark) and feature scale s

$\mathcal{O}_{wl}$ set $\mathcal{O}_{wl} = \{\mathbf{o}_k = (\Delta x, \Delta y, s, h_1, w_x, w_y, \eta) : 1 \le k \le R\}$ of observation vectors for word w and landmark l

$\mathcal{F}$ set $\mathcal{F} = \{\mathbf{f}_k = (f_x, f_y, f_s, \mathbf{d}, w) : 1 \le k \le K\}$ of local features computed for an image

$\mathcal{V}_l$ set of all votes $\mathcal{V}_l = \{\mathbf{v}^k = (v_r^k, v_x^k, v_y^k, v_s^k) : 1 \le k \le L\}$ for a POI l

Contents

1. Introduction

1.1. Why monocular 3D human pose estimation?

Why poses?

Automatic scene understanding is a challenging computer vision task that is mostly unsolved. Among the different object classes, persons are often of special interest in scene understanding systems, as, e.g., video surveillance systems. While person detection and tracking methods nowadays cross the border between research and application and are applied in an increasing number of products (e.g., car driver assistance systems), the scene understanding is limited often to a 2D or 3D bounding box view of the persons, i.e., the systems can only yield 2D or 3D locations and dimensions of the detected persons.

Fig. 1.1 (a) shows two different scenes from the SDHA (Semantic Description of Human Activities) dataset[1]. Fig. 1.1 (b) shows the bounding box for each person. This very limited view of the scenes does not contain enough information to discriminate between the boxing and handshaking scene. For a more detailed analysis of the scenes an automatic reconstruction of the 2D or even 3D poses – as shown in Fig. 1.1 (c) – of each detected person would be very helpful, because poses can reflect the differences in the interaction between the two persons in the two scenes much better than bounding boxes only.

Fig. 1.2 shows the image processing chain and processing modules that build the context for the work presented in this thesis. The first module detects

---

[1] http://cvrc.ece.utexas.edu/SDHA2010/Human_Interaction.html

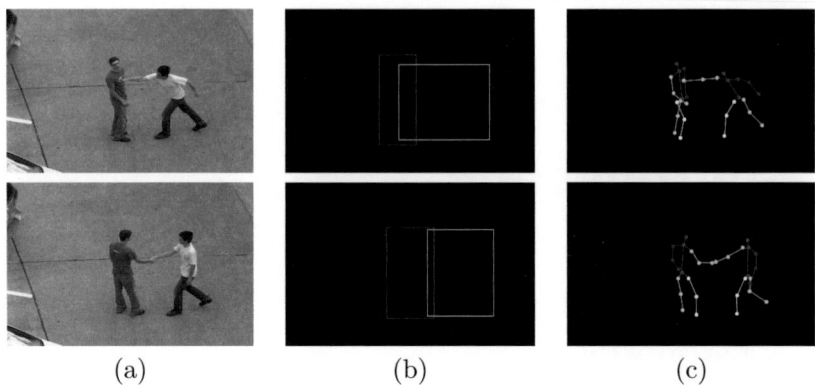

(a)   (b)   (c)

Figure 1.1.: Different levels of scene understanding. (a) Two example scenes (boxing and handshaking) (b) Person bounding box view of both scenes (c) 3D / 2D pose view of both scenes

and tracks persons. For each person hypothesis anatomical landmark (e.g., head, right shoulder, left knee) locations are estimated, which serve as input for another module that estimates 2D and 3D poses based on these landmark locations. Sequences of estimated 3D poses can then be used to recognize atomic actions for each person hypothesis (as e.g., *bending down, waving hands*). Finally, the set of person hypotheses together with the information about the poses and actions performed by each person can be used to recognize more complex situations such as person interactions, as e.g., *two persons meet and shake hands* or *one person hits another person*. This thesis presents solutions for the two highlighted modules, i.e., landmark localization and 2D / 3D pose estimation.

The image processing chain depicted here is only one possibility to analyze scenes automatically. Another possibility is to learn a mapping from image features retrieved from each person hypothesis to action labels. At a first glance it may look like a detour to localize landmarks and estimate 3D poses to recognize actions (*poses-to-action mapping*) instead of directly mapping image features belonging to persons to action labels (*features-to-action mapping*), but first estimating poses to be used as input for an action recognition step has a number of advantages.

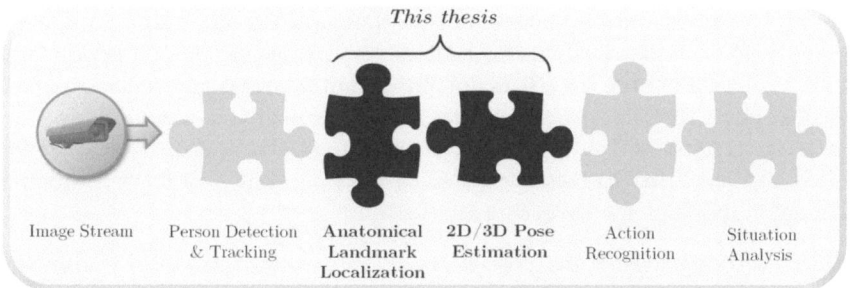

Figure 1.2.: Image processing chain for automatic scene understanding.
This thesis deals with two important processing steps for automatic scene
understanding which are anatomical landmark localization and 2D/3D pose
estimation.

First, poses – as described by a set of joint angles – are invariant to
viewpoint and person display size. For a features-to-action mapping
approach, the image features (e.g., local features, optical flow, etc.) will be
different if a person is recorded from a different viewpoint or at a different
distance. This means that the action recognition module does not only
have to be able to recognize actions but it also has to realize a difficult
invariance performance. Of course, this invariance performance does not
come for free for a poses-to-action mapping approach. The difference
is that this invariance performance is shifted partly to earlier modules
– namely the landmark localization and the pose estimation module –
such that multiple modules can realize this invariance performance in a
divide-and-conquer-manner jointly.

Second, new actions to be recognized can be added to the image processing
chain by manual specification. For a features-to-action mapping approach
adding new actions to the image processing chain means that we have to
re-learn or augment the mapping from the image features to the action
labels, which means that new example pairs (image features, action labels)
have to be provided. In contrast, for a poses-to-action mapping approach
new actions can be easily added to an action recognizer module by defining
directly a sequence of poses as a new action. E.g., for recognizing a new
action as *sitting down* we can directly specify how to recognize such an
action based on the change in the joint angles of the legs. Further, this

allows to provide more general action descriptions since we can specify that the joint angles in the arms are not important for such an action. For a sitting down action, e.g., it is not important whether the arms are lifted or not. For a features-to-action mapping approach this would mean that we have to provide training images of a sitting person where the arms are lifted and not lifted to generalize during learning that arm related features are not important for detecting this action.

Third, working within the pose description domain instead of within the feature domain allows to define easily inter-person situations without the need to record such situation examples for training. E.g., for recognizing a situation as *two persons shake hands* we can specify that two persons have to stand near to each other and stretch their right arms into the direction of each other. The poses-to-action mapping approach allows to define even more complex scenarios, where more than two persons are involved, by defining an expected sequence of poses for each person involved (e.g., two persons carrying a patient lying on a gurney).

Why monocular?

The task of recognizing human poses can be simplified if appropriate sensors are used.

HPE using a depth camera. One possibility to ease the task of human pose estimation[2] is to use a sensor that provides depth information. In this context, Microsoft launched the "Kinect" sensor in November 2010, which provides not only a RGB camera, but also an infrared laser projector and a monochrome CMOS sensor which is used to estimate a depth value for each pixel of the RGB image (RGB-D sensor). Together with the Kinect SDK, developers can retrieve reconstructed 3D poses with 50 frames per seconds on a modern 8 core desktop CPU (see [Shotton et al., 2011]). In Fig. 1.3 an example of a Kinect reconstructed 3D pose is shown. Unfortunately, the operation range of Kinect is limited to a range of 0.8m-4m, i.e., only for persons in this range 3D poses can be reconstructed. Further, the Kinect sensor cannot be used for outdoor applications, since depth estimation is based on the principle of structured light (infrared speckle pattern) and

---

[2]Abbreviated as "HPE" in the following.

direct exposure to infrared radiation from the sun perturbs the emitted pattern of structured light. This limits the application scenarios for Kinect to well controlled indoor scenarios, as e.g., Human-Computer-Interaction scenarios (HCI), where the person stands directly in front of the sensor.

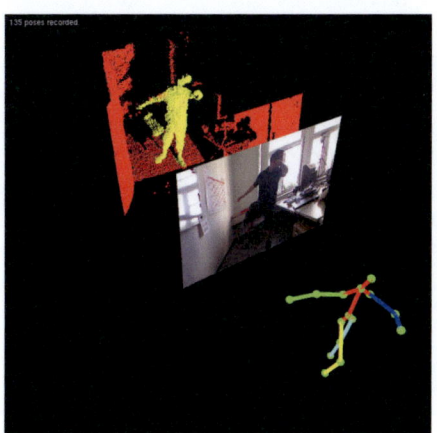

Figure 1.3.: Example of a 3D pose recorded with Kinect. Left: The red and yellow tiles are a visualization of the depth information provided for the frame shown. Yellow tiles correspond to pixels detected as being part of a person. Right: Kinect sensor with tripod.

HPE using multiple view images. Another possibility is to use multiple cameras that allow to monitor a scene and record a person from different view points. This allows to compute a voxel-model of the person. For this, first for each image the silhouette of the person is retrieved using a background vs. figure segmentation. For each silhouette a back-projection cone is computed, where the intersection of all these back-projection cones is the so called *visual hull*, which corresponds to a voxel-model of the person. Some authors do not only use multiple camera images, but other sensor modalities as well, e.g., inertia sensors. E.g., [Pons-Moll et al., 2011], restrict the pose search space by using additional orientation cues provided by inertia sensors (IMU).

HPE using single view images. Nevertheless, most of our video data sources nowadays are monocular (e.g., TV, movies, YouTube) and do not contain an additional depth information channel. Even for surveillance scenarios where multiple cameras are used, some areas might be visible only by one camera. E.g., for a parking lot surveillance system many places can be occluded by trees, allowing for being monitored by one camera only. Therefore, it is highly desirable to reconstruct 3D poses from monocular images as well. This could lead to a rich set of new applications by allowing to perform semantic searches in monocular video databases (e.g., searching for handshaking scenes). Also a more detailed analysis of person-object interactions would be possible if the 3D pose can be reconstructed in videos. For a parking lot surveillance system that describes persons at the level of bounding boxes it is hard to discriminate whether a person is just standing beside a car or taking an object out of the car. If additional 3D pose information is provided such a discrimination can be facilitated.

Why is it difficult?

There are a several reasons why monocular human pose estimation from images is difficult.

Figure 1.4.: Ambiguity due to missing depth information. Missing depth information can lead to left/right confusions. Considering only one monocular image, it is hard to decide which foot is nearer to the camera – even with slightly different appearances of the shoes due to different viewpoints. When considering all four images, it is slightly easier but still difficult to decide which is the right and which is the left foot.

Missing depth information. First, probably the main reason is the missing depth information. Humans are 3D objects and projecting the human body to 2D means that information is lost which can result in left / right ambiguities. In Fig. 1.4 we present as an example four successive frames of a sequence showing the legs of a person walking to the left. Even for humans it is not easy to decide which foot is nearer to the camera and therefore to decide which is the left foot. This example shows that left / right ambiguities can result directly as a consequence of the missing depth information. Humans can compensate for this missing depth information by using sequence information, i.e., watching multiple video frames, or by exploiting scene context information.

Occlusions. Second, occlusions make the task even more difficult. When only one camera is used, parts of the human body can be occluded by other persons and objects or by other body parts of the person itself. This means that information about the location of other body parts is missing and has to be inferred from the visible parts.

Pose and appearance variance. Third, the number of possible poses that humans can show is huge. Further, the same pose shown by two different persons can have a very different appearance due to different clothing, different person sizes, viewpoints from which the persons are recorded, lighting conditions, etc.

For these reasons, estimating human poses from monocular images is a highly under-determined problem. One aspect of the approach presented here is therefore to "fill up" the very limited information that is provided by monocular video sequences by using additional information about typical human poses. This additional information can be retrieved from large motion capture databases and can be added to the estimation process in the form of pose priors.

An important question is how precise the final 3D pose estimates have to be. This question cannot be answered in general. Instead the application background has to be considered. For a HCI scenario where a person wants to control an avatar in a video game, discriminating between fine graded differences concerning the poses might be important. E.g., estimating the wrist joint state exactly during a golf swing can be very important in an virtual golfing game. In contrast, for discriminating between standing and lying on a floor poses in a security application, rough 3D pose estimates can be sufficient.

1.2. Approach and contributions

The goal of this thesis is to estimate a 3D pose for each person hypothesis detected in an image. Formally, we want to find a mapping

$$f : (\mathbf{I}, \mathbf{h}_1, ..., \mathbf{h}_N) \mapsto (\mathbf{q}_1, ..., \mathbf{q}_N) \qquad (1.1)$$

where $\mathbf{I}$ is a gray-scale input image[3], $\mathbf{h}_i$ $(i = 1, ..., N)$ are detected persons in the image – represented by bounding box information or a set of local image features associated with each hypothesis – and $\mathbf{q}_i$ are the corresponding 3D pose description vectors for each person hypothesis.

The main idea of this work is to formulate the pose estimation process within the Implicit Shape Model[4] approach. An ISM represents the appearance of an object by storing the information for a given codebook at which locations and scales words appear on the object. One of the key contributions of this thesis is to show that the ISM can not only be used to detect a person but to estimate its pose as well.

In Fig. 1.5 we show a schematic overview of the approach presented in this thesis.

We assume that in a preceding step all persons in the input image have been detected. For each person hypothesis (green bounding box) a set of local feature (yellow circles) is computed or provided by the person detector. For each landmark a pre-trained ISM is used to cast votes (red circles) for its 2D location in the image. For this step several voting strategies are developed and presented in Chapter 6.

Although the new voting strategies place more of the votes near to the true landmark locations compared to the original vote generation method, often an unique final location estimate for a single landmark cannot be determined, i.e., the landmark vote distributions show several peaks. To deal with these location ambiguities and in order to compensate for wrongly estimated landmark locations we use knowledge about real 3D

---

[3]We do not use color information and do not exploit temporal information in the work here, i.e., the presented approaches can estimate 3D poses for single gray-scale images as well.

[4]Abbreviated as "ISM" in the following.

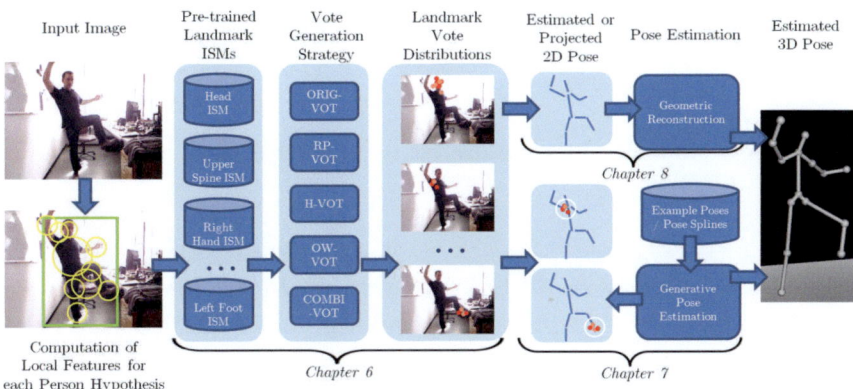

Figure 1.5.: Approach overview. Local features (yellow circles) cast votes (red dots) for landmark locations using one pre-trained ISM for each landmark. The pose estimation problem is then formulated as a geometric reconstruction based on a resulting 2D pose estimate, or by an optimization process that tries to find the 3D pose hypothesis such that the corresponding projected pose hypothesis matches best to the vote distributions.

poses by projecting example 3D poses directly onto the landmark vote distributions. This allows to score the different pose candidates according to the average vote density near to the projected landmark locations. The pose estimation process is then formulated as an optimization process over poses and projection parameters that maximizes the vote density near to the projected pose hypotheses. This generative pose estimation approach (top-down method) is presented in Chapter 7.

An alternative approach for 3D pose estimation on basis of generated vote distribution is presented in Chapter 8. Starting from a 2D pose estimate the bottom-up method described there uses a geometric reconstruction approach to compute possible corresponding 3D pose candidates in a first step, that can be filtered for the most probable one in a second step.

There are five main contributions made by this thesis:

Contribution #1:
Anatomical landmark localization using Implicit Shape Models

In Fig. 1.6 two example frames of the HumanEva dataset[5] are shown together with a visualization of SIFT features tracked by an ISM based person tracker and the ground truth locations of 15 anatomical landmarks.

A key question at the beginning of this work was whether the features that were assigned to each person hypothesis carry enough information in order to be used to estimate the locations of anatomical landmarks, and whether the landmark locations could be estimated within the same ISM framework as for the detection of the person center (person hypothesis). In [Müller and Arens, 2010] we showed that the features from the person detection step can indeed be "recycled" to vote for the landmark locations as well and that a rough 2D pose estimate is possible by using one ISM for each landmark we are interested to localize.

This result suggests that we can detect persons and landmark locations within the same framework: local features (e.g., SIFT or SURF) are first computed for the whole image, vote for person centers in a first step, and all features that are assigned to a person hypothesis vote in a second step for the landmark locations. This has several advantages:

- Figure-Ground-Segmentation. The person tracker already provides a separation between background image structures and image structures belonging to persons. By using only local features that supported a person hypothesis we avoid the need to perform an additional figure-ground segmentation in the pose estimation step. Many other approaches that do not couple the person detection and pose estimation process such closely need to deal with the problem of figure-ground segmentation explicitly, e.g., by assuming a static camera and applying background subtraction techniques (e.g., [Li et al., 2009]) or by learning to suppress background features by learning

---

[5]http://vision.cs.brown.edu/humaneva/

to discriminate between background and human-like features (e.g., [Agarwal and Triggs, 2006a]).

- Computational cost reduction. By using the same features for landmark localization that have already been computed for detecting persons, we avoid to recompute local features again that would only be used for the landmark localization step.

- Reuse of ISM framework. ISM implementation code used for detecting persons can be used for landmark localization as well since both steps are formulated as voting procedures within the same object detection framework.

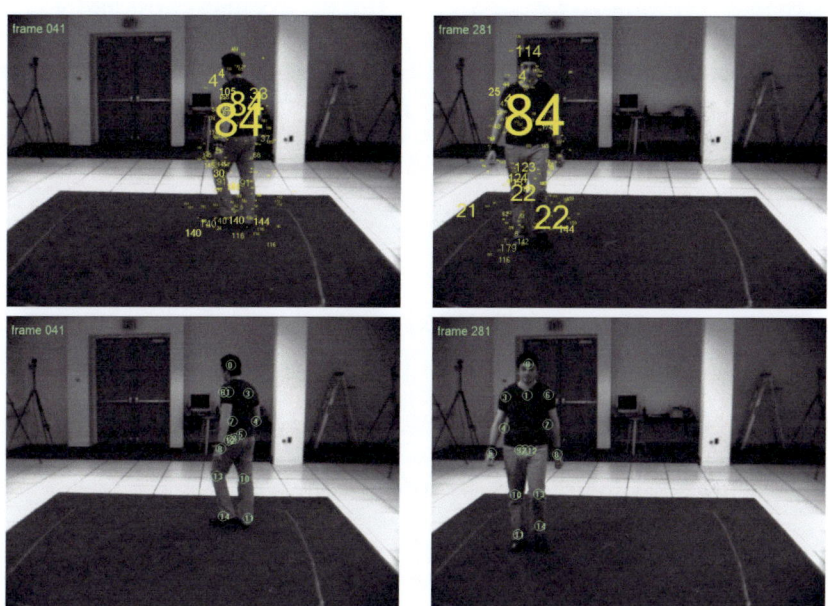

Figure 1.6.: Features tracked by an ISM based person tracker. Top row: two example frames of the HumanEva dataset. Each yellow number corresponds to a SIFT feature associated with the person hypothesis. The number corresponds to the ID of the best matching word found in the codebook used. The text size is chosen proportional to the scale of the feature. Bottom row: corresponding ground truth locations of 15 anatomical landmarks.

Contribution #2:
New voting strategies for the ISM

Unfortunately, the vote distributions resulting from the original ISM voting mechanism [Leibe et al., 2008b] are not much focused when trying to localize anatomical landmarks. For this, we explored alternative voting strategies. One of these strategies (RP-VOT) exploits the fact that the person detection step yields a reference point that can be used in the voting procedure: only words that occur at similar locations (observed during training) relative to this reference point are used. Another new voting strategy (H-VOT) can be used as a vote filter mechanism as well by restricting the words to cast votes only if they probably carry information about the landmark location. A third new voting strategy (OW-ISM) uses a second pass training step for the ISM model learning in which an individual vote weight is learned for each observation vector. These new voting strategies have recently been published in [Brauer et al., 2013a] and yield significantly much more focused vote distributions for the landmark localization task.

Contribution #3:
Fast generative 3D pose estimation approach using vote distributions

Given the output of the landmark localization process – one vote distribution for each landmark – we introduce a top-down method that is able to estimate 3D poses based on these vote distributions.

In the hypotheses search step of the original ISM approach locations of high vote densities are detected and considered as object hypotheses (e.g., detected persons). Since there are several (here: 15) landmarks and for each landmark an own vote distribution results with several location candidates to be considered, we have to reformulate this hypotheses search such that we find a 3D pose that maximizes the overall vote density in contrast to the single vote density maximization task in the person detection step. A key idea of this thesis is to project 3D hypotheses onto the vote distributions to compare projected landmark locations and vote distributions directly. For a single landmark a matching score can be defined by a Kernel weighted sum of the distances of the votes to the projected landmark location. For the overall 3D pose hypothesis a matching score can then be defined by the average of these matching scores and the whole 3D pose estimation process can be formulated as a search where the matching score is maximized. An important advantage of this approach is that a single 3D pose hypothesis can rapidly be evaluated, since projected landmark locations and votes can quickly be compared. This allows to test millions of 3D pose candidates per second. Nevertheless, due to the high dimensionality of the 3D pose search space, we cannot evaluate all possible 3D poses. For this, it is proposed to use a Particle Swarm Optimizer (PSO), which is a meta-heuristic optimization approach that has shown to work even for very high-dimensional search problems. Some of these ideas have been published in [Brauer et al., 2012] and [Brauer et al., 2013b].

Contribution #4:
Pose splines for compressing motion sequences

Example 3D poses are one possibility to restrict the search space to a limited set of pose candidates. Since they are very restrictive, an alternative is explored as well, which we call "pose splines". Motion capture databases typically contain hundreds or thousands of motion sequences. We compress each of these motion sequences, which typically consist of some thousands 3D poses, to a very limited number of 3D pose supporting points by detecting automatically which 3D poses can be discarded within the motion sequence since they can be linearly interpolated by two successive supporting poses in the motion sequence. By this procedure, we can compress a large motion capture database – as the CMU motion capture database with 2.7 million 3D poses – to approximately 3-4% of its original amount of 3D poses and formulate the 3D pose hypothesis search as a Particle Swarm Optimization on such pose splines. Compared to the limited, discrete set of example 3D poses this has the advantage that we allow for a whole continuum of 3D pose candidates during the search process. The comparison of the example based and the pose spline based pose prior knowledge representation shows that both representations yield similar 3D landmark localization errors while the PSO based optimization on pose splines needs significantly fewer pose candidate evaluations to converge to the final 3D pose estimate. The idea of pose splines has recently been published in [Brauer et al., 2013b].

Contribution #5:
Unique geometric reconstruction of 3D poses for perspective camera models

While the top-down method presented here relies on example poses, we also present a 3D pose estimation method that does not need any knowledge about example poses. A simple working principle is used to geometrically reconstruct possible 3D poses from a 2D pose estimate: the more a limb appears foreshortened in the 2D image, the larger is its displacement in the depth dimension. The idea to exploit this foreshortening information for 3D pose reconstruction was proposed in [Taylor, 2000] with several severe restrictions. First, a very limited camera model was used (weak perspective projection). Second, the reconstruction was not unique, i.e., instead of a single 3D pose estimate hundreds or even thousands of 3D poses candidates could result. Third, some of the input parameters for the geometric reconstruction had to be provided manually. In this thesis we show how to adopt the idea of geometric reconstruction of 3D poses to a more realistic camera model, namely the standard perspective camera model. In addition, a mechanism is proposed to filter for a single unique 3D pose estimate, resulting in a fully-automatic 3D pose estimator, compared to the semi-automatic 3D pose estimation approach presented originally. Important parameters needed for the geometric reconstruction method – namely the focal length and a camera to person distance estimate – are estimated automatically by computing the average probability of reconstructed poses for different parameter choices. These ideas and corresponding evaluation experiments have been published in [Brauer and Arens, 2011].

1.3. Thesis outline

Chapter 2 provides a short survey on HPE approaches. Previous surveys often divide approaches into bottom-up vs. top-down, which results in a very coarse discrimination of HPE methods. Here we present a finer graded discrimination based on the central ideas of the methods.

Chapter 3 presents a list of publicly available HPE evaluation datasets and state-of-the-art results reported in literature for different datasets and levels of difficulty regarding the conducted experiments.

Chapter 4 introduces the body model we use to represent a human pose.

Chapter 5 describes the original ISM as proposed in [Leibe et al., 2008b]. While the reader who is familiar with the ISM can skip this chapter, we introduce many notations around the voting scheme here used in later chapters.

The main contributions of this thesis can be found in **Chapter 6** (anatomical landmark localization), **Chapter 7** (top-down method to estimate 3D poses) and **Chapter 8** (bottom-up method to estimate 3D poses).

Chapter 6 presents the idea to use one ISM to localize each anatomical landmark. Several new voting strategies are introduced that can be used to generate much more focused vote distributions for the task of anatomical landmark localization compared to the original voting strategy of the ISM.

Chapter 7 shows how to use the landmark vote distributions to estimate 3D poses using a top-down approach: 3D pose hypotheses are projected to the 2D image plane and are compared directly with the vote distributions. In order to avoid to search the whole 3D pose space and to compensate for errors during the landmark localization process, we use example 3D poses extracted from motion capture databases. The 3D pose estimation task is formulated as an optimization process which can be solved with Particle Swarm Optimization (PSO). Further, pose splines are introduced as an alternative to the hard example based pose prior: they are a compact representation of motion sequences by a sparse set of supporting point poses.

Chapter 8 presents an alternative approach to estimate 3D poses that does not need to have knowledge about example poses. Starting from a 2D pose estimate a simple working principle can be used to geometrically reconstruct a 3D pose. While this idea was originally proposed for the very limited weak perspective camera model and was only semi-automatic, we show how to adopt this idea to a fully-automatic method with a more realistic camera model – the perspective camera model – and how to estimate important parameters needed as input for the reconstruction algorithm automatically.

Chapter 9 presents the conclusions and a list of promising ideas to continue and improve the work presented in this thesis.

2. Related work

In **Section 2.1** a compact survey on approaches used for HPE is provided, while **Section 2.2** highlights the differences of the approach presented in this thesis to previous methods.

2.1. Approaches

Surveys. There is a large amount of literature on HPE. In the last years, different authors have provided surveys which provide a good overview on HPE related publications: [Ji and Liu, 2010], [Hen and Paramesran, 2009], [Sminchisescu, 2007], [Poppe, 2007], [Moeslund et al., 2006], [Moeslund and Granum, 2001]. A common used classification for HPE approaches used in these surveys is bottom-up vs. top-down. While bottom-up approaches directly try to map the image representation to a 3D pose, top-down approaches use a 3D body model and compare hypothesized configurations of this body model with the image evidence. Since this is a very coarse classification of HPE approaches into two classes only, here we present a finer discrimination of the approaches based on the central idea proposed to cope with the problem of the very limited monocular information.

Action recognition. HPE is strongly connected to action recognition, since one of its main application is building a basis for action recognition by first trying to estimate 3D poses and then to predict action labels based on sequences of these 3D pose estimates [Ramirez, 2013]. But there are also approaches that directly try to predict an action label from input images. [Wang et al., 2009] e.g., extract different local spatio-temporal features (e.g., HOG3D, ESURF) from the video, represent the video with a Bag-of-Words (BoW) and use a SVM classifier to discriminate 25 different actions. [Kuehne et al., 2012] compute a sparse optical flow and represent each video frame by a global motion histogram. Low-level actions are modeled and recognized by HMMs, which can be combined according to a context-free grammar to recognize complex actions.

Different number of camera images used. Works on HPE differ depending on how many input cameras are used and how they are arranged relatively to each other. While some works use stereo-cameras mounted in the head of a humanoid robot with a small baseline, e.g., [Azad, 2008], other works use three cameras that allow to record a person from the front and both sides, e.g., [Hofmann and Gavrila, 2012], or even use four cameras, e.g., [Yao et al., 2012], that provide even more helpful input information to deal with pose ambiguities.

In contrast, this thesis is about monocular HPE and in particular not about action recognition or multiple view HPE. For this, we only focus on publications related to monocular (2D and 3D) HPE in the following.

2.1.1. Low-dimensional manifolds

The 3D human body configuration is typically described by a high-dimensional pose vector resulting in a high-dimensional search space for the correct 3D pose.

In [Agarwal and Triggs, 2006a] a 24 dimensional pose vector is used. [Wei and Chai, 2009] use 37 dimensions. 55 dimensions and 47 dimensions are used in [Sigal and Black, 2006a] depending on the experiment, while [Urtasun et al., 2005] even use 84 dimensional and 72 dimensional pose vectors for their experiments.

[Sidenbladh et al., 2002]

Figure 2.1.: Examples of estimated poses from a publication exploiting low-dimensional manifolds. Pose estimation results for a walking sequence.

The high dimensionality of the search space makes it difficult to explore the whole pose space. Fortunately, the number of poses that have to be considered can be limited significantly. First, only some locations in the pose space correspond to possible poses since joint constraints of the human body do not allow for all configurations. Second, while humans can move their joints in principle independently from each other, in practice, joint configurations are highly correlated. During a walking phase, e.g., the joint angles in the arm and leg joints change according to some typical pattern. Third, when considering certain application scenarios for a human pose estimator, we can exclude a large number of poses which we are not interested in. E.g., for estimating poses of soccer players within a soccer game we can ignore Yoga poses.

Since joint angles are highly correlated, in practice poses lie in a low dimensional subspace of the high dimensional pose space. It is therefore a natural idea to try to exploit this lower intrinsic dimensionality of the pose subspace.

Both, linear PCA [Sidenbladh et al., 2002] and non-linear Kernel PCA [Tangkuampien and Suter, 2006] have been used to reduce the dimension of pose vectors. Gaussian Process Latent Variable Models (GPLVM) have been used by several authors [Andriluka et al., 2010], [Gupta et al., 2008], [Ek et al., 2007] for dimensionality reduction of the pose space.

GPLVMs were introduced by Lawrence [Lawrence and Hyvärinen, 2005] and used, e.g., in [Urtasun et al., 2005] for constraining the pose estimation process. The mapping from the low dimensional latent space to the high dimensional pose space is modeled by a Gaussian Process[1] for each pose space dimension. The key idea of GPLVMs is to learn the low dimensional representation of the pose vectors in the latent space *and* the mapping from latent to pose space simultaneously by minimizing an objective function. A natural extension of the GPLVM is to model the chronological order of poses, i.e., motion priors, as well. Gaussian Process Dynamic Models (GPDM) were introduced by Wang et al. [Wang et al., 2005]. GPDMs

---

[1]Gaussian Processes provide a method for specifying a probability distribution over functions by specifying a mean and a covariance function for the function values $f(x)$. By training a Gaussian Process with sample data $\{x, f(x)\}$ the variance of the Gaussian Process becomes small for function values $f(x)$ near to supporting points x, which corresponds to an increased certainty about the function values at these points.

optimize the latent pose space representation and the mapping from latent
to pose space as GPLVMs do but additionally model the dynamics of
the poses within the latent space using a Gaussian Process by adding an
additional term to the GPLVM objective function for the latent space
dynamics.

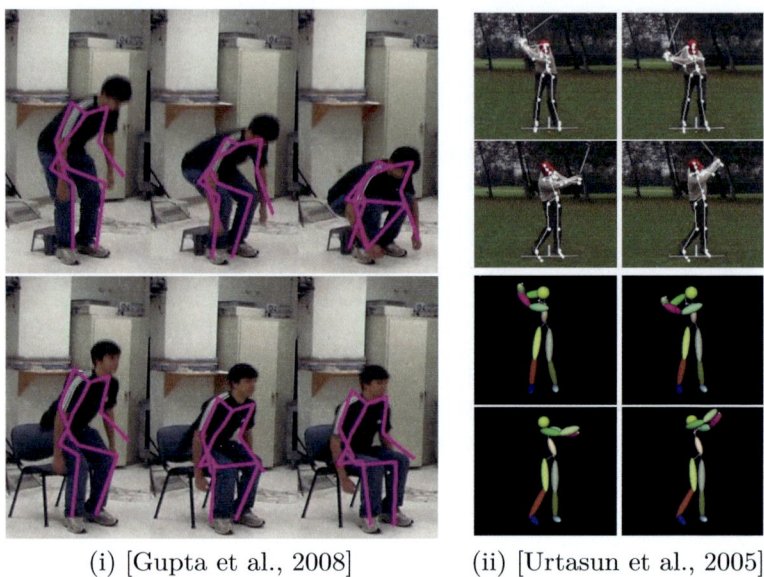

(i) [Gupta et al., 2008]   (ii) [Urtasun et al., 2005]

**Figure 2.2.: Examples of estimated poses from publications exploiting
low-dimensional manifolds**. Pose estimation results for a sitting down on a
step stool/chair (i) and a golf swing sequence (ii).

A major drawback of GPLVM is its time complexity of $O(N^3)$ during
learning where N is the number of sample poses which stems from the
inversion of a $N \times N$ kernel matrix. Some approaches have been proposed
that choose a proper subset of the original training data for the Gaussian
Process training (see [Quinonero-Candela et al., 2005] for an overview) to
tackle this problem.

Another drawback of the GPLVM approach is that the dimension d of the
latent space has to be chosen by the user. Typically d is set to 2 or 3 such
that it is possible to visualize the corresponding motions in latent space.

But this ignores the intrinsic dimensionality of the pose subspace which can be significantly higher (e.g., $d = 7$) and further ignores that different motions can have different intrinsic dimensions in their corresponding pose subspaces. The GPLVM approach is mostly used to learn a latent space model of only a single isolated motion (e.g., golfing, or a walking cycle as in [Urtasun et al., 2005]). This may be traced back to the reason that the method seems not to scale well to larger motion sets. [Shin and Lee, 2006] argue that this is probably true for dimension reduction methods that ignore the intrinsic dimension of large motion data sets which is higher than that of the target 2D space. This seems plausible since considering more than one motion and dealing especially with different motions where different joints are active for each motion means that there is a high variance in the data in different dimensions of the high-dimensional pose vectors which cannot be captured by using only two latent dimensions.

In computer graphics literature dimension reduction techniques have been introduced as well. Here the problem arises to edit motions of human avatars. Since it is not feasible for a user to specify each joint angle of a high dimensional pose vector explicitly when editing a motion, low dimensional pose spaces learned by PCA ([Safonova et al., 2004], [Mordatch et al., 2006]) and by GPLVM ([Levine et al., 2012]) have been used to control and edit the movement of avatars.

2.1.2. Context information

In computer vision, context information is often used to facilitate the pattern recognition task. E.g., scene information as ground planes is often used to ease the task of pedestrian detection [Sudowe and Leibe, 2011].

Object context. [Yao and Fei-Fei, 2010a] exploit the fact that objects and human poses can serve as mutual context to each other. They learn the spatial relationship between the object and the body parts. Their experiments on sport images show that the detection of an object (e.g., tennis racket, ball) can facilitate the estimation of the human pose, and vice versa: recognizing the pose (e.g., tennis volley) can ease the detection of an object (tennis ball). In a similar work, [Singh et al., 2010] augment their tree-structured human body model by an additional object node and

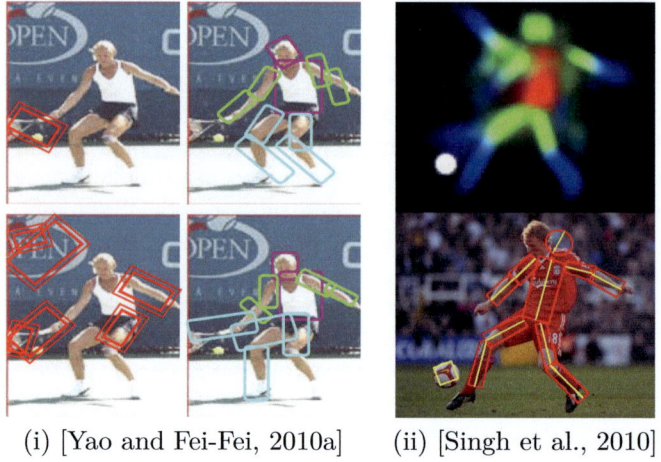

(i) [Yao and Fei-Fei, 2010a]   (ii) [Singh et al., 2010]

Figure 2.3.: Examples of estimated poses from publications exploiting context information. Exploitation of object context using (i) the location of the tennis racket and (ii) the location of the soccer ball.

estimate the pose in an image using a Bayesian framework by maximizing the likelihood for both the pose and object model parameters.

Human context. [Andriluka and Sigal, 2012] address the task of estimating poses for multiple persons jointly and use the pose of one person as context information for the estimation of the pose of the other person. Estimating the poses $\mathbf{q}_1, \mathbf{q}_2$ for two persons given the image evidence I is formulated as searching the maximum-a-posteriori (MAP) estimate: $P(\mathbf{q}_1, \mathbf{q}_2|\mathbf{I}) \propto P(\mathbf{I}|\mathbf{q}_1, \mathbf{q}_2)P(\mathbf{q}_1, \mathbf{q}_2)$. Here the 3D pose prior $P(\mathbf{q}_1, \mathbf{q}_2)$ reflects the correlations between the two poses of two subjects and depends on the action class (e.g., dancing vs. boxing). The approach was evaluated on sequences of cha-cha dancing couples, where the dancing pose of one person provides the context for the pose estimation of the other person.

Action context. Traditionally, 3D pose estimates are considered as input for action recognition. In [Yu et al., 2013] this order is reversed. The authors first use an off-the-shelf implementation of a deformable part model (DPM, [Yang and Ramanan, 2011]) to estimate a set of 2D pose hypotheses for each frame of a sequence based on 10 successive input frames. These

[Andriluka and Sigal, 2012]

Figure 2.4.: Examples of estimated poses from a publication exploiting context information. Here information about the pose of the dancing partner is exploited.

2D pose hypotheses are then used as input for an action detection forest, which is a decision forest with votes at the leaves for actions which are associated with 3D pose estimates. So, 2D pose hypotheses are used to recognize an action and each action is associated with possible 3D poses. These rough 3D pose estimates are then refined using a regression forest that outputs the 3D landmark locations as probability distributions in 3D space.

2.1.3. Regression approaches

Regression approaches for 3D HPE typically encode the image information within a person bounding box by some fixed-length descriptor and try to map this descriptor vector directly to a 3D pose vector using some regression method. Typically, the regression function is trained using a large set of example pairs of image descriptors and 3D pose vectors.

[Sedai et al., 2009] compute a set of 172-dimensional local shape context descriptors, project each descriptor vector to a 50-dimensional descriptor using PCA, and classify these lower dimensional descriptors according to a codebook of size 200. The global descriptor is a Bag-of-Words, i.e., histogram of these detected words which is mapped to a 31-dimensional pose vector using Relevance Vector Machine (RVM) regression.

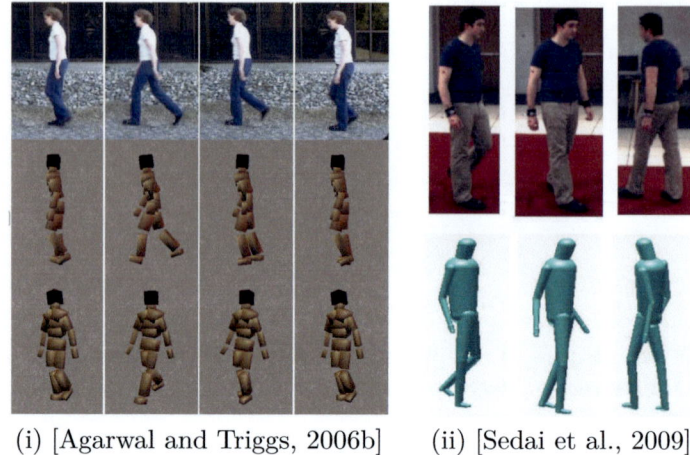

(i) [Agarwal and Triggs, 2006b]   (ii) [Sedai et al., 2009]

Figure 2.5.: Examples of estimated poses from publications using regression methods. Both publication examples use Relevance Vector Machine (RVM) regression.

Similar to this approach, [Agarwal and Triggs, 2006b] extract the silhouette from a person image, compute shape context descriptors, which are mapped to a codebook of size 100, and compute a Bag-of-Words. Three different regression approaches are evaluated in this work to map the Bag-of-Word image evidence representation to a 55-dimensional pose vector: ridge regression, Relevance Vector Machine (RVM) regression, and Support Vector Machine (SVM) regression over both linear and kernel bases. Their evaluation shows that RVM gives the best results in the pose tracking scenario with an average joint angle error of 4.1°.

The approach presented in [Bissacco et al., 2007] exploits both appearance and motion, by describing both through the help of rotated and scaled Haar-like features. These features are mapped to 26 dimensional pose vectors using a new variant of boosting regression.

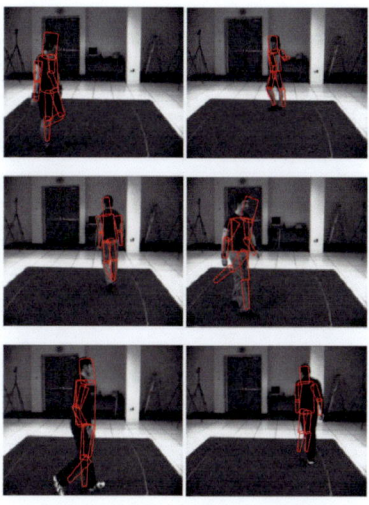

[Bissacco et al., 2007]

Figure 2.6.: Examples of estimated poses from a publication using regression methods. Boosting regression is used in this publication to estimate 3D poses.

2.1.4. Pictorial structures

Pictorial structures are based on the idea to represent an object by a set of parts arranged in a deformable configuration. The original idea was introduced in [Fischler and Elschlager, 1973].

The pictorial structures object model was first applied to HPE in [Felzenszwalb and Huttenlocher, 2005]. Given some image evidence D the posterior probability of the part configuration L is modeled by $p(L|D) \propto p(D|L)p(L)$. Here $p(L)$, i.e., the prior of a part configuration, can be learned using example poses. The main issue is to define a good likelihood function $p(D|L)$, i.e., the likelihood of the image evidence given a particular configuration.

While the work in [Felzenszwalb and Huttenlocher, 2005] used a simple appearance model requiring background subtraction, in [Andriluka et al.,

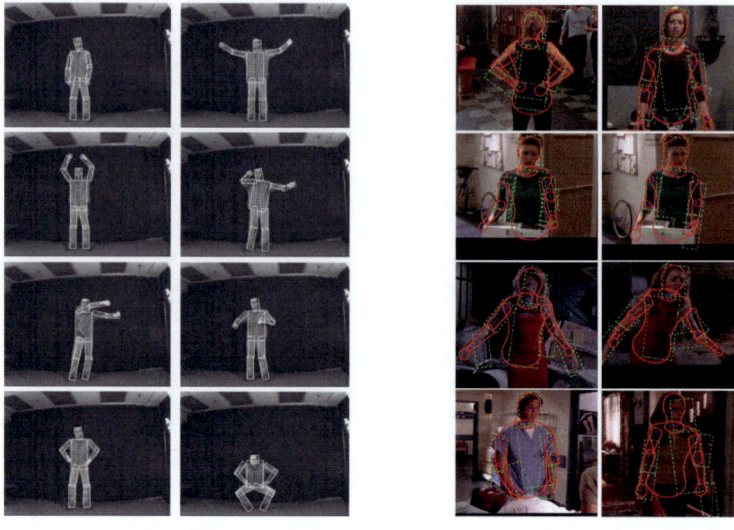

(i) [Felzenszwalb and Huttenlocher, 2005]   (ii) [Zuffi et al., 2012]

Figure 2.7.: Examples of estimated poses from publications using pictorial structures. (i) Pictorial structures (PS) model (ii) Deformable structures (DS) model

2009] the appearance of body parts was modeled using densely sampled shape context descriptors together with an AdaBoost discriminative part classifier, while the prior for part configurations is modeled using Gaussians.

Recently, [Zuffi et al., 2012] tried to replace the rigid part templates – typically used in the pictorial structures model – by deformable parts. The new proposed deformable structures (DS) model represents each part by a deformable contour and learns a low-dimensional linear subspace of the shapes of the contour using PCA. Further, the model allows to depend the shape of a part from its neighboring part and the relative angles between them and models this dependence using linear Gaussian models.

2.1.5. Superpart detection

The pictorial structures model method first detects possible locations of body parts and then resolves for ambiguities in the body part detection step by finding a good constellation of these parts. Since body parts are hard to detect only based on their appearance, this second step is crucial for the pictorial structures model. E.g., the image structure that corresponds to a lower arm can resemble many other image structures appearing in an image on objects. For this, it is a straightforward idea to try to detect larger image structures on the human body than just single body parts. Here we propose to call these parts "superparts".

(i) [Bourdev and Malik, 2009]

(ii) [Yao and Fei-Fei, 2010b]

Figure 2.8.: Examples of approaches using superparts. (i) Poselets, (ii) Grouplets

[Bourdev and Malik, 2009] do not define these superparts explicitly but propose an approach where these superparts – called "poselets" – are learned automatically. Poselets are image patches that correspond to a similar 2D or 3D body configuration. The actual detection step of such poselets is performed by a sliding-window SVM classifier.

[Yao and Fei-Fei, 2010b] introduced "grouplets" for classification of human-object interactions which can be used for pose estimation as well. Grouplets are discriminative sets of features that co-occur in a certain spatial configuration. A key contribution of their work is to propose an algorithm that automatically learns good grouplets for a pose class by finding grouplets that have a high computed grouplet score on images of this pose class and a low score on images of other pose classes.

2.1.6. Geometric reconstruction

Assuming we already have a 2D pose estimate from a previous 2D pose estimation step, it is an interesting question how we can use knowledge about the 3D to 2D projection process to try to invert this process and reconstruct a 3D pose geometrically.

[Taylor, 2000] showed that we can use a simple working principle to map a 2D pose to 3D which is to compare the actual 3D world limb lengths with the foreshortened projected 2D limb lengths in the image plane in order to reconstruct the missing depth information that does not come with a 2D pose. Unfortunately, there are two drawbacks of Taylor's work. First, the method assumes that the 2D pose is the result of a scaled orthographic projection of a 3D pose, which is an unrealistic assumption for real world cameras because in such a simple camera model the length of projected limbs do not depend on their distance to the camera. Second, the approach results only in a semi-automatic 3D pose reconstruction algorithm since the solution for the depth reconstruction provided is not unique. A user has to manually provide the information for each 2D limb which endpoint of the limb is closer to the camera and thereby implicitly selects one of the many mathematically possible 3D reconstruction solutions. Publications that build upon Taylor's work and try to tackle these two drawbacks are described in the following.

Non-uniqueness of reconstructed solutions. [Mori and Malik, 2006] store a number of example images with their corresponding 2D poses and the information for each limb of the 2D pose which limb endpoint

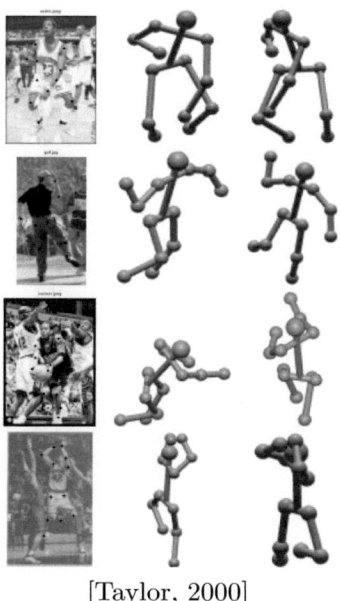

[Taylor, 2000]

**Figure 2.9.: Example of estimated poses from a publication using a
geometric reconstruction method.** Depicted 3D pose estimates are for
ground truth 2D poses where 2D landmarks were manually labeled.

is closer to the camera in a database. An unknown input image is then
compared with each stored image in the database using shape context
descriptor matching. For a found match, this allows not only to transfer
the corresponding body part labeling, but also to transfer the information
which limb is closer to the camera to the unknown input image.

[Jiang, 2010] compares each of the reconstructed pose candidate with
millions of 3D poses from the CMU motion capture database. In order to
allow for a fast comparison of each candidate pose with this huge set of
reference poses, poses are split up into upper and lower body poses and are
compared separately using an approximate nearest neighbor method. The
disadvantage of such an approach is that the method can only recognize
poses of actions already stored in the example database.

[Wei and Chai, 2009] do not only address the problem of non-uniqueness but also try to estimate the unknown scale parameter in the scaled or-thographic projection camera model automatically. Additionally to the bone projection constraints derived in Taylor's original work, the authors establish further constraints based on limb length symmetries and fixed lengths on some rigid subparts of the human body. The 3D pose estimation problem is then formulated as a continuous optimization problem guided by these constraints. Nevertheless, the authors could not guarantee that these additional constraints are sufficient to resolve the ambiguity in all cases. Then the pose reconstruction stops and the user has to resolve the ambiguity manually before the reconstruction can continue.

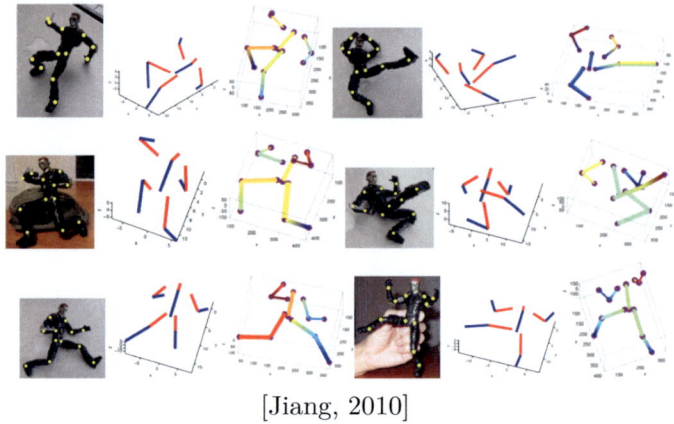

[Jiang, 2010]

Figure 2.10.: Example of estimated poses from a publication using a geometric reconstruction method. Depicted 3D pose estimates are for ground truth 2D poses where 2D landmarks were manually labeled.

Unrealistic camera model. [Parameswaran and Chellappa, 2004] tried to replace the limited scaled-orthographic camera model with a perspective camera model. First, the possible head orientations are reconstructed by setting up a system of polynomial equations, then the epipolar geometry is recovered, and in a recursive manner the rest of the body joint coordinates are computed using knowledge about the limb lengths. But in their approach the authors have to make two strong assumptions. First, the torso twist has to be small such that the hips and shoulders span up a plane, which means that the approach is not applicable to images of poses for which this assumption does not hold. Second, the approach assumes that the locations of four landmarks on the head are given (e.g., forehead, chin, nose and left or right ear), which is hard to be provided by a 2D pose estimator since it demands a very detailed localization performance.

2.1.7. Batch methods

While many HPE approaches estimate the poses on a per-frame basis or update its 3D pose iteratively with each new incoming frame, some approaches build the pose estimation process on top of multiple frames (batch of frames) extracted from a monocular video.

[Andriluka et al., 2010]

Figure 2.11.: Examples of estimated poses from a publication using a batch method (2D pose tracklets approach).

[Andriluka et al., 2010] is an example for the latter case. First, for each frame of the whole video sequence a 2D pose is estimated. Second, consistent sequences of 2D poses (2D pose "tracklets") are established for

a small number of consecutive frames. Third, 2D tracklets are lifted to 3D
pose tracklets. This is done by first assigning an initial 3D pose estimate
to each 2D pose using a set of example 3D poses by projecting the 3D
examples to 2D and comparing the projected part configurations with the
2D pose part configurations. Using these initial 3D pose estimates, the
actual pose estimation and tracking is done in a Bayesian framework.

[Ferrari et al., 2009] first detect humans using the HOG person detector
[Dalal and Triggs, 2005]. Single detections are associated over multiple
frames to build person tracks. A first pose estimate is then computed using
the iterative image parsing technique presented in [Ramanan, 2007]: at
the start of an iterative process only edge features are used to deliver soft
estimates of body part positions, which are used to build better appearance
models of the parts. These can be reused in the next iteration step for a
better localization of the body parts. Their key idea is then to determine
a set of frames where the system is confident about the poses using the
entropy of the posterior probability of the part positions. These pose
estimates are then used to improve the pose estimates from intermediate
frames with low confidence by including dependencies between body parts
over time (continuity of body part location changes).

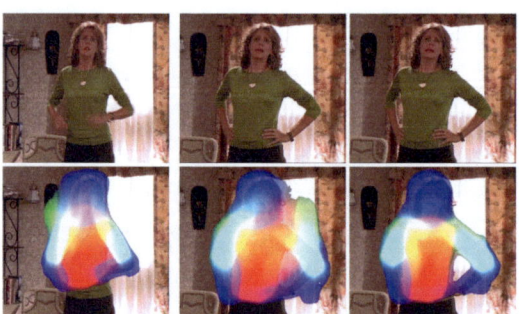

[Ferrari et al., 2009]

**Figure 2.12.: Examples of estimated poses from a publication using a
batch method (Iterative image parsing approach).**

Motion features are another variant to exploit a batch of frames for
monocular HPE. [Daubney et al., 2009] use as observational data a sparse
cloud of features extracted using the Kanade-Lucas-Tomasi (KLT) feature

tracker. The 3D trajectory of each tracked feature is estimated and used as input for the actual 3D pose estimation process.

2.1.8. Silhouette based approaches

A natural idea is to use the silhouette of a person as input to the pose estimation process. While the silhouette can be extracted using simple background subtraction techniques or more sophisticated adaptive background models, its usage often means that application scenarios for the corresponding pose estimation approaches are limited to static camera and single person scenarios.

Fig. 2.13 visualizes the key idea and shows some example pose estimates from own experiments of the author of this thesis using the silhouette based approach. Artificial silhouettes are generated by projecting 3D stick-figure hypotheses to 2D and rendering the limbs with thick lines and the head using an ellipse. While the first column shows the input images used, the second column in the image shows the foreground pixels resulting from an adaptive Gaussian mixture model described in [Zivkovic, 2004]. The third column shows the artificially generated silhouette of the best matching 3D pose that maximizes the similarity of the extracted person silhouette and the generated silhouette by minimizing the number of pixels that remain when computing the difference image between both images (see fourth column).

[Li et al., 2009] use a Gaussian mixture model to model the background and to extract the person silhouette in the first step. In a second step, they use a distance transform of the person silhouette to "skeletonize" the person silhouette. By exploiting the fact, that torso pixels have high values – since for pixels in the middle of the torso the distance to the next non-silhouette pixel is typically large – the location of the torso is estimated. Then, an iterative procedure is started using the EM (Expectation-Maximization) approach. Given the current pose estimate, for each silhouette pixel the most probable limb assignment is computed. Using all silhouette pixels assigned to the same limb class, PCA is used to extract the medial axis of this pixel set, which is used to update the orientation and location of all limbs, and thereby to update the 2D pose estimate.

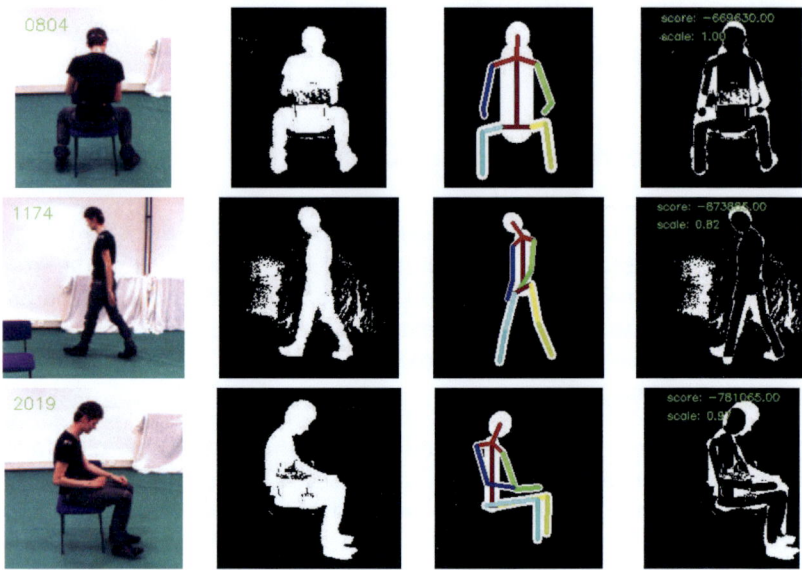

Figure 2.13.: Silhouette based pose estimation. 1st column: input images. 2nd column: silhouettes extracted from an adaptive background model. 3rd column: artificially generated silhouettes from 3D pose hypotheses. 4th column: difference images of 2nd and 3rd column images.

[Sminchisescu and Telea, 2002] use simple background subtraction to extract the person silhouette. Their work focuses on the definition of the observation likelihood that compares the projected person model with the person silhouette, such that local minima are avoided in an optimization based search process. Their likelihood term is based on two components: while the first component maximizes the model-image silhouette area overlap, the second component pushes the model inside the image silhouette. This two component objective function enforces the model to remain within the image silhouette, while simultaneously demanding that the image silhouette is entirely explained. The actual search for the best parameters is done in a framework that allows for a continuous switching between gradient descent steps and Newton-Raphson descent steps.

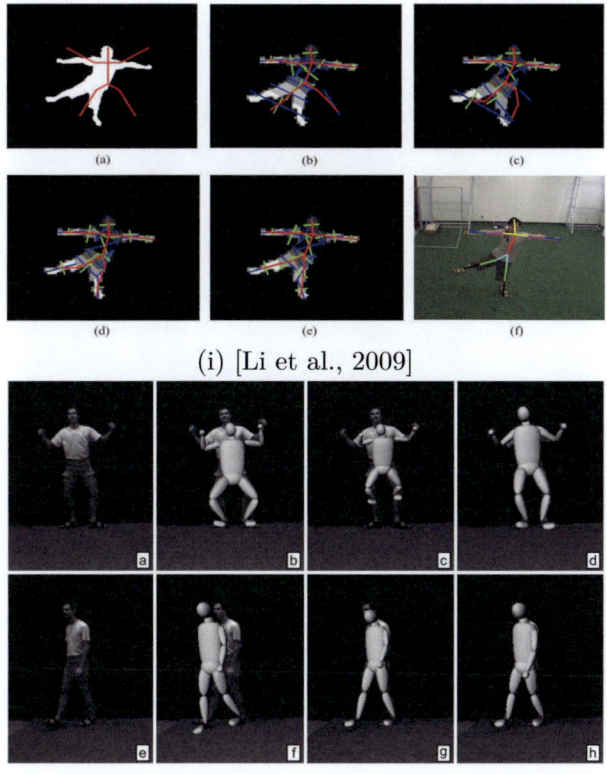

(i) [Li et al., 2009]

(ii) [Sminchisescu and Telea, 2002]

Figure 2.14.: Examples of estimated poses from publications using person silhouettes. (i) Distance transform based approach (ii) Approach that focuses on explaining the image silhouette completely.

[Delamarre and Faugeras, 1999] use an active contour model that incorporates optical flow and intensity measures to extract the silhouette of the person. The contour of the projected 3D model is then moved towards this extracted silhouette by using the Iterative Closest Points (ICP) algorithm: in each iteration of the algorithm and for each point on the model contour the closest point on the silhouette contour is computed and results in a

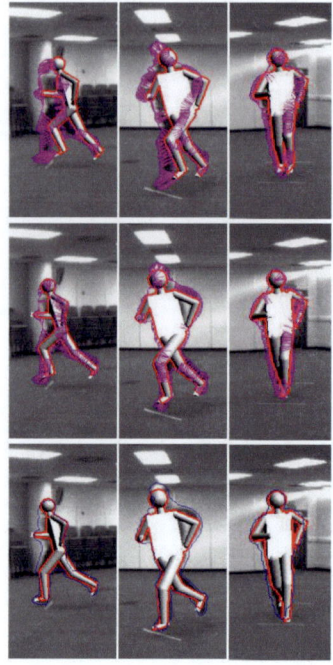

[Delamarre and Faugeras, 1999]

Figure 2.15.: Examples of estimated poses from a publication using person silhouettes (Iterative Closest Points approach).

small point-centric force. The average force vector is then used to move the model contour towards the silhouette contour.

2.2. Differences to previous approaches

Tight coupling of person detection and pose estimation

Most HPE methods consider the pose estimation step independently from the person detection step and use different algorithms to achieve both tasks. In this thesis we assume as well that all persons in the input image have already been detected. Nevertheless, the pose estimation method presented here can tightly be coupled with the person detection step, since it uses the ISM in a first step for localizing anatomical landmarks and the ISM is a common object model used for person detection [Leibe et al., 2008b]. More precisely, we can reuse local features that are considered as part of a person hypothesis to vote for the locations of anatomical landmarks, i.e., detect persons and estimate 2D landmark locations within the same object model framework which can result in reduced implementation costs.

Exploiting figure-ground-segmentation information provided by a person detector

Regression approaches as, e.g., [Sedai et al., 2009] that encode the person image with some global descriptor and try to map it directly to a pose vector do not provide a figure-ground-segmentation as input for the pose estimation process. In contrast, using the ISM to detect persons first and using only such local features that contributed to a person hypothesis, provides a figure-ground-segmentation on the level of local features for the pose estimation task: all local features of background structures can be discarded which do not contribute to the person hypothesis.

Dealing with occlusions

Most HPE estimation approaches as, e.g., many silhouette based and regression based approaches, do not to deal with occlusions. Silhouettes of two persons are hard to distinguish when they overlap. Regression based approaches often use a global descriptor of the person image that is mapped to a 3D pose vector, but a global descriptor will also contain image structures of another person or object if the actual person is occluded.

The method presented here allows to deal partly with occlusions by two procedures. First, by using the ISM local features vote for 2D locations of landmarks that are partly or completely occluded, i.e., visible image structures can vote for locations of landmarks belonging to image structures not visible. Second, the 3D pose estimation task is formulated as an optimization process based on maximizing the average vote density based on 15 landmark vote distributions. This allows to deal not only with wrongly estimated landmark locations, but also with landmarks that are occluded. The objective function to be maximized used in the optimization process is a weighted sum of the accumulated vote densities near to each of 15 different projected landmark locations of a 3D pose hypothesis which means that there is some incorporated robustness against missing landmarks. The UMPM evaluation data set sequences used in Chapter 6 and Chapter 7 contain many cases of persons partly occluded by objects or other persons.

Comparing pose hypotheses with image evidence quickly in the voting space

Previous top-down based methods which compare projected 3D pose hypotheses with the image evidence usually do the comparison in image space and use image features as, e.g., silhouettes [Sminchisescu and Telea, 2002], or contours [Delamarre and Faugeras, 1999] for computing a matching score between the projected pose hypothesis and the person image. While this is a straightforward approach, it results in a computational bottleneck which allows to check only a limited number of 3D pose hypotheses. The top-down 3D pose estimator presented in Chapter 7 first lifts the image evidence to the 2D voting space and uses this space to compare projected 3D pose hypotheses with the image evidence rapidly, which allows to test millions of pose hypotheses per second. While many methods have to approach the 3D pose estimation problem as a tracking problem, where starting from an initial 3D pose the pose is tracked by comparing a very limited set of pose hypotheses with the image evidence, the ability to test millions of 3D poses per second allows to test a huge set of pose candidates in each new frame again and again and thereby to avoid drift problems typical for pose tracking approaches.

Representing pose subspaces without low dimensional pose manifolds

For compensating for errors in the landmark localization process during the 3D pose estimation described in Chapter 7 we use example poses and "pose splines", which are a representation of motion sequences by a set of sparse supporting point poses. The latter representation is similar to the idea to model pose subspaces by low-dimensional manifolds (see approaches presented in Section 2.1.1) but has two advantages. First, we do not need to specify a dimension for the low-dimensional subspace in advance, which is often hard to provide since it is unclear what the intrinsic dimensionality of poses contained in a motion sequence is. Second, projecting 3D poses to some low-dimensional subspace corresponds to a compression step, where detail information (high frequency information) is lost: when re-projecting a point from the low-dimensional subspace to the original high-dimensional 3D pose space, the resulting 3D pose will be different. We avoid such compression artifacts by representing pose manifolds directly in the high-dimensional 3D pose space.

Fully automatic geometric reconstruction of 3D poses for perspective projections

An alternative to the top-down 3D pose estimator described in Chapter 7 is the bottom-up 3D pose estimator described in Chapter 8. It uses the working principle of exploiting limb foreshortening information to geometrically reconstruct the missing depth information up to an ambiguity. The idea was originally presented in [Taylor, 2000] for the very limited weak perspective camera model and was not fully automatically. In contrast, here we present an approach that allows to geometrically reconstruct 3D poses for the standard perspective camera model and resolves pose ambiguities automatically. Reconstruction parameters needed as input are estimated automatically as well by computing the average probability of reconstructed 3D poses for different parameter choices.

3. Evaluation datasets and State-of-the-art

In **Section 3.1** we briefly discuss how to measure the quality of estimated 3D poses. **Section 3.2** reviews the most important publicly available datasets for HPE evaluation. We further list some non-public proprietary datasets used by authors which report state-of-the-art results to compare the datasets used by these authors directly with the standard evaluation datasets. **Section 3.3** lists state-of-the-art results reported in the literature on public and non-public evaluation datasets.

3.1. 3D pose error measure

An important question is how to measure 3D pose estimation accuracy at all. Some authors do not present quantitative results, but only qualitative example results – i.e., images of estimated 3D poses – for proprietary and public available datasets: e.g., [Sidenbladh et al., 2002], [Parameswaran and Chellappa, 2004], [Urtasun et al., 2005], [Mori and Malik, 2006], [Jiang, 2010]. Some authors use the average joint angle error as a measure for 3D pose estimation accuracy, e.g., [Gupta et al., 2008], [Sedai et al., 2009].

The majority of the authors uses the 3D landmark location error (measured in cm) – i.e., the average Euclidean distance between 3D ground truth landmark locations and estimated 3D landmark locations – as a measure for the accuracy of estimated 3D poses: [Wang et al., 2005], [Andriluka and Sigal, 2012], [Andriluka et al., 2010], [Daubney et al., 2009]. Only rarely, authors report both joint angle and landmark location errors (e.g., [Ek et al., 2007]).

A main reason why many authors prefer the 3D landmark location error instead of the joint angle error might be traced back to the fact that this evaluation measure was proposed in [Sigal and Black, 2006b] and [Sigal et al., 2010], i.e., by the authors of the HumanEva dataset which was the first important evaluation dataset for HPE. Many authors that have chosen this dataset for a quantitative evaluation also have chosen the evaluation measure proposed there.

[Sigal et al., 2010] defines the 3D landmark location error μ_t' for a single frame t by the average of the Euclidean distances between the ground truth 3D landmark locations $\mathbf{m}_j^t$ and estimated 3D landmark locations $\tilde{\mathbf{m}}_j^t$:

$$\mu_t' = \frac{1}{J} \sum_{j=1}^{J} \|\mathbf{m}_j^t - \tilde{\mathbf{m}}_j^t\| \tag{3.1}$$

where J is the number of landmarks. Since most 3D pose estimation methods do not recover global landmark coordinates but only landmark coordinates relative to a root landmark [Sigal et al., 2010] proposed to use the following error definition:

$$\mu_t = \frac{1}{J} \sum_{j=1}^{J} \|(\mathbf{m}_j^t - \mathbf{m}_{root}^t) - \tilde{\mathbf{m}}_j^t\| \tag{3.2}$$

i.e., the 3D ground truth landmark locations $\mathbf{m}_j^t$ are now represented relative to the root landmark location $\mathbf{m}_{root}^t$ as well.

For a video sequence with T frames the average error μ_{seq} over all frames can be used to provide an overall measure for the 3D pose estimation accuracy of a 3D HPE approach:

$$\mu_{seq} = \frac{1}{T} \sum_{t=1}^{T} \mu_t \tag{3.3}$$

3.2. Evaluation datasets

There is only a small set of publicly available datasets that come both with video *and* synchronized 3D motion capture data and are appropriate for evaluating video based 3D pose estimation performance.

Figure 3.1.: **Example images from different public evaluation datasets.** While many datasets record the persons from the side, the TUM Kitchen dataset is of special interest, since cameras are mounted in the four top corners of the room (as many surveillance cameras), resulting in perspective foreshortening effects of the limbs.

[Aa et al., 2011] and [Sigal et al., 2010] provide both tables in their papers where the different available HPE evaluation datasets are compared regarding to the number of subjects, video sequences, frames, and different actions provided. We do not replicate these detailed numbers here but refer the reader to these publications. Here we provide another comparison regarding three key aspects for discriminating HPE evaluation datasets:

1. **Natural appearance of persons.** An appropriate dataset for the evaluation of estimated 3D poses should provide video sequences where people appear naturally. This condition can, e.g., be violated if persons need to wear a special suit necessary for capturing their motions.

2. **Possibility to test the method in cases of occlusions.** A dataset is desired that also provides video sequences showing persons partially occluded by other persons. This allows to test the body landmark localization and 3D pose estimation performance in such situations as well.

3. **Availability of camera calibration data.** Camera calibration information is necessary to project the 3D motion capture landmarks to the 2D image plane. This allows to test not only the 3D pose estimation performance, but also (i) to test the body part localization performance by generating ground truth 2D landmark locations by projecting 3D landmarks to the 2D image and (ii) to provide training data in form of ground truth 2D landmark locations for learning based landmark localization algorithms.

In Table 3.1 we provide a comparison regarding these three key aspects for HPE evaluation datasets.

CMU Mocap. The CMU Graphics Lab Motion Capture Database[1] is a large motion capture database recorded for a large set of different subjects and action types. Unfortunately, only for some few motion capture sequences corresponding videos are provided. Further, video frames sometimes contain video information overlayed (e.g., video recording time, see top left image in Fig. 3.1). Persons also had to wear a black suite while their motions were captured which leads to an unnatural appearance of persons and additionally all persons appear very similar. Therefore this dataset is not very helpful for the evaluation of HPE methods. Nevertheless, the rich set of recorded motion capture data can be used in order to learn a set of example poses and pose splines as done in Chapter 7.

CMU MMAC. The newer CMU Multi-Modal Activity Database (CMU-MMAC)[2] [Fernando De la Torre et al., 2008] provides both video and

---

[1]http://mocap.cs.cmu.edu/
[2]http://kitchen.cs.cmu.edu

Dataset name	Year	No. subjects	No. seqs.	No. actions	(i) Nat.	(ii) Occl.	(iii) Cali.
PUBLIC DATASETS							
CMU MoCap	2003	>100	2605	>100	−	+	−
CMU-MMAC	2009	48	185	1	−	+	+
HumanEva	2006	4	44	6	+	−	+
TUM Kitchen	2009	4	20	1	+	−	+
UMPM	2011	30	68	9	+	+	+
NON-PUBLIC DATASETS							
APE	2013	7	245	7	+	−	−
cha-cha couples	2012	4	3	1	+	−	−

Table 3.1.: Comparison of HPE evaluation datasets. Beside the number of subjects, sequences, and different actions a dataset provides, further important criteria are whether (i) persons appear natural, (ii) video sequences are contained that show persons occluded by other persons, and (iii) camera calibration information is provided.

motion capture data for all sequences in a kitchen scenario where different subjects prepare food and cook recipes. Nevertheless, persons still appear unnatural, since the same black motion capture suite had to be used by the subjects and additionally a special backpack for motion capturing.

HumanEva. The HumanEva dataset[3] was introduced in [Sigal and Black, 2006b]. In their more recent publication [Sigal et al., 2010] the authors do not only describe the dataset, but also present an own pose estimation method based on annealed particle filtering. While persons appear natural since they wear usual clothing and only some few small motion capture landmarks are visible, all sequences contain only a single person which means that this dataset does not allow to test occlusion scenarios where one person is occluded by another. Nevertheless, HumanEva is probably the most important HPE evaluation dataset since it is used by many authors. We therefore provide evaluation results on this dataset for both the top-down 3D pose estimation method presented in Chapter 7 and the bottom-up 3D pose estimation method presented in Chapter 8.

---

[3]http://vision.cs.brown.edu/humaneva/

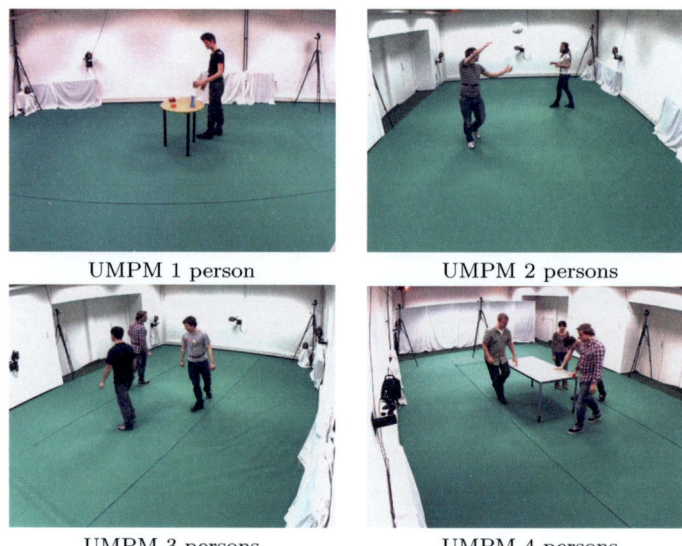

UMPM 1 person   UMPM 2 persons

UMPM 3 persons   UMPM 4 persons

Figure 3.2.: Example images from the UMPM evaluation dataset. The dataset contains different sequences showing one to four persons which allows to test the pose estimation in cases of occlusions.

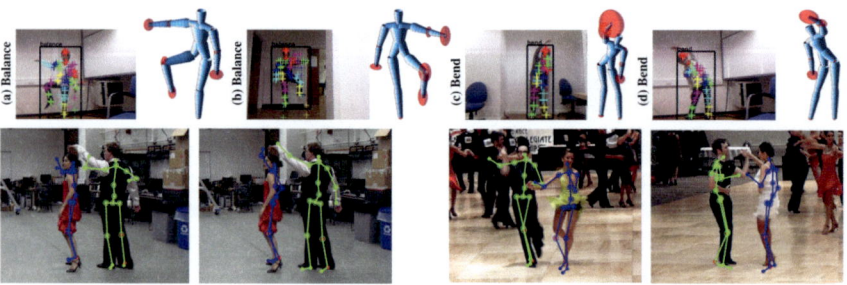

Figure 3.3.: Example images from two non-public evaluation datasets. Top row: from [Yu et al., 2013]. Bottom row: from [Andriluka and Sigal, 2012]

TUM Kitchen. The same holds for the TUM Kitchen dataset[4] [Tenorth et al., 2009] where persons appear natural since no motion capture suits

---

[4]https://ias.cs.tum.edu/software/kitchen-activity-data

or landmarks are worn and camera calibration information is provided as well. Unfortunately, in all sequences only a single person is visible which might be traced back to the limitations of the vision based (marker-less) motion capture system. Nevertheless, this dataset is interesting for experiments where one wants to test on strong perspective foreshortening effects, since the cameras are mounted in the top four corners of a room facing downwards. For this, we choose this dataset to test the geometric reconstruction method for perspective projection camera models presented in Chapter 8.

UMPM. Since persons appear natural and both camera calibration data and sequences with occlusion cases are present, the new UMPM bench-mark[5] [Aa et al., 2011] is probably the best available 3D HPE evaluation dataset currently available. It contains sequences recorded for 30 different subjects, which allows to define experiments, where we can train on some subjects and sequences and test on other sequences of other subjects show-ing similar actions[6]. We use it for evaluating the landmark localization accuracy in Chapter 6 and the 3D top-down pose estimator in Chapter 7. Since the dataset is relatively new (published at the end of 2011, see [Aa et al., 2011]), there are no reported results on this dataset so far. While we can still use this dataset for evaluation and compare the 3D pose estimation error with pose estimation errors on other datasets, we also report 3D pose estimation results on the most often used HumanEva dataset in Chapter 7 and Chapter 8 to make the results better comparable to other works.

APE and cha-cha couples. The APE ("Action-Pose-Estimation") and cha-cha dancing couples datasets are both non-public datasets[7] recorded and used for evaluation by the authors in [Yu et al., 2013] and [Andriluka and Sigal, 2012] respectively. While these are non-standard evaluation datasets we list them in Table 3.1 as well to allow for a direct comparison of the dataset features with the standard evaluation datasets.

---

[5]http://www.projects.science.uu.nl/umpm/

[6]While there are between one and four persons visible in each video sequence, see Fig. 3.2, motion capture data is provided only for up to two persons due to the limitations of the marker based motion capture system.

[7]In their paper [Yu et al., 2013] the authors announced to make the APE dataset public, but at the time of submitting this thesis in November 2013 this dataset was still not publicly available.

3.3. State-of-the-art results

How to compare results? Since different authors have tested their approaches on different datasets, including also proprietary data sets[8], one has to keep in mind how challenging each dataset is when comparing reported 3D pose estimation errors. Even for errors reported on the same publicly available dataset as, e.g., HumanEva, errors are often not directly comparable, since one author may use, e.g., only one training sequence and test on multiple other sequences showing new persons, while another author may use a large set of sequences to train and test only on a few sequences showing the same persons observed during training.

For this, we have to consider for each reported pose estimation error at least the following two questions when comparing reported numbers on pose estimation errors:

- **How challenging is the dataset used?** While some authors evaluate on publicly available datasets, other authors use proprietary (self-recorded) datasets which are often not publicly available. Human pose estimation in cases of occlusions is of special importance since in many scenes containing persons some of the persons are occluded. Some datasets do only show persons from one viewpoint (e.g., from the front) while other datasets contain images from persons from very different viewpoints. The datasets also differ concerning the display size of persons. E.g., HumanEva images show persons at a size of approx. 300 pixels, while TUM kitchen persons are shown at a size of approx. 200 pixels. Robust HPE in cases of background clutter is an import aspect for real applications. Most datasets were recorded in rooms where at least a few objects are present in the background. Together with the fact that the persons moved through these rooms while the poses were recorded it is guaranteed that there is a minimum amount of background clutter within the person bounding boxes. But for some datasets the persons do not even move through the room but stand in front of a homogeneous background (see, e.g., Fig. 3.3 top row). In the ideal case cross evaluation

---

[8]Typically self-recorded images and videos, or collection of images downloaded from image databases.

experiments are conducted as well, i.e., the pose estimation approach
is trained on one dataset and tested on another.

- **How challenging are the experiments?** An important aspect
  here is whether the test persons are different from the training persons.
  Further, test poses can be different or similar to the training poses.
  Some approaches need temporal information by using multiple input
  frames, while other approaches can estimate poses on a single frame
  basis. The number of training sequences used to train the approaches
  can be very different. Further, the number of test sequences used
  and the number of test experiments conducted can vary even for two
  different publications that use the same evaluation dataset.

In Table 3.2 we list the best known pose estimation results[9] for the average
landmark localization error μ_{seq} (cmp. eqn. (3.3)). Note that the dataset
and experiment challenges are very different which can explain the large
range of reported errors. We also list computation times if specified in the
publication, i.e., the time needed to estimate a single 3D pose[10]. With the
"overall difficulty" measure, which is the sum of challenges due to the chosen
dataset and the conducted experiments, we try to provide one number that
can be used to rank the publications according to the challenges faced in
the corresponding evaluations. In the following we describe the evaluation
settings provided by each of the referenced publication in more details and
explain why we rank a challenge to be present (+) or not to be present (-)
in the evaluation.

[Yu et al., 2013] exploit the idea of action context for estimating 3D
poses by first detecting actions which massively limits the search space
for possible 3D poses and then estimating 3D poses (see related work
section 2.1.2). While the authors report the most smallest pose estimation
error in literature compared to other publications (3.8-6.6cm), the difficulty
of the evaluation dataset used and their experiments can be ranked as low

---

[9]For the UMPM, TUM kitchen, and the CMU-MMAC dataset we could not find any
publication that uses a monocular approach to 3D pose estimation and reports
landmark localization errors.

[10]Computation times are typically specified in seconds needed to estimate a single 3D
pose on a state-of-the-art desktop PC using the implementation of the author. Time
complexity specifications using the $\mathcal{O}()$ notation is not used, since most 3D pose
estimation methods are complex algorithms for which the number of computation
steps depending on some input size is hard to specify.

	Yu 2013	Daubney 2009	Andriluka 2010	Tian 2010	Andriluka 2012
Dataset(s)	APE	Human Eva	Human Eva	CMU + Synthetic	Cha-Cha couples
Pose vector dim.	45	45	23	93	?
DATASET CHALLENGES					
1. cross evaluation	−	−	−	−	−
2. public	−	+	+	+	−
3. occlusions	−	−	−	−	+
4. non frontal poses	−	+	+	+	+
5. low resolution	−	−	−	−	−
6. backgr. clutter	−	+	+	+	+
EXPERIMENTS CHALLENGES					
7. test persons new	+	−	−	−	−
8. test poses new	−	−	−	+	−
9. large pose variety	−	−	−	−	−
10. single images	−	−	−	+	−
11. small train. sets	−	+	−	−	+
12. large evaluation	+	−	−	−	−
Overall difficulty	2 of 12	4 of 12	3 of 12	5 of 12	4 of 12
Error [cm]	3.8-6-6	7	10-11	17.5	19-25
Comput. time [s]	3.2	2.0	?	1.14	?

Table 3.2.: State-of-the-art in monocular HPE. 3D landmark location errors in cm from different recent publications (all numbers rounded). Publications sorted by reported 3D landmark localization error.

compared to other publications: The authors evaluate on their self-recorded APE dataset (currently non-public) and do not show any quantitative results on a standard publicly available dataset (1,2). Persons are never occluded in this dataset (3) are shown always from the front (4), and appear at high resolution (5) (cmp. Fig. 3.3 top row). The background is rather homogeneously, since mostly white walls (6). The evaluation was done always on new persons (7), while the test poses are already contained in the set of training poses (8). The poses do not vary much – only 7 different poses are used: balance, bend, box, clap, dance, wave1, wave2 (9). Image sequences are used (10) as input to first detect actions, then estimate poses. Nearly all of the 245 sequences are used for training: training is done on 86% (210 of 245) of the sequences, while only 14% (35 of 245) of the sequences are used for testing. For this, the training sets are not small (11). Using the one-leave-out strategy, pose estimation was evaluated for each of the 7 persons: training was done using 6*35 sequences, while testing was done on the remaining 35 sequences. For this we consider it as a large evaluation (12).

[Daubney et al., 2009] use 2D motion features for 3D pose estimation (see related work section 2.1.7). The authors report an error of approximately 7cm evaluated on the HumanEva dataset (1,2). Subjects in the HumanEva dataset are never occluded (3), but are often shown from the side as well (4). While the persons appear at high resolution (5), background clutter is contained (6): the persons move around while performing the actions such that the background in the person bounding boxes changes continuously. Persons and poses are not different between training and testing (7,8) and only two types of poses are evaluated (9): walking and jogging. Image sequences are exploited, since the approach uses feature trajectories as input for the 3D pose estimation process (10). Only few training data is necessary (11): no video material is used in the training phase, since the method uses only the motion of tracked points (corners) and no person appearance information. Evaluation was done only for 3 persons, for this we rank it as a small evaluation (12), compared, e.g., to [Yu et al., 2013].

[Andriluka et al., 2010] use 2D pose sequences as input for a 3D pose estimation process (see related work section 2.1.7). The authors report evaluation errors on the HumanEva dataset in the range of 10-11cm (1,2). As mentioned before, the HumanEva dataset contains no sequences where persons are occluded (3), but non-frontal poses (4), persons occur at high resolution only (5), and background clutter is contained since different background image structures appear in the person bounding boxes while the persons move through the room (6). The two test sequences that were used show subject S2. Since images of subject S2 were used to train an initial viewpoint classifier as well, training and test persons are not different (7). Further, training and test poses are not different (8) and only walking poses are used, i.e., there is no large variety of test poses (9). In the experiments image sequences are used as input (10). A large amount of training data was used, containing not only images and motion capture data from the HumanEva sequences, but also from two other datasets (11). In contrast, the evaluation data is quite limited, since only two sequences are used showing the same subject S2 (12).

[**Andriluka and Sigal, 2012**] exploit the key idea to use the pose of one person to limit the pose search space of another (see related work section 2.1.2). In order to evaluate their idea, the authors report 3D pose estimation errors on a proprietary dataset which shows cha-cha dancing couples (1,2). The persons frequently occlude each other (3), while they are recorded not only from the front (4). The high resolution images of the persons (5) contain a lot of background clutter, e.g., by other dancing couples (6). The appearance models for part detectors and the spatial priors of the body parts in a pictorial structures (PS) model were trained on another dataset. Nevertheless, a Gaussian Process Dynamical Model (GPDM) was trained on the same subjects as a model for the typical sequences of poses while dancing cha-cha, on which the approach was later tested (7). Training and test poses are both cha-cha dancing poses (8) and there are no other poses considered in the evaluation (9). Sequences of images are used as input (10). On the one hand, the training data set used is rather small (11): only two annotated cha-cha dancing couples were used. This situation can be traced back to the fact that the cha-cha couples dataset had to be annotated manually for generating ground truth 3D poses, since no motion capture system was used for ground-truth generation. On the other hand this means that the evaluation data set is very small as well: it consists of 120 annotated 3D frames only (12).

[**Tian et al., 2010**] use Gaussian Mixture Regression to map a 60 dimensional global descriptor vector – that encodes the form of the person silhouette – to a 93 dimensional pose vector, encoding the 3D locations of 31 landmarks relative to a root landmark (located in the pelvis). The authors evaluate their approach on synthetic images of persons generated using Poser and real images from the CMU motion capture database (1,2) and report an average error of 17.5cm on the CMU experiments. While there are CMU motion capture sequences with occlusions, non-occlusion sequences were used for the evaluation (3). Persons are shown not only from the front (4) at high resolution (5), while containing some background clutter (6). For training their approach the authors used sequences of subject 2. Testing was done on sequences of other subjects (1,8,15, and 17), but the appearance of the subjects does not really change between training and testing since all persons wear a black motion capture suit, such that the test persons are very similar to the one in the training phase (7). There are new test poses (8) which show quite a large variety

(9) compared to other works (e.g., various playground poses). For the experiments, poses were estimated on a per frame basis (10). The training data contains only one subject, but a large set of sequences were used to train the method (11). The evaluation set consists of $4 * 3 = 21$ sequences which is substantially less (12) compared to, e.g., the 245 test sequences used in [Yu et al., 2013].

4. Body model

In this chapter we introduce the model used in this work to represent the human body.

Section 4.1 gives a brief overview on body models used in other works on HPE. In **Section 4.2** we introduce our body model, while **Section 4.3** discusses how to represent the state of a joint.

4.1. Body models in literature

There is a wide variety of models used in literature for representing the human body. Most publications model the human body as a stick-figure, since it allows to reflect the main characteristics of a pose. But there are also approaches that use volumetric body models with different geometric primitives: [Bregler and Malik, 1998] use ellipsoids, [Roth et al., 2004] use cylinders, [Sminchisescu and Triggs, 2003] use super-quadrics, and [Sigal et al., 2007] use a polymesh based shape model with 25,000 polygons.

A further major difference between the body models is whether 3D coordinates or joint angles are used. [Agarwal and Triggs, 2006a], e.g., use a 24 dimensional pose vector to encode the 3D locations of 8 key upper body joint centers. Thereby not only the articulation is represented, but also the relative orientation of the (upper body of the) person to the camera.

Many approaches do not try to estimate the relative orientation of the person to the camera and use joint angles to describe only the articulation part. [Urtasun et al., 2005], e.g., uses a 84 dimensional vector to model walking poses and 72 dimensional vectors to model golfing poses.

While most publications define a body model, some authors do not use a predefined body model, but learn such a model within some training procedure.

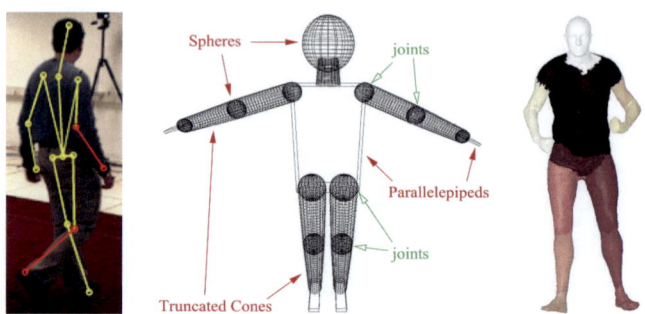

Figure 4.1.: Examples of body models. Three examples of different types of body models used in literature for HPE. (i) Stick figure model used in [Andriluka et al., 2010], (ii) Volumetric model consisting of volumetric primitives used in [Delamarre and Faugeras, 1999], (iii) Polymesh model used in [Sigal et al., 2007].

E.g., [Cheung et al., 2003] use multiple camera images, from which the Shape-From-Silhouette (SFS, other term: visual hull) is computed. While a person is instructed to move each joint independently after each other, corresponding points in the individual silhouette images are used to segment the voxels and based on the movement of the voxel segments, joint locations for the body model are estimated to compute a skeleton model and the shape of each segment (see Fig. 4.2).

4.2. Body model used here

Dual representation of 3D poses

For both the top-down 3D pose estimation method presented in Chapter 7 and the bottom-up 3D pose estimation method presented in Chapter 8 we use 3D landmark coordinates of 15 anatomical landmarks to represent a 3D pose, i.e., the 3D pose vector has a length of 45.

Nevertheless, we use the joint angle representation for 3D poses as well for both proposed 3D pose estimation methods.

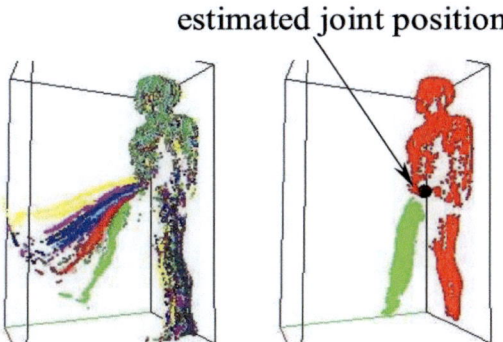

Figure 4.2.: Learning a body model. Example of a work that learns a human body model by estimating joint locations in the reconstructed voxel set. Image from: [Cheung et al., 2003]

In Chapter 7 example poses are stored by normalized 3D landmark coordinates relative to a root landmark. Rotated, tilted, and scaled versions of these 3D example poses are projected to the image to be compared with 2D landmark vote distributions. For both variants of representing a pose prior by example poses and pose splines we compute joint angles. For the example based representation of the pose prior, we traverse a motion capture dataset, compute for each 3D pose contained in the motion capture dataset the joint angles and check whether this 3D pose is already contained in the set of example poses on basis of joint angle comparisons. For the spline based representation of the pose prior, we generate the pose splines using example motion capture sequences as well. There we try to omit 3D poses by linear interpolation. For checking whether a 3D pose can be linearly interpolated by two other poses, we first compute linearly interpolated versions given two supporting point poses and then check for each interpolated version whether it is similar to the 3D pose we want to omit.

In Chapter 8 global 3D landmark coordinates are reconstructed. Nevertheless, joint angles are needed here as well. First, in order to prune the reconstruction tree we want to detect impossible 3D poses on basis of joint angle violations. Second, in order to rank the remaining geometrically reconstructed 3D pose candidates, a probability for each 3D pose candidate

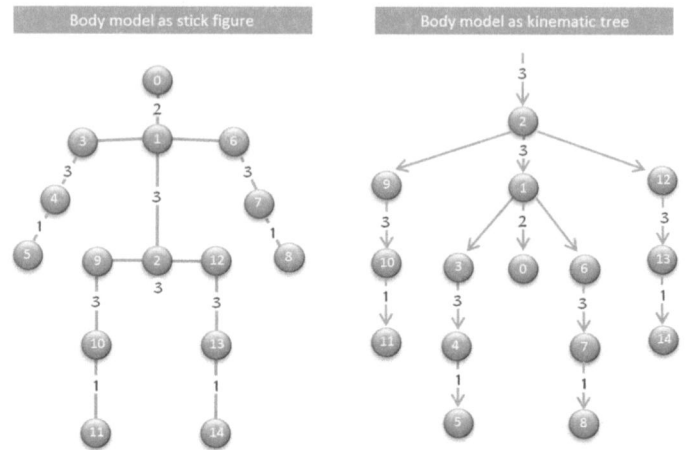

Figure 4.3.: Body model used. Left: body model as stick figure. Circles with numbers: landmark IDs. Numbers on lines: numbers of DoF of the joint that connects two landmarks. Our body model consists of 15 landmarks, connected by 1,2, or 3 DoF joints, resulting in a total of 24 joint angles. Right: body model as kinematic tree. Landmark 2 (lower spine) is the root of all kinematic chains.

is computed on basis of the probabilities of each joint state represented by joint angles.

Stick figure model

The stick figure model used in this thesis to represent the human body and 3D poses is depicted in Fig. 4.3. It consists of 15 anatomical landmarks[1] arranged within a kinematic tree, where some landmarks are connected by joints which are modeled with different number of DoF. For the name of each landmark see Table 4.1 (a). The connection between the elbows and the hands and the connection between the knees and the feet is modeled by a 1 DOF hinge joint, while the connection between the upper spine

---

[1]The terms "anatomical landmark", "landmark", and "marker" are used as synonyms in the following.

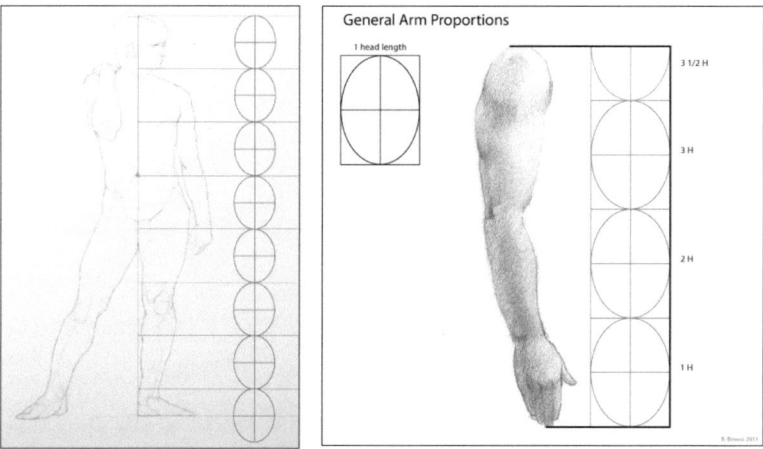

Figure 4.4.: Proportions used in drawing basics. Left: a person is typically 7.5 heads tall. right: size of the upper arm is typically 1.5 heads. Source: [http://www.paintdrawpaint.com/2011/01/drawing-basics-proportions-of-arm.html]

and the head is modeled by a 2 DOF joint, and other joints as, e.g., the connection between the hips and the knees are modeled by 3 DOF joints.

Normalizing limb lengths

Since we want to use example poses from different motion capture databases we have to deal with the problem that landmarks as, e.g., the hand landmarks, are often positioned at slightly different locations. One way to deal with this problem is to store direction vectors only pointing from each parent to child landmark and to use normalized limb lengths, if we want to compute absolute 3D landmark coordinates.

In this context we can exploit the fact that the ratio of limb lengths $r = l_{ij}/l_{km}$ of two selected limbs l_{ij} (connecting landmark i with landmark j) and l_{km} (connecting landmark k with landmark m) is very similar for different persons and therefore also the ratio $r_{ij} = l_{ij}/L$ of the length of limb l_{ij} compared to the sum $L = \sum_{(i,j)\in\mathcal{T}} l_{ij}$ of all limb lengths. With $\mathcal{T}$ we denote the kinematic tree, such that $(i,j) \in \mathcal{T}$ if there is a segment

Landmark ID	Landmark name
0	head
1	upper spine
2	lower spine
3	right shoulder
4	right elbow
5	right hand
6	left shoulder
7	left elbow
8	left hand
9	right hip
10	right knee
11	right foot
12	left hip
13	left knee
14	left foot

(a)

Limb	l_{ij}/L
$2 \rightarrow 1$	0.131
$1 \rightarrow 0$	0.039
$1 \rightarrow 3$	0.052
$3 \rightarrow 4$	0.075
$4 \rightarrow 5$	0.057
$1 \rightarrow 6$	0.052
$6 \rightarrow 7$	0.075
$7 \rightarrow 8$	0.057
$2 \rightarrow 9$	0.031
$9 \rightarrow 10$	0.120
$10 \rightarrow 11$	0.080
$2 \rightarrow 12$	0.031
$12 \rightarrow 13$	0.120
$13 \rightarrow 14$	0.080

(b)

Table 4.1.: Landmark names and typical relative limb lengths. (a) landmark names (b) typical relative limb lengths measured in sum of all limb length L units.

starting at landmark i and ending in landmark j within the body model. This allows to model all absolute limb lengths by a single scale factor s, which can be used to compute each individual absolute limb length by $l_{ij} = s\, r_{ij}$.

Typical relative limb lengths can be taken from standard proportions used in drawing basics, as shown in Fig. 4.4, or computed using motion capture data. Table 4.1 (b) shows the typical relative limb lengths we computed from the CMU motion capture database.

4.3. Joint state representation

For computing joint angles we have to answer the question how to represent the state of a joint.

Representing the joint state by a rotation matrix

If we place a local coordinate system (LCS) into each landmark of our body model, we can define the joint state by the rotation matrix[2] that rotates the LCS in the parent landmark into the LCS in the child landmark. Fig. 4.5 shows the LCS in the hip and the right elbow for some example frames.

Since a LCS is nothing more than three orthonormal vectors, we can represent the LCS by a rotation matrix as well. The relative rotation matrix R_{ij} that rotates the LCS R_i in parent landmark i into the LCS R_j in child landmark j – i.e., $R_j = R_i \, R_{ij}$ – can then be computed by (see [Craig, 2005], p. 22):

$$
R_{ij} = \begin{bmatrix} \mathbf{x}_b \circ \mathbf{x}_a & \mathbf{y}_b \circ \mathbf{x}_a & \mathbf{z}_b \circ \mathbf{x}_a \\ \mathbf{x}_b \circ \mathbf{y}_a & \mathbf{y}_b \circ \mathbf{y}_a & \mathbf{z}_b \circ \mathbf{y}_a \\ \mathbf{x}_b \circ \mathbf{z}_a & \mathbf{y}_b \circ \mathbf{z}_a & \mathbf{z}_b \circ \mathbf{z}_a \end{bmatrix} \tag{4.1}
$$

where the 3x3 rotation matrices R_i and R_j are denoted here with the help of 3x1 column vectors $\mathbf{x}_a, \mathbf{y}_a, \mathbf{z}_a$ ($\mathbf{x}_b, \mathbf{y}_b, \mathbf{z}_b$ respectively):

$$
R_i = \begin{bmatrix} \mathbf{x}_a & \mathbf{y}_a & \mathbf{z}_a \end{bmatrix} \tag{4.2}
$$

$$
R_j = \begin{bmatrix} \mathbf{x}_b & \mathbf{y}_b & \mathbf{z}_b \end{bmatrix} \tag{4.3}
$$

---

[2] A rotation matrix $R \in \mathbb{R}^{N \times N}$ is an orthogonal matrix with $\det(R) = 1$. A matrix R is called orthogonal, if it is a square matrix with real entries and its columns and rows are orthogonal unit vectors. An equivalent description is that the transpose of R is equal to its inverse, i.e., $R^T = R^{-1}$, which means that $R^T R = R R^T = I$, where I is the identity matrix. Rotation matrices preserve lengths and angles of vectors, i.e. $\|Rv\| = \|v\|$ and $Rv \circ Rw = v \circ w$ ($v, w \in \mathbb{R}^N$), where $\circ$ is the inner product.

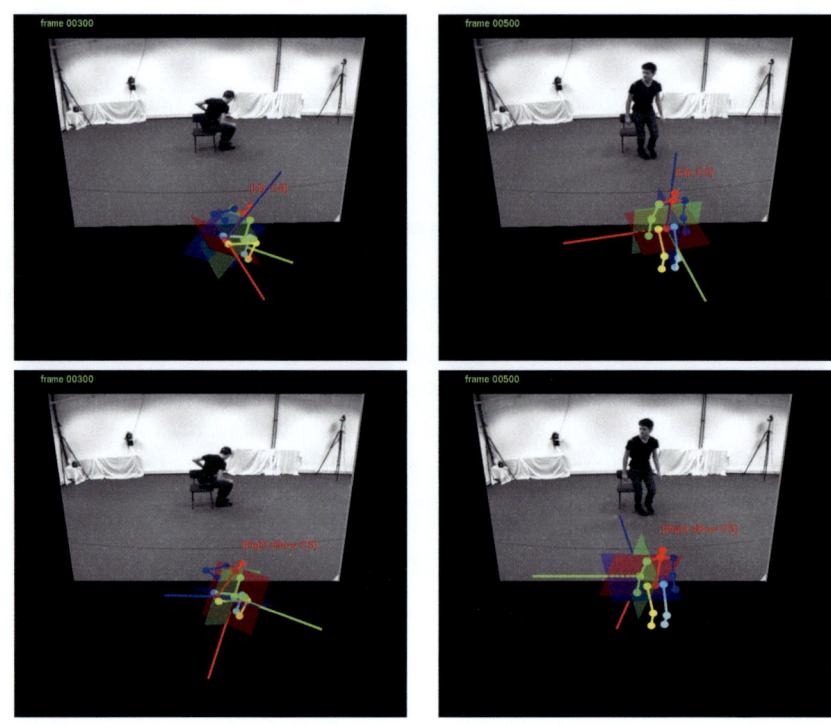

Figure 4.5.: Local Coordinate System Examples. Top row: LCS in hip landmark. Bottom row: LCS in right elbow landmark.

This relative rotation matrix $R_{ij} \in \mathbb{R}^{3x3}$ is one possible representation for the joint state. Though since it consists of 9 scalar values and a 3D orientation has only 3 independent degrees of freedom, it is a non-minimal representation for the joint state.

Representing the joint state by Euler angles

A minimal representation for a 3D rotation is an Euler angle triplet (α, β, γ) which encodes three successive elementary rotations about the axes of a coordinate system. While Euler angles describe successive rotations of a moving coordinate system (intrinsic rotations), we can in principle also describe rotations about fixed axes, i.e., within a fixed coordinate system (extrinsic rotations). A rotation about the x-,y-, or z-axis by α degrees can be represented by a corresponding 3x3 rotation matrix:

$$R_x(\alpha) = \begin{bmatrix} 1 & 0 & 0 \\ 0 & \cos(\alpha) & -\sin(\alpha) \\ 0 & \sin(\alpha) & \cos(\alpha) \end{bmatrix} \tag{4.4}$$

$$R_y(\alpha) = \begin{bmatrix} \cos(\alpha) & 0 & -\sin(\alpha) \\ 0 & 1 & 0 \\ \sin(\alpha) & 0 & \cos(\alpha) \end{bmatrix} \tag{4.5}$$

$$R_z(\alpha) = \begin{bmatrix} \cos(\alpha) & -\sin(\alpha) & 0 \\ \sin(\alpha) & \cos(\alpha) & 0 \\ 0 & 0 & 1 \end{bmatrix} \tag{4.6}$$

Since rotations are not commutative, the order is important and must be specified if we talk about Euler angles. In our case, we use the Z-Y-X order: i.e., we first rotate around the z-axis of the initial coordinate system by α degrees, then about the resulting new y-axis by β degrees, and finally about the new resulting x-axis by γ degrees.

The overall rotation matrix can be computed by a multiplicative concatenation of the elementary rotation matrices[3]

$$R_{zyx} = R_z(\alpha)R_y(\beta)R_x(\gamma) \tag{4.7}$$

Given a LCS in a parent landmark and a child landmark, we can compute the relative rotation matrix R according to 4.1 and then retrieve the Euler angles as a minimal representation of the joint state. For a rotation matrix R

---

[3]Note the interesting result mentioned in [Craig, 2005], p.45: "three rotations taken about fixed axes yield the same final orientation as the same three rotations taken in opposite order about the axes of the moving frame", i.e., rotating in the order ZYX with a moving coordinate system results in the same rotation as rotating in the order XYZ within a fixed coordinate system.

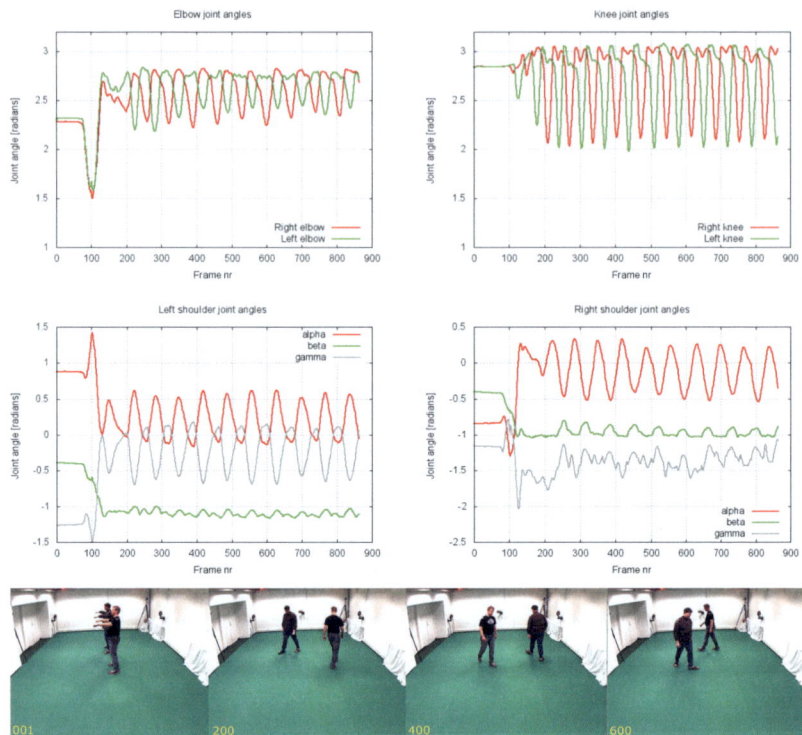

Figure 4.6.: Example joint angles for a walking sequence. Selected joint angles for the person with the T-shirt are plotted. The sequence starts with both arms stretched for some seconds (corresponding to the start interval in the plots where the joint angles are constant), followed by a hand clapping pose sequence, and then the actual walking in a circle sequence.

$$R = \begin{bmatrix} r_{11} & r_{12} & r_{13} \\ r_{21} & r_{22} & r_{23} \\ r_{31} & r_{32} & r_{33} \end{bmatrix} \tag{4.8}$$

we can compute the Euler angles for the Z-Y-X order by (see [Craig, 2005], p. 43):

$$\beta = \text{atan2}(-r_{31}, \sqrt{r_{11}^2 + r_{21}^2}) \tag{4.9}$$
$$\alpha = \text{atan2}(r_{21}/\cos(\beta), r_{11}/\cos(\beta)) \tag{4.10}$$
$$\gamma = \text{atan2}(r_{32}/\cos(\beta), r_{33}/\cos(\beta)) \tag{4.11}$$

Note that the Euler angles are only defined if $\beta \neq \pm\pi/2$. If $\beta = \pm\pi/2$, then $\cos(\beta) = 0$, i.e., in this case α and γ are not defined uniquely. One possible convention is then to define (see [Craig, 2005], p. 43) the Euler angles for $\beta = \pi/2$:

$$\beta = \pi/2 \tag{4.12}$$
$$\alpha = 0.0 \tag{4.13}$$
$$\gamma = \text{atan2}(r_{12}, r_{22}) \tag{4.14}$$

and for $\beta = -\pi/2$:

$$\beta = -\pi/2 \tag{4.15}$$
$$\alpha = 0.0 \tag{4.16}$$
$$\gamma = -\text{atan2}(r_{12}, r_{22}) \tag{4.17}$$

While they are a minimal representation, Euler angles have two disadvantages: if one of the rotation axes aligns during the successive rotations with another rotation axis, one degree of freedom for rotating the coordinate system is lost. This situation is called "singularity" or "gimbal lock". Another drawback are possible discontinuities, i.e., an angle near to $-\pi/2$ can "jump" to $+\pi/2$ and reverse, which has to be regarded when comparing joint angles[4].

---

[4]Quaternions are an alternative representation for rotations which does not suffer from these problems at the cost of a non-minimal representation for 3D rotations: quaternions are 4D vectors. We also experimented with quaternions as joint state representation. Nevertheless, the usage of quaternions did not result in better 3D pose estimation results, which seems to indicate that the gimbal lock and

The 1, 2, and 3 DoF joints are modeled by allowing for 1, 2, or 3 Euler angles to be adjustable. Fig. 4.6 shows examples of joint angles computed for a sequence in which a person walks in a circle. The plots show that the joint angle representation is independent of the orientation of the person to the camera and clearly reflects the periodic nature of the walking movement pattern.

---

discontinuity problem of Euler angles seems not to play a major role concerning the overall results in our context.

5. Implicit Shape Model

In this chapter we introduce the Implicit Shape Model (ISM) which we use and extend in Chapter 6 for localizing anatomical landmarks. Many notations that are used in the next chapters in the context of the ISM are introduced.

Section 5.1 provides a short survey on object models used in computer vision. We then continue with an explanation of the components of the ISM in **Section 5.2**. **Section 5.3** describes the first step of the ISM training, the codebook generation, i.e., the learning of a set of prototypical image structures. In **Section 5.4** the second step of the ISM training is explained, which is the learning of a probability distribution that models the occurrence probability of local features at a certain feature scale and location relative to an object center. **Section 5.5** shows how this learned probability distributions can be used to vote for the object center location given a set of local features. **Section 5.6** is dedicated to the question of how the influence of the individual votes can be modulated to achieve two types of normalizations. **Section 5.7** explains how the generated vote distributions are finally used to detect object instances in an image. **Section 5.8** lists up some extensions of the ISM proposed in literature.

5.1. Object models in computer vision

For modeling object categories there are two main classes of models used in computer vision: window based and part-based models [Grauman and Leibe, 2011].

Window based models represent the appearance of an object category by a single descriptor[1]. E.g., the person detector proposed in [Dalal

---
[1]Often called "holistic" descriptor.

and Triggs, 2005] computes a histogram of oriented gradients ("HOG descriptor") within a sliding window located at different image locations and at different scales and uses a Support Vector Machine (SVM, [Cortes and Vapnik, 1995]) to discriminate between persons and all other image structures based on the computed HOG descriptor vector for each window. There are several disadvantages of window based models. First, the model can only partly deal with occlusions: if a large part of the object is occluded, the single appearance descriptor often represents too much non-object related image structure information to yield a correct classification result. Second, a single model is often not sufficient to represent the appearance of the object for different viewpoints. Even for slight viewpoint changes it can be necessary to represent the appearance of the same object class by an additional model.

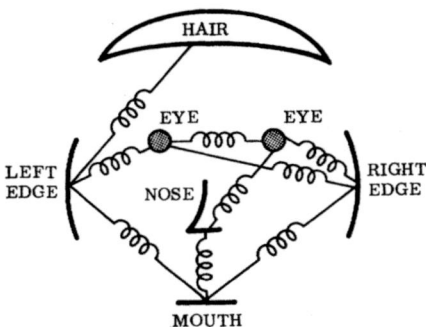

Figure 5.1.: Pictorial structures model by Fischler and Elschlager. Objects (as, e.g., faces) are modeled as a set of parts that appear in some typical spatial relationship with some flexibility concerning the relative locations. Image source: [Fischler and Elschlager, 1973]

Part-based models try to overcome these drawbacks by modeling each object as a set of parts that can appear in a flexible spatial configuration. The idea goes back to the "Pictorial Structures" model of [Fischler and Elschlager, 1973] which models the appearance of objects as a set of parts where some of the parts are connected by springs which allow for some limited variance concerning the relative locations of two such connected parts (see Fig. 5.1).

While the Pictorial Structures model uses semantically meaningful (manually defined) object parts, as e.g., "eye" or "hair", and assumes that each
object in the image will appear with these parts, these parts are often hard
to detect. Instead, it is easier to work with image features that are not
directly associated with a semantic meaning, but can easily be detected
based on keypoint detectors. The image patch corresponding to each
keypoint is described by some descriptor vector which is then mapped to
one of N prototypes ("words").

Different models for modeling the spatial relationships of these words have
been proposed (see Fig. 5.2). At the one end of the spectrum there is
the **Bag of Words** (BoW) object model where no spatial relationship
is modeled at all. This has the advantage that – as long as the words
themselves do not change, but only their spatial relationship – the object
model is invariant to viewpoint changes. The disadvantage of the Bag of
Words approach is that it is not very discriminative: two different object
classes can be associated with a similar set of words, while the spatial
relationships at which they occur can be very different. At the other end
of the spectrum we can see the **constellation model** [Fergus et al., 2003]
which models the relative location between each two words. While this
model represents the spatial relationships at a high degree of detail, it
has the disadvantage that the number of parameters grows quadratically
with the number of words. This demands a large training set in order to
estimate these parameters from the training data. A **tree model** (used,
e.g., in [Felzenszwalb and Huttenlocher, 2005]) needs less parameters by
modeling the spatial relationship in a hierarchical way: the location of a
word is only dependent on the location of its parent.

A compromise between precision in modeling the spatial relationships
and number of model parameters are **star models** of words. Here only
the spatial relationship of each word to a specific location on the object
(e.g., the object center) is modeled, while the spatial relationships between
words are not modeled directly. While the number of parameters grows
only linearly with the number of words in star models, star models have
another advantage: the object detection procedure can be formulated using
a simple voting scheme, as was shown in [Leibe and Schiele, 2003] and is
described in Section 5.5.

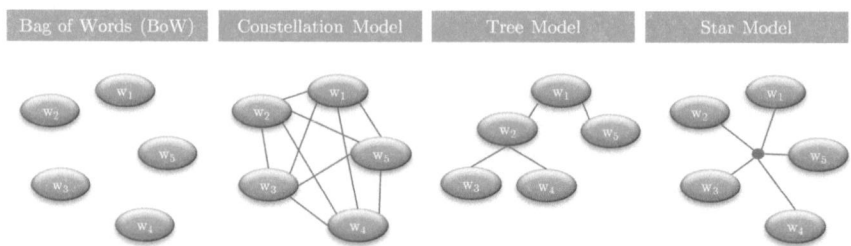

Figure 5.2.: Part-based object models. Different models haven been proposed for modeling the spatial relationship between words associated with an object category.

5.2. ISM object model components

In [Leibe and Schiele, 2003] the *Implicit Shape Model* (ISM) model was introduced. A star model is used to represent the spatial relationship of local scale-invariant features, e.g., SIFT [Lowe, 2004] or SURF [Bay et al., 2006], relative to the object center. An ISM

$$\mathcal{I} = (\mathcal{C}, \mathcal{P}) \tag{5.1}$$

for an object category (e.g., persons) consists of a set $\mathcal{C}$ (codebook) of prototypical image structures w (words, visual words, codewords) together with a set $\mathcal{P}$ of 3D probability distributions

$$\mathcal{P} = \{P_1, ..., P_{|\mathcal{C}|}\} \tag{5.2}$$

where P_i ($i = 1, ..., |\mathcal{C}|$) specifies where we find the word w typically on the object and at which scale, i.e.

$$P_i : \mathbb{R}^3 \to \mathbb{R}, \ (x, y, s) \mapsto [0, 1] \tag{5.3}$$

and

$$\int\limits_{x} \int\limits_{y} \int\limits_{s} P_i(x, y, s) \, ds \, dy \, dx \;=\; 1 \tag{5.4}$$

Note that the probability distributions P_i are defined independently for each word of the codebook which reflects the star model design choice. In other words, we do not try to model the joint probability distribution (co-occurrence) of the words explicitly, since this would require a significantly larger number of training data to sample from this high dimensional probability distribution. On the one hand, ignoring the co-occurrence properties of words is clearly an oversimplification. On the other hand, it allows to learn a model of the object using only small training data sets. Further, a fast object detection procedure is feasible, since words can cast votes according to their corresponding probability distribution P_i independently, i.e., hints from different words for the location of the object can be accumulated independently, allowing, e.g., for a parallel implementation of the voting procedure.

In the following we describe the steps for learning an ISM and how we can use it for detecting objects of that class more detailed.

5.3. Codebook generation

For learning an object class specific codebook $\mathcal{C}$, a set of example images showing instances of the object is needed. For each of these images local scale-invariant keypoints (x, y, s) are computed and for each keypoint region a descriptor vector $\mathbf{d}$ is extracted that encodes the corresponding image patch information. Then, the descriptor vectors are clustered, resulting in descriptor vector centroids, which are called "visual words" or simply "words" (see Fig. 5.3). In [Leibe et al., 2008b] SIFT keypoints and descriptor vectors are used, but in principle we can use any combination of a local scale-invariant keypoint detector and a descriptor vector, e.g., SURF keypoints in combination with Shape Context Descriptors [Belongie et al., 2000].

Since we do not know the number of clusters N in advance, a cluster technique as k-means clustering is inappropriate, because we have to

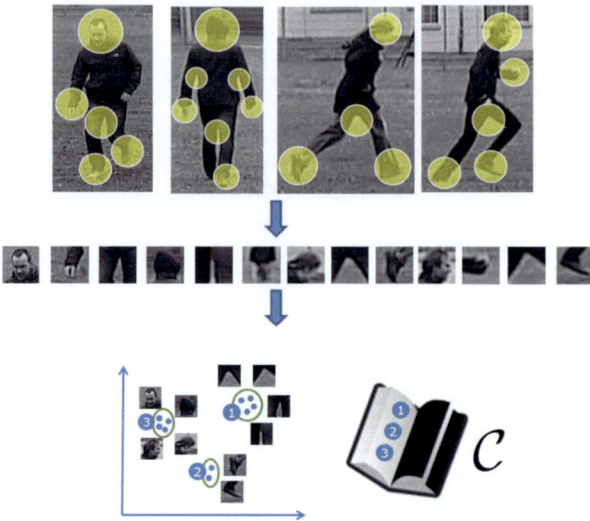

Figure 5.3.: Codebook generation. For each object image we compute a set of local scale-invariant keypoints and compute descriptor vectors for the corresponding image patches. The descriptor vectors (blue dots) are then clustered, resulting in a set of prototypical descriptor vectors (blue circles with numbers) – the words – which together build the codebook $\mathcal{C}$.

specify the number of clusters in advance. Instead, clustering techniques as, e.g., Mean Shift Clustering [Cheng, 1995] where the number of clusters is determined automatically and only indirectly controlled by clustering parameters are more appropriate. In [Leibe et al., 2008b] hierarchical clustering is used, where the number of clusters is controlled indirectly by a cluster compactness threshold.

5.4. Probability distribution representation

A direct approach to model the probability distributions P_i is to record sample locations $(\Delta x, \Delta y)$ and scales s of the local features (matched against word w) relative to the object center and to store these observation

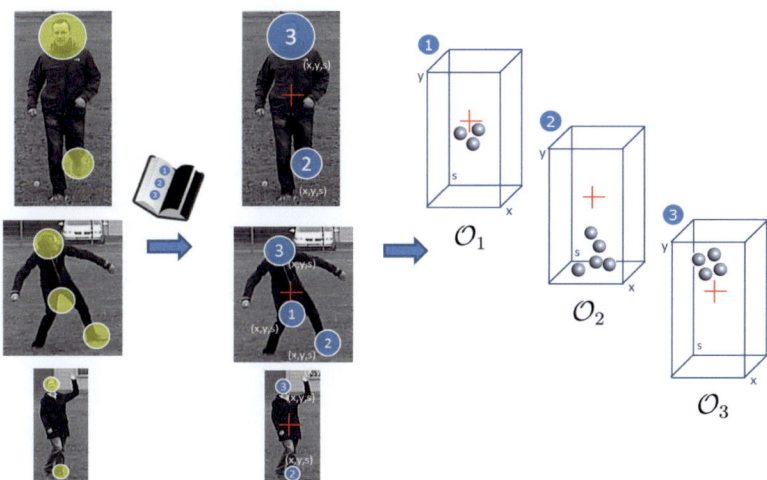

Figure 5.4.: Implicit Shape Model Learning. For a set of example images of the object, we compute keypoints (x, y, s) and descriptor vectors $\mathbf{d}$ and match these to the codebook. The $(\Delta x, \Delta y)$ keypoint location relative to the POI (here: person center) and the scale s of each matched feature is stored as an observation example $\mathbf{o} = (\Delta x, \Delta y, s)$ associated with the corresponding word.

vectors $\mathbf{o}_k = (\Delta x, \Delta y, s)$ associated with each word within a list $\mathcal{O}_w$ of R observation vectors in total:

$$\mathcal{O}_w = \{\mathbf{o}_k = (\Delta x_k, \Delta y_k, s_k) : 1 \leq k \leq R\} \qquad (5.5)$$

Leibe et al. argue that encoding the spatial probability distribution in this non-parametric manner *"enables the method to model the true distribution in as much detail as the training data permits instead of making a possibly oversimplifying Gaussian assumption"* – see [Leibe et al., 2008b], p.7. In order to collect such location/scale samples $\mathbf{o}_k$ we need ground truth annotated images, i.e., example images have to be provided in conjunction with annotated object centers (see Fig. 5.4).

The relative orientation between object center and feature can be described *object centric* or *feature centric*. Here we use a feature centric description, where we store the location of the object center relative to the feature location, since in the object detection phase we first detect features and then cast votes for the object center.

5.5. Voting procedure

In the application phase, we match features against words of the codebook and use the relative location and scale information recorded in the training phase to cast votes for the object center relative to the detected features.

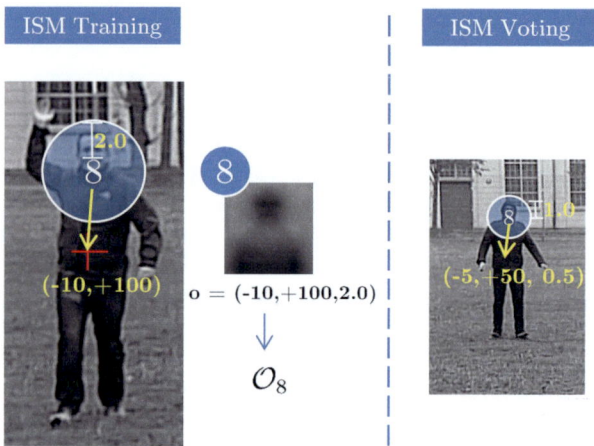

Figure 5.5.: Adaptation of observation vectors during voting procedure. Left: a feature **f** is observed at scale 2.0, object center at $(-10, +100)$ relative to this feature. Right: during voting a feature **f'** is observed at half of the scale (1.0), which means that the vote for the object center location has to be adapted accordingly to location $(-5, +50)$ and object size 0.5 (relative to training object size).

For the vote generation, for each feature and observation vector $\mathbf{o} = (\Delta x, \Delta y, s)$ associated with the word that matches to the feature a vote is generated where the location and scale of the vote corresponds to the observation vector but adapted to the feature scale f_s. Fig. 5.5 shows a motivating example for this need of adaptation.

Vote generation example

Imagine we find a feature $\mathbf{f}' = (f'_x, f'_y, f'_s, \mathbf{d}', w')$ during training at scale $f'_s = 2.0$ which best matches to word id $w' = 8$. During training the object center could be found at $(\Delta x, \Delta y) = (-10, +100)$ relative to the feature location (f'_x, f'_y). So we add an observation vector $\mathbf{o} = (-10, +100, 2.0)$ to $\mathcal{O}_8$. If we find a feature $\mathbf{f} = (f_x, f_y, f_s, \mathbf{d}, w)$ during the application phase, which matches to word id $w = w' = 8$ again and its scale is $f_s = 1.0$, we have to adapt the offset vector $\mathbf{o}$ for generating a vote, since the image structure only appears at half of its size compared to the training phase. For this, the object center can be found at $(-5, +50)$ relative to the detected location of feature $\mathbf{f}$ and we know that the object has probably half of its size compared to training, i.e., we cast a vote at $(f_x - 5, f_y + 50, 1.0/2.0)$ into the 3D voting space.

More generally, a feature $\mathbf{f} = (f_x, f_y, f_s, \mathbf{d}, w)$ that is matched to a word w casts votes $\mathbf{v} = (v_r, v_x, v_y, v_s)$ according to the offset vectors $\mathbf{o} = (\Delta x, \Delta y, o_s) \in \mathcal{O}_w$:

$$v_r = \frac{1}{|\mathcal{O}_w|} P(w|\mathbf{d}) \tag{5.6}$$

$$v_x = f_x + \Delta x \frac{f_s}{o_s} \tag{5.7}$$

$$v_y = f_y + \Delta y \frac{f_s}{o_s} \tag{5.8}$$

$$v_s = \frac{f_s}{o_s} \tag{5.9}$$

Generalized Hough Transform

The ISM is sometimes also called Generalized Hough Transform. The original Hough transform was introduced and patented in [Hough, 1962] as a method for the detection of lines. For this, a dual space – the Hough voting space – is introduced that consists of the parameters used to represent a straight line. The basic idea for detecting lines is to let each detected edge pixel in an image vote for all possible corresponding lines, i.e., possible parameters of a line parametrized by y-axis intercept and slope. Later, [Duda and Hart, 1972] replaced the unbounded intercept-slope parameters of a straight line by bounded 2D polar parameters. [Ballard, 1981] showed that the method could be used for detecting even arbitrary shapes that are not described in an analytic form. For this, for each boundary edge pixel of the arbitrary shape, an offset vector to a reference point (e.g., shape center) is computed, and stored in a table indexed by the gradient orientation at this boundary point. For detecting instances of such shapes, first edge pixels and gradient orientation at each edge pixel are computed and using the previously stored table, the offset vectors are used to vote for the reference point location. Nevertheless, the method of Ballard only allows to detect non-scaled and non-rotated versions of the prototype shape, i.e., translation is the only transformation allowed.

The ISM introduced in [Leibe et al., 2008b] extends the idea of the Generalized Hough Transform (GHT) in many ways. First, it is not based on edge pixels, but uses scale-invariant local features. Instead of indexing the offset vectors by gradient orientations, the offset vectors are indexed by the words of a codebook. Second, it can deal with scaled and rotated versions of the object, by using the scale of each local feature in order to compute a scale-normalized vote. Third, it is a probabilistic version of the GHT. Each vote has a weight which allows to incorporate the probability of how good a local feature matches to a word of the codebook.

5.6. Vote weighting

The vote strength v_r can be used to modulate the influence of a single vote and to realize the following two types of normalizations.

Assign each feature the same vote mass

First, the number $|\mathcal{O}_{w_1}|$ of offset vectors collected for one word w_1 during the ISM training phase, can be significantly smaller or larger compared to the number $|\mathcal{O}_{w_2}|$ of offset vectors collected for another word w_2. This could be, e.g., due to a bias in the set of training images which show less (or more) instances of word w_1 than instances of word w_2. To compensate for these different numbers we can set v_r to $1/|\mathcal{O}_w|$ to compensate for such a bias. This means, each detected local feature in the image will cast the same "vote mass" into the 3D voting space.

This normalization is also necessary to make sure that the collected offset vectors $\mathcal{O}_w$ can be interpreted as a non-parametric and discrete representation of the probability distribution P_w. For a discrete variant of eqn. (5.4), where the voting space is binned in all dimensions x, y, s, we have to make sure that the individual probabilities $P_w(\mathbf{a})$ for each location $\mathbf{a} = (x, y, s)$ in the 3D vote space sum up to 1:

$$\sum_x \sum_y \sum_s P_w(x, y, s) = 1 \tag{5.10}$$

This is true if we set

$$P_w(x, y, s) := \left\{ \begin{array}{ll} \frac{1}{|\mathcal{O}_w|} & , \mathbf{o} = (x, y, s) \in \mathcal{O}_w \\ 0 & , \text{else} \end{array} \right. \tag{5.11}$$

Then

$$\sum_x \sum_y \sum_s P_w(x, y, s) = \sum_{\mathbf{o}=(x,y,s) \in \mathcal{O}_w} P_w(\mathbf{o}) = |\mathcal{O}_w| \frac{1}{|\mathcal{O}_w|} = 1 \tag{5.12}$$

Soft matching vs. hard matching

Second, the vote weights can be used if we use *soft matching*. Soft matching means that the descriptor vector $\mathbf{d}$ of a detected feature $\mathbf{f}$ is not only matched to a single word w (*hard matching*), but to a set of words $S = \{w_1, ..., w_M\}$, e.g., to all words w such that the Euclidean distance between the descriptor vector and the word centroid vector $\mathbf{w}$ is below some threshold:

$$S = \{w : \|\mathbf{w} - \mathbf{d}\|_2 \leq \Theta, \ i \in \{1, ..., |\mathcal{C}|\}\} \tag{5.13}$$

To compensate for the different number M of matching words, we can then define the vote weight v_r as:

$$v_r = \frac{1}{|\mathcal{O}_w|} \frac{1}{M} \tag{5.14}$$

If we further have a word matching probability distribution $P(w|\mathbf{d})$, that yields the probability that descriptor vector $\mathbf{d}$ matches to word w, we can define the weight vote as:

$$v_r = \frac{1}{|\mathcal{O}_w|} P(w|\mathbf{d}) \tag{5.15}$$

In other words, in soft matching we have to distribute the "vote mass" of 1 among all possible interpretations $S = \{w_1, ..., w_M\}$ of the descriptor vector $\mathbf{d}$, while in hard matching there is only one interpretation w of the descriptor vector $\mathbf{d}$.

5.7. Object detection

For detecting objects, locations of high vote density in the 3D voting space are identified (see Fig. 5.6).

For quickly finding regions within the 3D vote space that contain promising candidates for local maxima, the 3D vote space is divided into 3D grid cells and within each cell the sum of all containing votes is computed. Then, a Mean Shift [Fukunaga and Hostetler, 1975] mode search is performed on all the votes of candidate regions in order to find locations in the 3D vote space of high vote density.

For estimating the vote density ρ at some location $\mathbf{a} = (x, y, s)$ in the 3D vote space, we can use a weighted kernel density estimator:

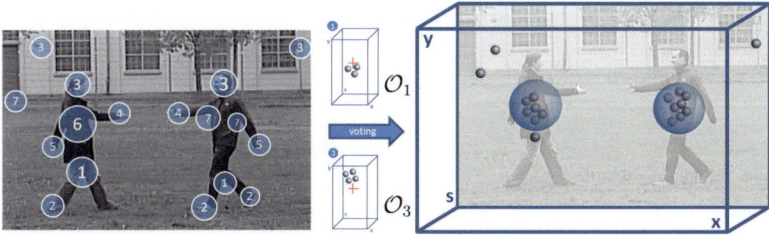

Figure 5.6.: ISM voting and object detection. For a new image for which we want to detect objects, keypoint and descriptors are computed and matched against the codebook. Corresponding to the previously learned probability distributions P_i we cast votes at different image locations (x,y) and scales s. Locations in this 3D voting space with a large number of assigned votes are considered as detected instances of the object class.

$$\rho(\mathbf{a}) \quad = \quad \frac{1}{Wh} \sum_{k=1}^{|\mathcal{V}|} v_r^k K \left(\frac{\|\mathbf{v}_3^k - \mathbf{a}\|_2}{h} \right) \tag{5.16}$$

$$W \quad = \quad \sum_{k=1}^{|\mathcal{V}|} v_r^k \tag{5.17}$$

where $\mathcal{V}$ is the set of all votes $\mathbf{v}^k = (v_r^k, v_x^k, v_y^k, v_s^k)$ $(k = 1, ..., |\mathcal{V}|)$ casted from all features for the POI[2], $|\mathcal{V}|$ is the number of total votes casted, $\mathbf{v}_3^k = (v_x, v_y, v_s)$ is the 3D vote space location of a vote $\mathbf{v}^k$, W is the sum of weights of all votes casted, h is the bandwidth (smoothing parameter) of the kernel, and K is some kernel function. Typically a Gaussian kernel is used for K, i.e.

$$K(d) = \frac{1}{\sqrt{2\pi}} \exp(-\frac{d^2}{2}) \tag{5.18}$$

---

[2]Point Of Interest, e.g., the person center, or an anatomical landmark as the head, right shoulder, etc.

[Leibe et al., 2008b] argue not to use a constant bandwidth h, but a bandwidth that depends on the scale coordinate of the vote location $\mathbf{a}$, i.e., $h(\mathbf{a}) = h(s)$. Such a kernel density estimator is called a balloon density estimator [Comaniciu et al., 2001]. The argumentation is that as the object size increases in the application phase relative to the object size in the training phase, the votes will be spread over a larger area around the hypothesized object center, such that we should make the kernel bandwidth larger to compensate for this effect in the local maxima detection step. For this, the final kernel density estimator is:

$$\rho(\mathbf{a}) = \frac{1}{Wh(s)} \sum_{k=1}^{|\mathcal{V}|} v_r^k K \left(\frac{\|\mathbf{v}_3^k - \mathbf{a}\|_2}{h(s)} \right) \tag{5.19}$$

For vote space locations $\mathbf{a} = (x, y, s)$ where the vote density $\rho(\mathbf{a})$ is above some minimal threshold θ we consider $\mathbf{a}' = (x, y)$ as a detected instance of the object class at image position (x, y) and define a hypothesis score $S(\mathbf{a}') = \rho(\mathbf{a})$ for this detection. The scale s is only a relative scale, namely the scale of the features that occurred in the detection phase relative to the scale of the features in the training phase. This scale dimension of the voting space is used to identify clusters of *scale consistent* votes, i.e., for an object instance in a new image, the features that vote for this object instance should have scales that are proportional to the scales of the features belonging to the object class as found during ISM training.

Probability vs. Hypothesis Score

The ISM does not yield probability estimates $P(\mathbf{a}')$ for each image location $\mathbf{a}' = (x, y)$ but only a hypothesis score $S(\mathbf{a}')$. Although the density $\rho(\mathbf{a})$ integrates to one (as a property of densities):

$$\int_{\mathbf{a}=(x,y,s)} \rho(\mathbf{a}) \, d\mathbf{a} = 1 \tag{5.20}$$

and could be used to define a corresponding probability distribution, such a definition would be inappropriate. The reason is that the vote density only reflects how many of all votes casted we can find at some location **a** in the 3D vote space (with a weighting of these locations by the vote weights). For two persons present in an image, the corresponding vote densities can be significantly different. For a first person which stands frontal to the camera we could detect a multiple of more local features than for another person, which is viewed from the side or which bends down. The large differences in number of features can result in a large difference of number of votes and an eventually large difference in the "vote mass" casted for each person. The resulting vote densities at these two locations in the vote space can be very different and therefore cannot be used a measure for the probability that an object is present here. For this, vote densities cannot be mapped directly to probabilities.

5.8. Extensions of the original ISM

Since its original publication [Leibe and Schiele, 2003] a number of extensions of the ISM have been proposed.

[Seemann et al., 2006] address the problem of detecting non-rigid objects recorded from different viewpoints, which is difficult, since the appearance can change not only due to different viewpoints, but also due to deformations of the object (e.g., different articulation of persons). In a first step, different possible 2D appearance shapes (person silhouettes) of the object are learned by clustering the shapes using a Chamfer distance metric. The ISM is then extended from a 3D to a 4D voting space, where a word is not only associated with a 3D location in (x, y, s) voting space, but also with one of the shape clusters. By this extension, a person detection corresponds to a vote cluster in 4D space, which means that the image evidence has to be consistent not only concerning the location and scale of the person, but also regarding its shape.

In [Seemann et al., 2007] the authors tackle the problem of learning an object-instance specific online model for a detected object starting from a generic ISM object model. The key idea here is to exploit the information provided by a single detection of the generic object model, namely, which words occurred and at which locations relative to the person center. Since this set of words builds up an appearance model of a person, we can use it to detect the person in subsequent frames more reliably using this instance specific model compared to using the generic object model.

In [Leibe et al., 2008a] the authors propose to group features not only based on their visual similarity during codebook generation process, but also to learn high-level object parts. Based on the co-occurrence information of words, i.e., the information which words appear reliably near to each other on the same object class, high-level object parts consisting of combinations of such features are learned and used for detecting objects.

[Gall and Lempitsky, 2009] replace the codebook by Hough forests in which each image patch is mapped directly to votes for the object centers. More specifically, each leaf node of a Hough tree in the forest makes a probabilistic decision whether an image patch belongs to a part of the object or the background and casts a probabilistic vote for the location of the object.

[Lehmann et al., 2009] underline the similarities between the sliding window based and Hough transform based worlds for object detection. While the sliding window based object detection methods first iterate over all possible object hypotheses (possible object locations) and then over all features within a sliding window to compute a classifier result for each window, the Hough transform based object detector methods iterate over all features and then over all object hypotheses. For reducing the computation time during voting, the authors replace the discrete representation of possible object locations relative to a word by Gaussian Mixture Models (GMM): large sets of sample observation vectors are represented by some few Gaussians that model the typical location of a landmark relative to a word. The authors further showed that soft matching during the voting procedure is not necessary since the same results can be obtained by (i) using a simple nearest neighbor matching (hard matching) during voting which is faster and (ii) moving the soft matching step to the ISM training phase: for recording possible object locations relative to words, features are matched probabilistically to multiple words here. In another work [Lehmann et al., 2011] showed how to integrate the idea of Efficient Sub-window Search (ESS) [Lampert et al., 2008], which is a branch-and-bound strategy to reduce the image search space subsequently, to the ISM framework.

6. Anatomical landmark localization

In this chapter we show how the Implicit Shape Model can be used to localize anatomical landmarks on the human body. Alternatives to the original voting strategy are presented which can be used to significantly improve the landmark localization accuracy in terms of correct votes.

Section 6.1 presents the approach idea which is to train one ISM for each anatomical landmark and to use these pre-trained ISMs in the landmark localization step. In the following sections 6.2.1-6.2.4 new voting strategies are presented for an increased landmark localization accuracy.

Section 6.2.1 introduces the first voting strategy (RP-VOT) which is to exploit knowledge about the person center for filtering observation vectors within the voting procedure. In **Section 6.2.2** another observation vector filter mechanism is proposed (H-VOT) which focuses on the question which local features are allowed to vote for which landmarks. **Section 6.2.3** presents a voting strategy (OW-VOT) which introduces a second pass for the ISM training procedure, where for each observation vector an individual weight is learned based on the reliability of the observation vector to predict the location of the landmark. In **Section 6.2.4** we show that the three previously described voting strategies (RP/H/OW-VOT) can be combined in one algorithm (COMBI-VOT).

Section 6.2.5 discusses an alternative to the use of discrete votes which is to represent the probability distributions of the locations of the landmarks relative to the words using Gaussian Mixture Models (GMMs)[1].

---

[1]Such an approach was explored as the topic of a diploma thesis supervised by the author of this thesis and results from this diploma thesis are briefly presented in this section.

Section 6.3 evaluates the proposed voting strategies and shows their benefit in the context of landmark localization. **Section 6.4** summarizes the results obtained in this chapter and presents the conclusions.

6.1. Introduction

In the previous Chapter 5 we introduced the Implicit Shape Model for object recognition using local features. This model was introduced in [Leibe and Schiele, 2003] for the detection of objects such as persons, cars, etc. The key idea presented here is to re-use the features that were used in the initial ISM object detection step together with one ISM learned for each point of interest (POI) for a fine-graded localization of this POI on the object. Here the objects are persons and the POIs are anatomical landmarks, but the same idea can be applied to other object classes (e.g., cars) and POIs (e.g., car door, rear window, etc.).

More formally, for each landmark l $(1 \leq l \leq J)$ an ISM $\mathcal{I}_l = (\mathcal{P}_l, \mathcal{C})$ is trained with a corresponding set $\mathcal{P}_l$ of probability distributions $\mathcal{P}_l = \{P_{1l}, ..., P_{|\mathcal{C}|l}\}$. Each P_{wl} models the location of landmark l relative to word w $(1 \leq w \leq |\mathcal{C}|)$ and at which scale the word appears on the object.

There are two main advantages of this voting for landmarks approach. First, local features that voted for the object center typically belong to the object only, i.e., the set of local features associated with the object hypothesis do not contain (much) background image structures. In other words: we do not need to care about figure-background-segmentation in successive processing steps. Second, re-using the same local features that were used to detect the object for detecting landmarks saves computation time, since no extra features have to be computed for the landmark localization step.

The voting strategies described in this chapter can also be applied in combination with other person detectors, e.g., sliding-window based person detectors as the "Fastest Pedestrian Detector in the West" (FPDW) [Dollár et al., 2010] or the HOG person detector [Dalal and Triggs, 2005]. A detected person is then described by a detection bounding box $\mathbf{b} = (x, y, width, height)$. For sliding window based person detectors we can

Figure 6.1.: Words associated with landmark locations. Small images on right: examples of image patches and ground truth landmark locations. Large images on left: words (visualized by the mean image of the corresponding image patches on the right, where all image patches were resized to 50x50 pixels) overlayed with associated ground truth landmark locations. Source: [Brauer et al., 2012]

compute a set of local features that have their keypoint location within the person bounding box. Thus, the input for the landmark localization step is in both cases (ISM based person detector or sliding window based person detector) a set of local features. But the main advantages – benefiting from the figure-background segmentation and saving of computation costs if the local features are provided by the ISM based person detector – vanish if we use a sliding window based person detector.

Fig. 6.1 visualizes the key idea of landmark localization. The small images on the right are sample image patches extracted from the KTH dataset[2]. The colored dots represent anatomical landmark locations as, e.g., head, right shoulder, etc. The large image on the left represents the word of a codebook that best matches to the image patches to the right. While the word itself is difficult to visualize since it is a 128 dimensional SURF descriptor vector, here we visualize it by the mean image of all image patches that were used to generate it during the codebook generation step. For each word of the codebook and each landmark a set of discrete locations is stored. E.g., the white dots in the top left image represent the typical head locations observed during training. These locations can be

---

[2]http://www.nada.kth.se/cvap/actions/

used to vote for the head location if the word is observed in a new person image for which we want to localize the landmarks.

While [Thomas et al., 2008] showed that detecting subparts of an rigid object is possible using the ISM, in [Müller and Arens, 2010] we showed that the local features of the person detection and tracking step can indeed be used to roughly estimate landmark locations on a person as well, i.e., subparts of a non-rigid object. In [Brauer et al., 2013a] we further showed that the landmark localization accuracy can significantly be increased when using alternative voting strategies which are described in the following sections.

6.2. Method

6.2.1. Reference point voting (RP-VOT)

6.2.1.1. Providing a reference point

For estimating the poses of persons in the image we assume a preceding step in which all persons are detected in the image. For an ISM based person detector [Leibe et al., 2008b] local features vote directly for the person center location which can be used as a reference point.

For bounding box based person detectors the center of the bounding box can be used as the person center – at least for upright standing persons that are fully visible in the image. Note that the bounding box center cannot be used as an estimate for the person center if the person is only partially visible in the image or is not standing upright (see Fig. 6.5 iii)).

In Fig. 6.2 we show an example track of the person center provided by an ISM based person tracker [Jüngling and Arens, 2009] on a 320 frame sequence of the UCF-ARG[3] person dataset. Such a reference point can be exploited during the landmark voting procedure to improve the landmark localization accuracy.

---

[3]http://crcv.ucf.edu/data/UCF-ARG.php

Figure 6.2.: Example track of person center. The red dots correspond to the person center – estimated by the ISM based person tracker introduced in [Jüngling and Arens, 2009] – at each frame of a sequence of 320 frames in total.

6.2.1.2. Key idea of RP-VOT

For the original ISM approach, features cast votes for the object center location (e.g., person center) independent of their location in the image. While there are no reference points in the initial person detection step, we have a different situation for the successive landmark localization step: we can try to make use of the person center as a reference point while voting in order to better place the votes for the landmarks. Fig. 6.3 depicts a visualization of the motivation for the usage of reference points. The same image structure can appear at different locations on the human body, or in other words: different parts of the human body can have the same appearance locally. Therefore it is problematic to let the corresponding words cast votes independent of their location on the human body.

In Fig. 6.3 the word #3 – a vertical bar like image structure – appears on the legs and the arms as well. During ISM training we record two example locations of this word relative to the person center. If we detect such a word in the application phase, we would cast two votes according to the original ISM voting strategy (ORIG-VOT). In Reference Point Voting (RP-VOT) we first compare the current word location (w_x, w_y) relative to the reference point (person center) with the word location relative to the

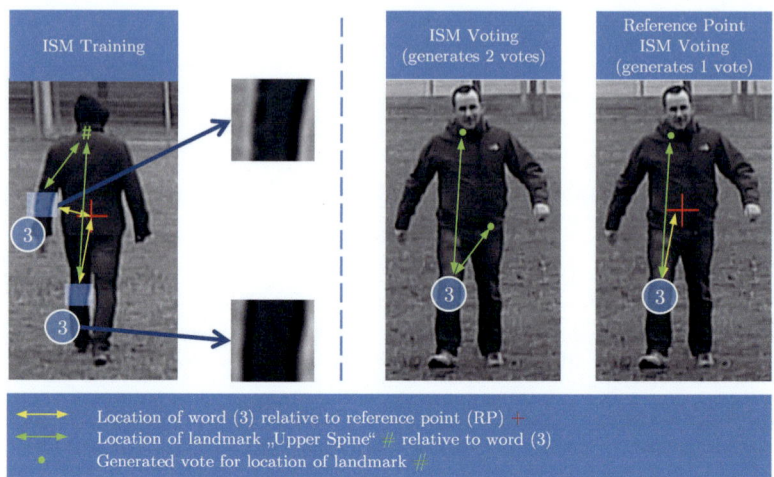

Figure 6.3.: Motivation for Reference Point Voting (RP-VOT). Left: similar instances of an image structure – here: a vertical bar-like structure – can appear at very different locations on the human body. Right: while original ISM voting procedure casts two votes (green dots) in this scenario, reference point ISM acts like a vote filter which only casts votes if the word location is similar to the training situation.

reference point during training and only cast a vote for the position of the landmark if the location is similar.

More precisely, we augment the observation vectors of each landmark ISM to $\mathbf{o} = (\Delta x, \Delta y, s, h_1, w_x, w_y)$ such that we also record where (w_x, w_y) we observed the word relative to the reference point and at which height h_1 (in pixels) we observed the person during training. The word location relative to the reference point during training (w_x, w_y) can then be represented in person height units $\mathbf{a} = (w_x/h_1, w_y/h_1)$. For a new image, $\mathbf{a}$ can be compared with the new detected word location relative to the reference point during voting (R_x, R_y) in person height units as well: $\mathbf{b} = ((f_x - R_x)/h_2, (f_y - R_y)/h_2)$, where h_2 is the estimated person height in the landmark localization phase (see Fig. 6.4). For each feature $\mathbf{f}$ and observation vector $\mathbf{o}_j$ we then cast a vote only, if the location difference is below some threshold, i.e., $\|\mathbf{a} - \mathbf{b}\|_2 < \theta$. Here we use $\theta = 0.05$ which

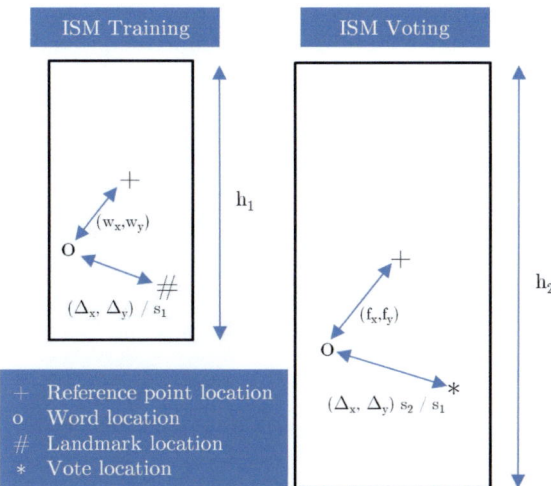

Figure 6.4.: Word location comparison during training and testing.
Schematic visualization of word location comparison during training and testing.
The word locations are normalized by an estimate of the person height to describe
the location invariant to the person's height.

means that we use the observation vector only if the distance between the
location of the word during training and testing is below 5% of the height
of the person.

6.2.1.3. Detecting a similar location

A first key issue for the RP-VOT voting strategy is the stability of the
reference point. It is important to choose a point on the human body
that can be detected as stable as possible, such that the location of the
word relative to this reference point is described as stable as possible. The
person center provided by an ISM based person detector is typically a
relative stable point. Nevertheless, as we will see later, the head is also a
good candidate for the reference point, compared to less appropriate points
as, e.g., the knees or elbows, since they cannot be localized comparably
reliable.

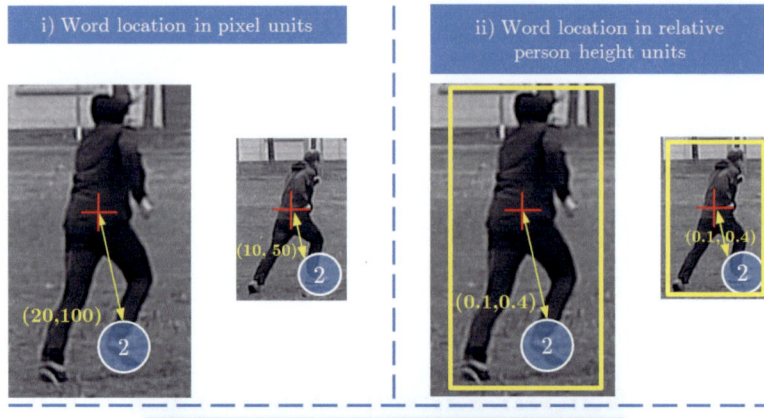

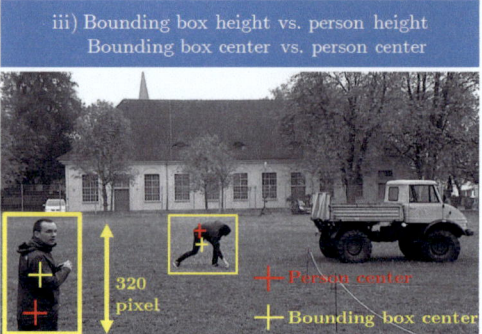

Figure 6.5.: Encoding word locations. i) pixel units are not invariant to person display height in image, ii) word location encoded in relative person height units is invariant to person display height, iii) simple estimation of person height based on bounding box height fails if person is only partially visible or bends down

A second issue is how to encode the location of the words relative to this reference point. Pixel unit coordinates are not appropriate since a person that will appear two times smaller compared to the training will show, e.g., its right foot also roughly two times nearer to the reference point in the image (see Fig. 6.5 i)). For this, it is better to encode the word locations in units relative to the projected height of the person. The question is then how to estimate the height of a person. For upright standing persons the bounding box height can be a simple estimate of the height of a person (see Fig. 6.5 ii)). But when considering also poses in which persons, e.g., bend down or images where the person is only partially visible in the image the bounding box height is not a good estimate for the actual height of a person. In Fig. 6.5 iii) the bounding box has a height of 320 pixels, but the true height of a person at this distance would correspond roughly to 600 pixels.

6.2.1.4. Person height estimation

Idea. The before mentioned drawbacks of using the bounding box height as a simple estimate for the person height motivate an alternative approach for estimating the height of a person (in pixels). The key idea is to use the set of local features that appear on the person to estimate its height using an ISM as well. I.e., the same local features that are associated with a person hypothesis, do not only vote for the landmark locations, but vote for the person height.

Even in situations where the lower body of the person is not visible or where the person bends down as shown in Fig. 6.5 iii) local features will appear on the visible parts of the person and should allow to estimate its height independently of the bounding box height which fails in such situations to estimate the height.

More precisely, we learn an ISM for person height estimation, where we collect for each word a list at which scales the word occurred together with the ground truth person height at this time. In the application phase, we then let the words vote for the height of the person in pixels, i.e., in this case the voting space is a 1D space.

Final height estimate. To determine a final height estimate, we compared two approaches. First, a simple averaging of all height votes. Second, a 1D Mean Shift maximum search using a 1D Gaussian kernel (with standard deviation $\sigma = 30$). In theory, the latter approach should be superior to the simple averaging approach in the case of multiple local maxima in the 1D voting space.

Evaluation. To test this approach for person height estimation, we used the 614 training person images (some showing multiple persons, 1234

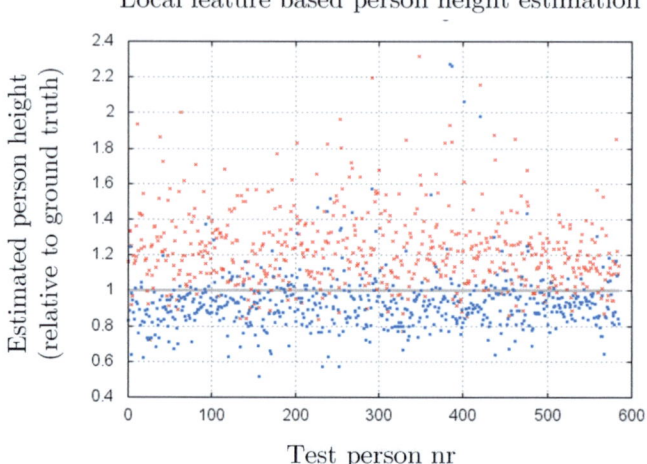

Figure 6.6.: Local feature based person height estimation. The same local
features that were used to detect the person and vote for landmark locations
are used to vote for the height of the person as well. Red dots: final estimated
person height by simple averaging of all height votes in the 1D voting space.
Blue: estimated person height by 1D Mean Shift maximum search in the 1D
voting space.

training persons in total) of the INRIA person dataset[4] which contains
images of persons with very different sizes. First a codebook was learned
using the dataset, then a person height ISM was trained. Evaluation was
done on the 288 test images of the test dataset (some showing multiple
persons, 585 test persons in total). Each feature within the person bounding
box of the test person is matched to a word of the codebook and then
casts (1D) votes for the person height.

Results. Fig. 6.6 shows the results. For each test person number (x-axis)
the estimated person height of both methods (red=averaging, blue=1D
Mean Shift maximum search) is plotted – normalized by the ground truth
height of the person. A value of, e.g., 1.5 means that the estimated person
height was 150% of the ground truth person size. At a first glance, the

---

[4]http://pascal.inrialpes.fr/data/human/

Figure 6.7.: Examples of person height ISM training/testing images.
Top: three example training images with detected SURF features within the
person bounding box from the INRIA training data set used to train the ISM
based person height estimator. Bottom: three example test images from the
INRIA test data set used to evaluate the person height estimator.

1D Mean Shift maximum search approach seems to yield better person
height estimates compared to the simple averaging approach. This first
impression is verified by a quantitative evaluation: the mean error of the
simple averaging approach is 23% (standard deviation: 21%), while the
mean error for the 1D Mean Shift maximum search is only 7% (standard
deviation: 17%). So, the 1D Mean Shift maximum search approach for
determining a final height estimate is significantly superior to a simple
averaging of all person height votes and can be used to estimate the height
of a person quite stable without relying on a bounding box height with an
average person height error of 7%.

6.2.2. Heuristic voting (H-VOT)

In the voting procedure of the original ISM (ORIG-VOT), features also
cast votes for object center locations outside the descriptor region of the
feature. Fig. 6.8 i) shows such an example situation. Two features –
here: corresponding each to word #8 – that appear on the object vote for
locations outside their corresponding descriptor region. Since the truck is

a rigid object with a fixed center, two of the generated votes are placed near to the true object center.

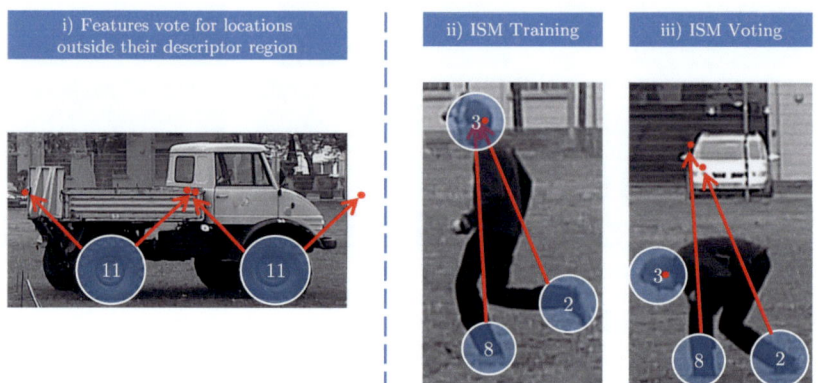

Figure 6.8.: Features casting votes outside their descriptor regions. i) two features cast votes for the truck (rigid object) center location. ii) head and word locations during ISM training iii) three features cast votes for the person (non-rigid object) head during ISM voting location.

While this approach makes sense for rigid objects as, e.g., a truck or a relative rigid part of a person as the torso, it makes less sense for non-rigid objects, especially if we want to vote for the location of a highly articulated point on that object. As an example see Fig. 6.8 iii). Three features that appear on the person cast votes for the head location according to learned feature to head locations observed in ISM training phase. Though due to the fact that a person is a non-rigid object, the head location relative to the features that appear on the feet (#2 and #8) can change dramatically, resulting in wrong votes for this example situation.

For this, we have to rethink whether each feature should vote for all landmark locations. In principle, when using a very large set of training examples, we could learn that there is strong spatial relationship between the occurrence of words #2 and #8 and the location of the head, since these image structures do not include image structures that occur on the head.

Nevertheless, in practice the number of training examples is often very limited and we observe only a real subset of possible head locations that co-occur with word #2 and #8. If we allow all words to vote for all landmarks, the votes of words that really show the landmark-corresponding parts of the human body can easily be dominated by words that do not contain direct image information about the corresponding body parts.

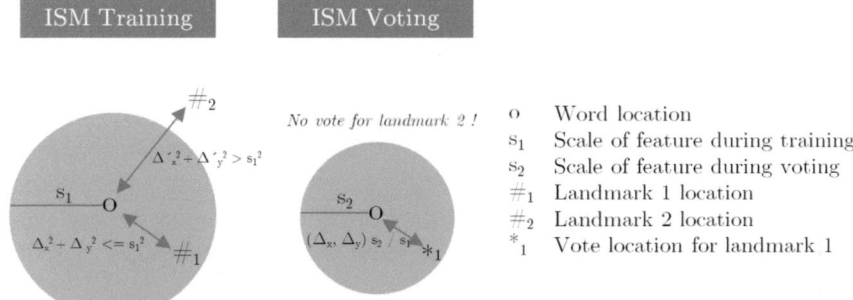

Figure 6.9.: Schematic description of H-VOT. Left: during training two observation vectors are recorded: $\mathbf{o}_1 = (\Delta_x, \Delta_y, s_1)$ for landmark 1, and $\mathbf{o}_2 = (\Delta_x', \Delta_y', s_2)$ for landmark 2. While landmark 1 is within the descriptor region of the feature, landmark 2 is not. Right: during voting, only observation vector $\mathbf{o}_1$ is used, since the descriptor region corresponding to the observed feature during training, included landmark 1, but not landmark 2.

A straightforward solution to this problem is to exploit the information for each observation vector, whether the landmark location was observed within the descriptor region of the corresponding detected feature during the ISM training step. In this case we know that the sub-image that corresponds to the feature shows the landmark (if it is not occluded). H-VOT only uses such observation vectors for which this was the case during training. This avoids the domination of wrong votes casted by features that do not directly show the corresponding landmark which we try to localize during the voting phase. In the above example, during the ISM training phase, we would record for the observation vector from word #3 to the head landmark that the head landmark was within the descriptor region, but not for both the observation vectors from word #2 and word #8 to the head landmark.

It is not necessary to augment the observation vectors by this information, since they already contain this information: the landmark location is within the descriptor region of the feature during training for an observation vector $\mathbf{o} = (\Delta x, \Delta y, s)$ if $\sqrt{\Delta x^2 + \Delta y^2} < s$ (see Fig. 6.9). Therefore – as an advantage of H-ISM compared to RP-ISM – the training procedure does not need to be adapted, but only the voting procedure that makes use the observation vectors stored.

6.2.3. Observation vector weighting voting (OW-VOT)

6.2.3.1. Key idea

As shown in eqn. (5.12) we can define the vote weights such that each feature will cast the same "vote mass" into the 3D vote space.

A problem of this normalization approach is that it introduces strong peaks in the 3D vote space for words w_1 that have stored only one or a few offset vectors $\mathbf{o} \in \mathcal{O}_{w_1}$ compared to words w_2 that can have stored a multiple of more offset vectors in their corresponding offset lists $\mathcal{O}_{w_2}$ compared to w_1. If word w_1 was observed only once during the ISM training and has therefore only one associated offset vector to the POI, a corresponding vote $\mathbf{v}^k$ will have a large weight $v_r^k = 1$ (in hard matching scenario), resulting in a peak in the 3D vote space. In contrast, a word w_2 that was observed 1000 times, will produce votes with small weights $v_r^k = 1/1000$. Such large differences in the number $|\mathcal{O}|$ of observed relative locations between a word and the POI heavily depend on the ISM training data. But these differences are common since we can not guarantee that each word of the codebook $\mathcal{C}$ will occur equally often. This problem is also mentioned in [Jüngling, 2011] (p.29).

An even worse problem is that the vote weights do not take into account that some words of a codebook $\mathcal{C}$ allow to localize the POI better than others. For the case of pose estimation, where we try to localize J different landmarks (POIs), we can further be confronted with scenarios in which one word w_1 is better suited to localize a POI l_1 compared to a word w_2, but at the same time, w_2 could better be suited to localize a POI l_2 compared to word w_1.

This problem can roughly be tackled by the heuristic presented in Section 6.2.2, where we restrict words to vote only for POIs which were within the descriptor region of the corresponding feature during training.

The key idea presented next is a more general approach to solve this problem. More precisely, we try to learn appropriate word and landmark specific vote weights such that the majority of the vote density is located near to the true POIs locations. This can be realized by learning a weight η_{wl} for each combination of a word w, POI l, and the k-th observation vector and modify the vote strength definition in eqn. (5.15) to:

$$v_r^{k,l} := \eta_{wlk} \frac{1}{|\mathcal{O}_w|} P(w|\mathbf{d}) \qquad (6.1)$$

6.2.3.2. Learning the weights

The idea for learning the weights is to give an observation vector a large weight if it successfully allows to detect landmarks and to give it a smaller weight if this is not the case.

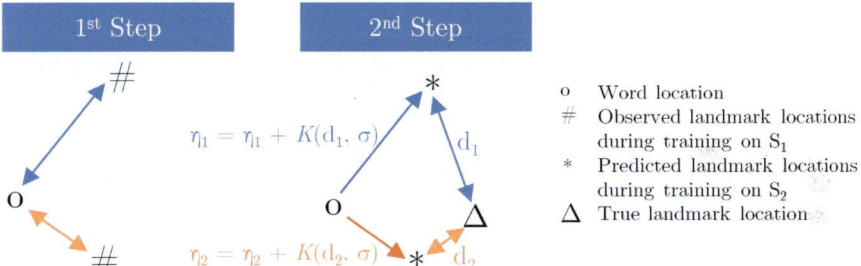

Figure 6.10.: Schematic description of OW-VOT. Left: during training on S_1 two observation vectors are recorded for a landmark. Right: during training on S_2 the true landmark location is visualized by $\triangle$. The orange observation vector predicts the true landmark location better than the blue observation vector ($d_2 < d_1$) and its weight η_2 will be increased larger compared to η_1, since $K(d_2, \sigma) > K(d_1, \sigma)$ (with a Gaussian kernel K).

For this, the training of the ISM is split into three steps. The training data S is divided into two equally sized subsets S_1 and S_2, comparable to the principle of cross-validation. The first set S_1 is used to collect the observation vectors $\mathbf{o}_j$. The second set S_2 is used to estimate the weights η_j.

In the first step, we collect observation vectors using S_1 as in original ISM training step.

In the second step of the learning procedure, we traverse S_2 and augment each observation vector $\mathbf{o} = (\Delta x, \Delta y, s, h_1, w_x, w_y, \eta)$ by a weight η which is initially set to 0. For each sample image contained in S_2 we compute local features $\mathbf{f}$, match them to words, and for each word iterate over all the observation vectors associated with the words. We compute the corresponding vote location $\mathbf{v}_2$ and compare it with the ground truth landmark location $\mathbf{t}$. The weight is increased by $K(\|\mathbf{v}_2 - \mathbf{t}\|_2, \sigma^2)$ where K is a Gaussian kernel with a standard deviation of $\sigma = 0.1h$, and h is the current projected person height. This ensures that observation weights are increased largely if the corresponding vote location is near to the ground truth landmark location. In contrast, for observation vectors that badly predict the landmark location $\mathbf{t}$, the weight is increased only little or near to 0 (see Fig. 6.10).

In the third step, each weight η_{wlk} is normalized by S_{wl}, i.e., $\eta_{wlk} \leftarrow \frac{\eta}{S_{wl}}$, where S_{wl} is the sum of all R observation weights of word w and landmark l, i.e., $S_{wl} = \sum_{k=1}^{R} \eta_{wlk}$. During voting the vote weight formula in eqn. (5.15) is then modified by the observation vectors weights, i.e., $v_r = \eta P(w_i|\mathbf{d})$. Note that the original vote weight normalization by $\frac{1}{|\mathcal{O}_w|}$ (compare eqn. (6.1)) – which was introduced in ORIG-VOT to give each feature the same weight when voting – can be skipped, since the new weights η are already normalized to sum up to 1 for a fixed word w_i and landmark j. Thus OW-VOT replaces the uniform weighting of all observation vectors by a relative weighting in dependence on their capability to predict a corresponding landmark location. The complete observation vector weight learning procedure is presented in algorithm 1 as pseudo code[5].

---

[5] While we learn a confidence weight for each single observation vector here, it might be interesting to introduce a similar approach on the word level. E.g., a straightforward idea is to measure the variance of observed landmark locations relative to a word and use this variance as a confidence measure for the landmark location prediction reliability of the word. Nevertheless, using a confidence weight for each single

6.2.4. Combined voting strategy (COMBI-VOT)

The voting strategies RP-VOT, H-VOT, and OW-VOT have the advantage that they can freely be combined. This allows to define the original voting strategy ORIG-VOT used in [Leibe et al., 2008b] together with these three new strategies in one compact generic voting algorithm where we can switch on or off each presented voting strategy in a flexible way. The corresponding pseudo-code is presented in algorithm 2.

RP-VOT and H-VOT mainly act as a filter for observation vectors. If used, each observation vector $\mathbf{o}$ associated with a word w and landmark l is checked during the voting procedure whether to be used or not. If RP-VOT is used (line 9), the location $\mathbf{a}$ of a feature during training is compared with the location $\mathbf{b}$ during voting and $\mathbf{o}$ is discarded, if the location difference is larger than some threshold θ. If H-VOT is used (line 17), the information is exploited, whether the landmark was within the descriptor region of the feature during training. If this was not the case, the corresponding observation vector $\mathbf{o}$ will not result in a vote neither. If H-VOT is used, we could in principle discard such observation vectors and do not store them in the set $\mathcal{O}_{wl}$ already during the ISM training phase, but storing them as well, preserves the option to turn on or off this filtering mechanism flexibly within the generic voting algorithm.

If OW-VOT is used (line 27), the resulting vote weight v_r will be computed according to eqn. (6.1) (which exploits the precomputed weight modifiers η_{wlk} from algorithm 1) and not according to eqn. (5.15) and observation vectors will have larger weight, if they have shown to be appropriate for predicting landmarks.

---

observation vector allows a finer graded weighting during voting than using a confidence weight for a word (which is associated with a large list of single observation vectors).

Algorithm 1 OW-VOT Training: learns an individual weight per observation vector

input: training data sets S_1, S_2, Codebook $\mathcal{C}$, number of landmarks L
output: one set of observation vectors $\mathcal{O}_{wl}$ for each combination of word w and landmark l, where each observation vector $\mathbf{o}_k = (\Delta x, \Delta y, s, h_1, w_x, w_y, \eta_{wlk}) \in \mathcal{O}_{wl}$ has a landmark prediction confidence weight η_{wlk}

```
 1:                                                    ▷ Step #1: collect observation vectors
 2:  for w=1 to |C| do                                                         ▷ for all words
 3:      for l=1 to L do                                                   ▷ for all landmarks
 4:          O_wl ← ∅
 5:          for j=1 to |S_1| do                      ▷ for all training images in training set S_1
 6:              compute local feature set F = {f_i = (f_x, f_y, f_s, d, w)} for image j
 7:              for i=1 to |F| do                                 ▷ for all detected features
 8:                  compile observation vector o = (Δx, Δy, s, h_1, w_x, w_y, 0)
 9:                  O_wl ← O_wl ∪ {o}
10:              end for
11:          end for
12:      end for
13:  end for
14:  for l=1 to L do                                          ▷ Step #2: compute weights
15:      for j=1 to |S_2| do
16:          compute local feature set F = {f_i = (f_x, f_y, f_s, d, w)} for image j
17:          for i=1 to |F| do                                 ▷ for all detected features
18:              for k=1 to |O_wl| do                    ▷ for all associated observations vectors
19:                  get observation vector o_k = (Δx, Δy, s, h_1, w_x, w_y, η_wlk)
20:                  compute vote location v_2^k given o according to eqn. (5.7)-(5.9)
21:                  get true landmark location t for landmark l
22:                  d = ||v_2^k − t||_2 ▷ compare vote location with true landmark location
23:                  η_wlk ← η_wlk + N(d, σ^2)                     ▷ increase observation weight
24:              end for
25:          end for
26:      end for
27:  end for
28:  for w=1 to |C| do                                        ▷ Step #3: normalize weights
29:      for l=1 to L do
30:          S ← 0
31:          for k=1 to |O_wl| do
32:              S ← S + η_wlk                         ▷ sum up all observation vector weights ...
33:          end for                                      ▷ ... for fixed word w and landmark l
34:          for k=1 to |O_wl| do                                                ▷ normalize
35:              η_wlk ← (1/S) η_wlk
36:          end for
37:      end for
38:  end for
39:
40:  return {O_wl : w = 1, ..., |C|, l = 1, ..., L}
```

Algorithm 2 COMBI-VOT: generates votes for location of landmark l

---

input: set of features $\mathcal{F} = \{\mathbf{f}_i = (f_x, f_y, f_s, \mathbf{d}, w)\}$ associated with a person hypothesis, id l of landmark to localize, ISM $\mathcal{I}_l = (\mathcal{P}_l, \mathcal{C})$, reference point (R_x, R_y), feature location similarity threshold $\theta = 0.05$, person height estimate h_2, boolean flags RP-VOT, H-VOT, OW-VOT
output: set of votes $\mathcal{V}_l$ for landmark l

1: $\mathcal{V}_l \leftarrow \varnothing$
2:
3: **for** $i=1$ to $|\mathcal{F}|$ **do**   ▷ for all detected features
4:     get next detected feature $\mathbf{f}_i = (f_x, f_y, f_s, \mathbf{d}, w)$
5:     **for** $k=1$ to $|\mathcal{O}_{wl}|$ **do** ▷ for all observations associated with word w / landmark l
6:
7:         get next observation vector $\mathbf{o}_k = (\Delta x, \Delta y, s, h_1, w_x, w_y, \eta_{wlk})$
8:
9:         **if** RP-VOT **then**
10:             $\mathbf{a} = (w_x/h_1, w_y/h_1)$
11:             $\mathbf{b} = ((f_x - R_x)/h_2, (f_y - R_y)/h_2)$
12:             **if** $\|\mathbf{a} - \mathbf{b}\|_2 > \theta$ **then**   ▷ feature location similar to training?
13:                 continue   ▷ do not use observation vector
14:             **end if**
15:         **end if**
16:
17:         **if** H-VOT **then**
18:             **if** $\sqrt{\Delta x^2 + \Delta y^2} > s$ **then**   ▷ landmark within descriptor region?
19:                 continue   ▷ do not use observation vector
20:             **end if**
21:         **end if**
22:
23:         $v_s = f_s/s$ ▷ use observation vector
24:         $v_x = f_x + v_s \Delta x$
25:         $v_y = f_y + v_s \Delta y$
26:
27:         **if** OW-VOT **then**
28:             $v_r = \eta_{wlk} P(w|\mathbf{d})$ ▷ use observation vector weights from Section 6.2.3.2
29:         **else**
30:             $v_r = \frac{1}{|\mathcal{O}_w|} P(w|\mathbf{d})$ ▷ use ORIG-VOT vote weight according to eqn. (5.15)
31:         **end if**
32:
33:         generate vote $\mathbf{v} = (v_r, v_x, v_y, v_s)$ for landmark l
34:         $\mathcal{V}_l \leftarrow \mathcal{V}_l \cup \{\mathbf{v}\}$
35:
36:     **end for**
37: **end for**
38:
39: **return** $\mathcal{V}_l$

6.2.5. Gaussian Mixture Model voting (GMM-VOT)

The above presented voting strategies represent the probability distribution P_{wl} that encode where the landmark l can be found relative to word w in a non-parametric manner as in [Leibe et al., 2008b], namely by a set of discrete observation vectors: for each P_{wl} we store a set $\mathcal{O}_{wl}$ of observed locations (and scales) of the landmark l relative to word w.

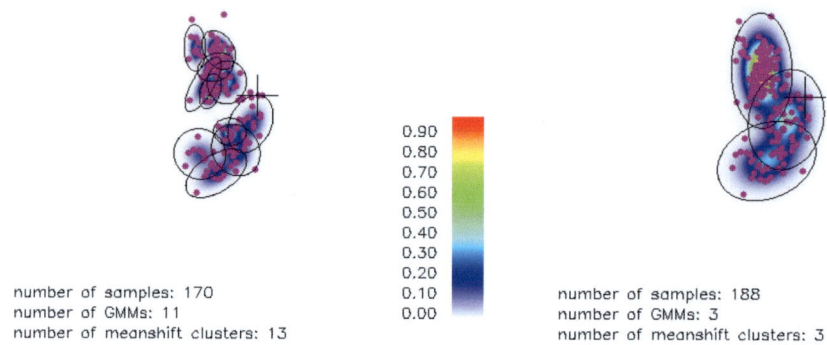

```
0.90
0.80
0.70
0.60
0.50
0.40
0.30
0.20
0.10
0.00
```

number of samples: 170
number of GMMs: 11
number of meanshift clusters: 13

number of samples: 188
number of GMMs: 3
number of meanshift clusters: 3

Figure 6.11.: Examples of learned GMMs. Cross: word location. Purple dots: observed (x, y) locations of the landmark. Black ellipses: Gaussians. Left: Resulting GMM for representing the landmark locations if 11 Gaussians are used[6]. Right: Resulting GMM if 3 Gaussians are used. Source: [Dobler, 2012a]

While this is a straightforward approach to represent the P_{wl} probability distributions, it has one drawback: for large training data sets where millions of observation vectors **o** can be recorded, these lists can get very large. Further, during the voting procedure, we have to transform each observation vector **o** into a vote **v** – the loop in algorithm 2 / line 5 runs over all observation vectors – and this can result in a bottleneck regarding the computation time if $|\mathcal{O}_{wl}|$ is large.

In order to represent the landmark location probabilities P_{wl} in a much more compact way, one could therefore represent the distributions of the

---

[6]The number of Gaussians to use within the GMM is determined using Mean-shift clustering. While there are 13 resulting clusters found for the depicted samples, only 11 Gaussians are used for the GMM, since 2 samples are isolated in an individual cluster each and cannot be used for computing a covariance matrix (singularity case).

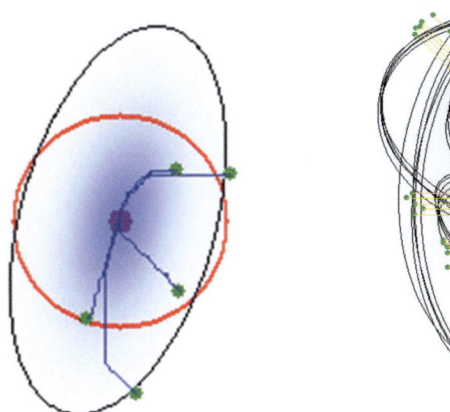

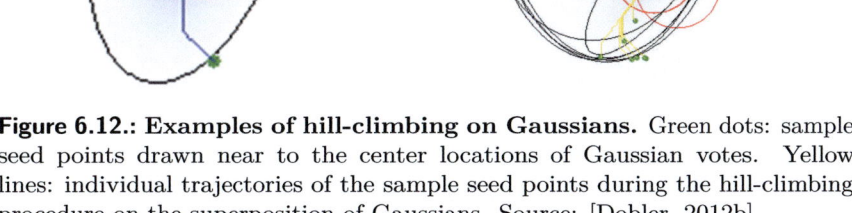

Figure 6.12.: Examples of hill-climbing on Gaussians. Green dots: sample seed points drawn near to the center locations of Gaussian votes. Yellow lines: individual trajectories of the sample seed points during the hill-climbing procedure on the superposition of Gaussians. Source: [Dobler, 2012b]

3D observation location samples $(\Delta x, \Delta y, s)$ using a Gaussian Mixture Model (GMM), i.e., instead of a set of discrete observation vectors $\mathcal{O}_{wl}$, a GMM $\mathcal{M} = \sum_i^N \omega_i \mathcal{N}(\mu_i, \Sigma_i)$ represents where we can find the landmark and at which scale, where μ_i represents the 3D location (x, y, s) of the i-th Gaussian and Σ_i is its corresponding 3x3 covariance matrix.

In [Dobler, 2012a][7] this idea was picked up. Though instead of modeling the distribution in 3D (x, y, s) space, only its projection in (x, y) image space was modeled by a GMM, i.e., μ_i represents the 2D location (x, y) of the i-th Gaussian and Σ_i is its corresponding 2x2 covariance matrix.

Fig. 6.11 shows an example where a large set of observed landmark locations (purple dots) is represented by a GMM with 11 components (left), and by a GMM with 3 Gaussians (right), i.e., the large list of individual observations is compressed to a short list of GMM parameters (number of Gaussians, 2D location of each Gaussian, 2x2 covariance matrix for each Gaussian).

---

[7]Diploma thesis supervised by the author of this thesis at Fraunhofer IOSB.

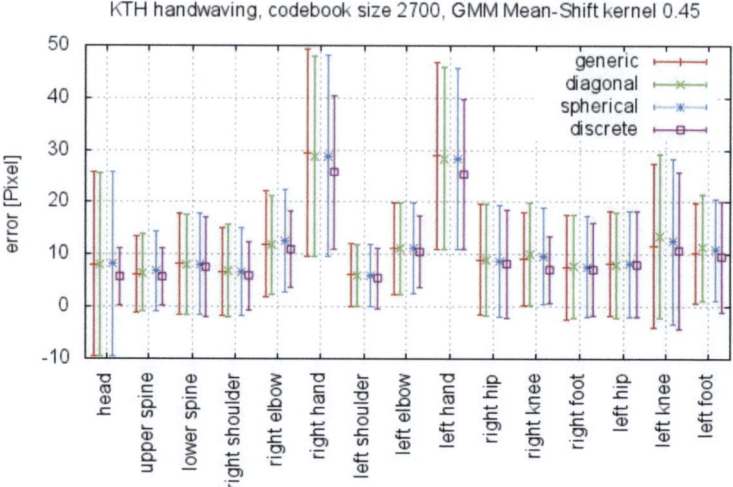

Figure 6.13.: Results for landmark localization using GMM-VOT. For each landmark the average localization error and its standard deviation is plotted depending on the voting strategy used: discrete voting vs. GMM-VOT with spherical, diagonal, and generic covariance matrices for the Gaussians. Source: [Dobler, 2012a]

For transforming the sample distributions of observed landmark locations (x, y) into GMMs, first the number of Gaussians for each GMM has to be determined. For this, in [Dobler, 2012a] Mean-Shift clustering was used to cluster the samples (purple dots). The resulting number of generated clusters was then used to set the number N of Gaussians in the corresponding GMM representation of these samples (see Fig. 6.11). Then the EM algorithm [Dempster et al., 1977] is used to learn the GMM parameters, i.e., determine the μ_i and Σ_i. During voting, instead of discrete votes, Gaussians are casted as votes and the final probability distribution for the landmarks are the result of the superposition of the Gaussians casted. For determining final potential landmark locations, sample seed points were drawn from the Gaussian votes (green dots in Fig. 6.12) – i.e., near potential local maxima – and for each seed point a hill-climbing procedure was started to determine local maxima, which were considered as final landmark location candidates.

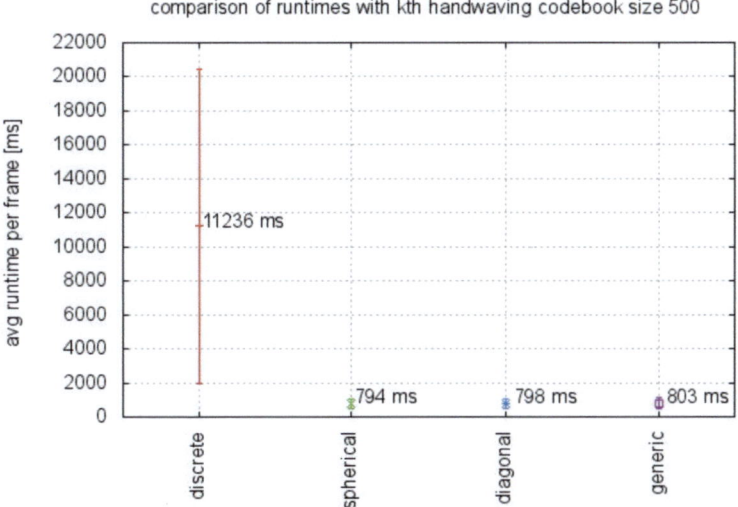

Figure 6.14.: Landmark localization computation time of GMM-VOT.
The GMM-VOT voting strategies (using spherical, diagonal, and generic
covariance matrices for the Gaussians) that cast Gaussians are much faster
than the original ISM voting strategy that casts discrete votes. Source: [Dobler,
2012a]

For the evaluation of the GMM-VOT strategy, the KTH[8] and the UMPM
dataset were used. For each landmark the location candidate with the
highest probability was chosen and the Euclidean distance (measured in
pixels) to the corresponding ground truth landmark location was computed.
Three different subtypes of GMM models were evaluated depending on
which type of covariance matrix was allowed for a single Gaussian (spherical,
diagonal, and generic covariance matrix). Fig. 6.13 shows the error of
landmark localization for the KTH dataset: the GMM-VOT strategy that
casts Gaussians as votes, results in a nearly identical landmark localization
accuracy as when using the original ISM voting that casts discrete votes.
Fig. 6.14 further compares the mean and standard deviations of runtimes
of the original ISM voting strategy with the GMM-VOT strategies. The
speed-up for the average runtime is in the order of 14 since we do not

---

[8]http://www.nada.kth.se/cvap/actions/

need to cast a large set of discrete votes stored with each word. This number further increases linearly with the number of landmark locations observed during training, i.e., the training data size. Instead, in GMM-VOT a few Gaussians are casted that represent the typical locations of the landmark relative to a word. Further, the standard deviation of the runtimes is reduced significantly: while in the original ISM voting the number of generated votes can vary dramatically depending on the set of words that are detected – since the number of sample locations that are stored with each word can vary significantly from word to word – there is not such a large variety of number of Gaussians stored with each word, since sets of large sample landmark locations recorded during ISM training are compressed to a few Gaussians in the GMM representation.

The main result from these experiments can be summarized as follows: voting becomes much more faster with Gaussians and we do not loose landmark location accuracy. The same idea – using Gaussians to represent the landmark locations and to vote – was tried in [Lehmann et al., 2011] with some differences in determining the number of mixture components and searching local maxima. Interestingly, the authors came to exactly the same conclusion: "[...] that the GMM makes it possible to speed up the search with no, or only little loss of accuracy" ([Lehmann et al., 2011], section 3).

Since GMM-VOT does not improve the landmark localization accuracy but is only an option to speed up the voting procedure, we do not include it in the evaluation of the landmark localization accuracy of the different voting strategies in the following.

6.3. Evaluation

6.3.1. Experiments conducted

Evaluation datasets

For comparing the new voting strategies with the original ISM voting strategy we need an evaluation dataset that provides ground truth 2D landmark locations. These can be generated automatically for all datasets that provide 3D motion capture data and additionally camera calibration data such that it is possible to project the 3D landmarks into the image. Since we further want natural appearing test persons and we would like to test the landmark localization in cases of partial occlusions of persons, from the list of publicly available evaluation datasets in Chapter 3 there is only one dataset that fulfills all these three requirements, namely the UMPM dataset.

The large number of UMPM video sequences allows to define a rich set of experiments with which we can test the landmark localization accuracy in different training and testing conditions. An overview of all 40 experiments conducted on the UMPM dataset is shown in Table 6.1.

Since the HumanEva dataset is used by the majority of authors reporting results for monocular HPE, we also include 24 further experiments (experiments 41-64) on the HumanEva dataset which are listed in Table 6.2.

Example experiment

E.g., in exp. 10 we first train a landmark localizer using the precomputed generic codebook and extract person images and ground truth 2D poses from the "p2 grab 1" and "p3 grab 1" video sequence showing four persons walking around a table and grabbing different objects from it (actually 5 persons are shown, but motion capture data is only provided for 4 persons in the two videos). While learning we observe typically about 1 to 3 million locations of a landmark relative to a word. This large number can be explained by the fact that we have 15 landmarks in our body model and typically about 30 features per person detection. Therefore, we observe typically about $30 \cdot 15 = 450$ locations of a landmark relative to a word already for one frame and a single training video approximately consist of 3000 frames. In exp. 10 we then test the landmark localization performance using the sequence "p1 grab 3" showing another person different from the 4 persons in the training phase.

The "experiment code", e.g., "U-chair-2-1", encodes the experiment settings briefly using the encoding:
[codebook used]-[action class]-[number of training persons]-[number of test persons]

Exp No.	Exp code	Training sequences	N	Test sequence	N
01	U-chair-2-1	p2 chair1	2	p1 chair2	1
02	G-chair-2-1	p2 chair1	2	p1 chair2	1
03	U-chair-4-1	p2 chair1/p3 chair1	4	p1 chair2	1
04	G-chair-4-1	p2 chair1/p3 chair1	4	p1 chair2	1
05	U-chair-3-2	p1 chair2/p3 chair1	3	p2 chair1	2
06	G-chair-3-2	p1 chair2/p3 chair1	3	p2 chair1	2
07	U-grab-2-1	p2 grab1	2	p1 grab3	1
08	G-grab-2-1	p2 grab1	2	p1 grab3	1
09	U-grab-4-1	p2 grab1/p3 grab1	4	p1 grab3	1
10	G-grab-4-1	p2 grab1/p3 grab1	4	p1 grab3	1
11	U-grab-3-2	p1 grab3/p3 grab1	3	p2 grab1	2
12	G-grab-3-2	p1 grab3/p3 grab1	3	p2 grab1	2
13	U-ball-2-2	p3 ball2	2	p2 ball1	2
14	G-ball-2-2	p3 ball2	2	p2 ball1	2
15	U-free-2-2	p3 free1	2	p2 free1	2
16	G-free-2-2	p3 free1	2	p2 free1	2
17	U-free-4-2	p3 free1/p3 free11	4	p2 free1	2
18	G-free-4-2	p3 free1/p3 free11	4	p2 free1	2
19	U-ortho-2-1	p2 orthosyn1	2	p1 orthosyn1	1
20	G-ortho-2-1	p2 orthosyn1	2	p1 orthosyn1	1
21	U-ortho-4-1	p2 orthosyn1/p3 orthosyn11	4	p1 orthosyn1	1
22	G-ortho-4-1	p2 orthosyn1/p3 orthosyn11	4	p1 orthosyn1	1
23	U-ortho-3-2	p1 orthosyn1/p3 orthosyn11	3	p2 orthosyn1	2
24	G-ortho-3-2	p1 orthosyn1/p3 orthosyn11	3	p2 orthosyn1	2
25	U-table-2-1	p2 table1	2	p1 table2	1
26	G-table-2-1	p2 table1	2	p1 table2	1
27	U-table-4-1	p2 table1/p3 table11	4	p1 table2	1
28	G-table-4-1	p2 table1/p3 table11	4	p1 table2	1
29	U-table-3-2	p1 table2/p3 table11	3	p2 table1	2
30	G-table-3-2	p1 table2/p3 table11	3	p2 table1	2
31	U-tria-2-1	p3 triangle1	2	p1 triangle1	1
32	G-tria-2-1	p3 triangle1	2	p1 triangle1	1
33	U-tria-4-1	p3 triangle1/p3 triangle11	4	p1 triangle1	1
34	G-tria-4-1	p3 triangle1/p3 triangle11	4	p1 triangle1	1
35	U-tria-3-2	p1 triangle1/p3 triangle11	3	p3 triangle1	2
36	G-tria-3-2	p1 triangle1/p3 triangle11	3	p3 triangle1	2
37	U-meet-2-2	p3 meet1	2	p3 meet2	2
38	G-meet-2-2	p3 meet1	2	p3 meet2	2
39	U-meet-4-2	p3 meet1 + p3 meet11	4	p3 meet2	2
40	G-meet-4-2	p3 meet1 + p3 meet11	4	p3 meet2	2

Table 6.1.: Definition of UMPM experiments. 40 different experiments are conducted on the UMPM dataset for a comparative evaluation of the voting strategies. N specifies the number of persons in the training and test sequences. If the experiment code starts with U, the UMPM codebook is used, else the generic codebook.

To give a better impression of the training and test data used, we show one randomly selected example image from each training and test sequence in Appendix A.

Exp No.	Exp code	Training sequences	N	Test sequence	N
41	H-walk-1-1	S2 walk	1	S1 walk	1
42	G-walk-1-1	S2 walk	1	S1 walk	1
43	H-walk-2-1	S2 walk, S3 walk	2	S1 walk	1
44	G-walk-2-1	S2 walk, S3 walk	2	S1 walk	1
45	H-box-1-1	S2 box	1	S1 box	1
46	G-box-1-1	S2 box	1	S1 box	1
47	H-box-2-1	S2 box, S3 box	2	S1 box	1
48	G-box-2-1	S2 box, S3 box	2	S1 box	1
49	H-walk-1-1	S1 walk	1	S2 walk	1
50	G-walk-1-1	S1 walk	1	S2 walk	1
51	H-walk-2-1	S1 walk, S3 walk	2	S2 walk	1
52	G-walk-2-1	S1 walk, S3 walk	2	S2 walk	1
53	H-box-1-1	S1 box	1	S2 box	1
54	G-box-1-1	S1 box	1	S2 box	1
55	H-box-2-1	S1 box, S3 box	2	S2 box	1
56	G-box-2-1	S1 box, S3 box	2	S2 box	1
57	H-walk-1-1	S1 walk	1	S3 walk	1
58	G-walk-1-1	S1 walk	1	S3 walk	1
59	H-walk-2-1	S1 walk, S2 walk	2	S3 walk	1
60	G-walk-2-1	S1 walk, S2 walk	2	S3 walk	1
61	H-box-1-1	S1 box	1	S3 box	1
62	G-box-1-1	S1 box	1	S3 box	1
63	H-box-2-1	S1 box, S2 box	2	S3 box	1
64	G-box-2-1	S1 box, S2 box	2	S3 box	1

Table 6.2.: Definition of HumanEva experiments. 24 experiments are conducted on the HumanEva dataset for a comparative evaluation of the voting strategies. N specifies the number of persons in the training and test sequences. If the experiment code starts with H, the HumanEva codebook is used, else the generic codebook.

Input/Output for each experiment

For the person input image provided to the landmark localizer we use the person bounding box computed by the minimal bounding box that surrounds all 2D ground truth landmarks. We explicitly do not use person bounding boxes from a person detector here since we want to test the landmark localization performance independently from the chosen person detector. For the complete image SURF features are sampled and all features are used for the landmark localization step for which the keypoint center is within the person bounding box. This set of local features is the input for the landmark localizer, while the output is a set of votes for each of 15 anatomical landmarks. For RP-VOT as person height estimate the height of the bounding box is used and as reference point the bounding box center is used.

The landmark vote generation experiments are designed in order to evaluate the influence of five different aspects (I-V):

I. Voting strategy

Each experiment is conducted with each of the five voting strategies (ORIG, RP, H, OW, COMBI) in order to compare the landmark localization accuracy in dependence of the selected vote generation mechanism.

II. Codebooks

The landmark localization in this thesis matches local features to prototypes (words) stored in a codebook.

To test the influence of this codebook on the overall performance, three different codebooks were used for the experiments: two application specific codebooks and one generic codebook. While the application specific codebooks were generated on images from the same dataset we use for testing (UMPM and HumanEva dataset), the generic codebook was trained on another dataset (ETHZ Pedestrian dataset).

For the generation of the (application specific) UMPM codebook 178 of the 272 UMPM video sequences were used. All video sequences were skipped where persons occurred on which we later tested in the experiments. This ensures, that we do not include image structures in the codebook generation process on which the body part localization is later tested. SURF keypoints were computed for each video frame using the OpenCV library[9]. From 1000 frames showing 1747 persons we collected 109458 descriptor vectors

---

[9]http://opencv.org/

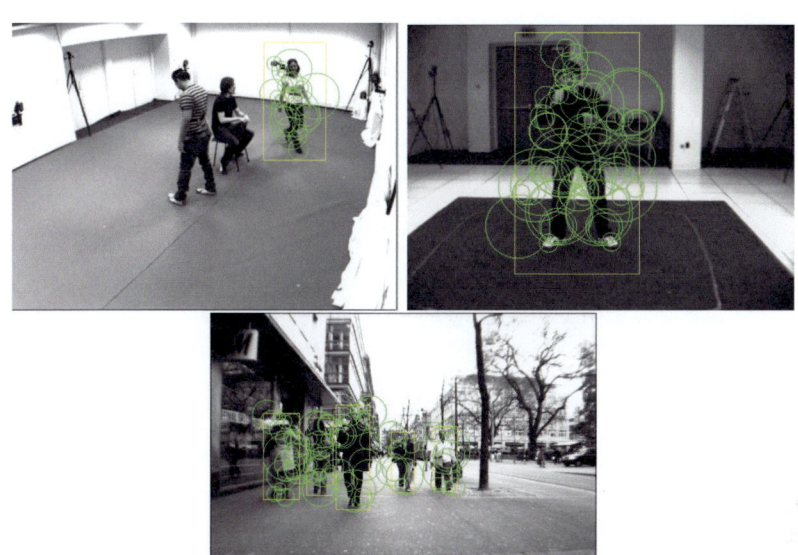

Figure 6.15.: Example images used for codebook generation. Left: example image used for UMPM codebook generation and detected SURF features with keypoint center within one of ground truth person bounding boxes. Right: example image used for generic codebook generation with SURF features within all ground truth person bounding boxes.

of keypoints that had their center location within a person bounding box. The 128 dimensional descriptor vectors were clustered using Reciprocal Nearest Neighbor (RNN) clustering. The resulting codebook has a size of 1315 clusters (codewords).

The HumanEva codebook was generated using 6 video sequences of walking and boxing persons. Since the dataset is small, it was not possible to skip persons on which we later tested in the experiments. From 55 frames showing 3 different persons 4056 SURF descriptor vectors were collected and clustered using RNN clustering into a codebook of size 301.

The generic codebook was generated using the ETHZ Pedestrian dataset[10] used in [Ess et al., 2008]. It shows hundreds of different persons in street scenes. From 5346 frames showing 17721 persons we computed SURF keypoints again, collected 56234 descriptor vectors and clustered these vectors using RNN clustering. The resulting codebook has a size of 843 codewords[11].

The main difference between the application specific codebooks and the generic codebook is that the UMPM and HumanEva codebooks contain image structures from similar poses that will appear during evaluation while the generic codebook does not. Further, although there is a larger number of different persons in the dataset used for the generation of the generic codebook, the persons in the street scenes typically do not show much variance in their poses.

III. Number of persons in training data

The influence of the number of different persons in the training data on the performance of the landmark localization is another important aspect which we want to test. For this we train in some experiments on a single person (e.g., exps. 41+42), two persons (e.g., exps. 01+02), three persons (e.g., exps. 05+06), or four persons (e.g., exps. 03+04).

IV. Occlusion cases

Landmark localization while body parts are occluded is an important issue for real-world scenarios. Note that the training data used in the UMPM experiments 01-40 also contain image structures resulting from occlusions of two or three persons. The first reason to include image structures from occlusion cases into the ISM training is that the number of UMPM video sequences where only one person is present is very small. More precisely, there is only one subject for 1-person-videos. We use these video sequences already for testing to have test videos where a single person is present, i.e., never occluded. Thus, video sequences where only one subject is present

---

[10]http://www.vision.ee.ethz.ch/~aess/dataset/

[11]For all three codebooks (UMPM, HumanEva, generic) the same clustering compactness threshold was used.

and is therefore not occluded by other persons, is not available for training. The second and more important reason is, that we explicitly want to train on image structures resulting from occlusion cases, in order to be able to estimate landmark locations in such cases as well.

E.g., in experiments 01-04 only one person is visible in the test data, i.e., no occlusions of this person by other persons are present in the test data. In experiments 05-06 there are two persons visible in the test data which occlude each other frequently for some time.

Note that motion capture data is provided for each sequence only for a maximum of two persons due to restrictions of the landmark based motion capture system used by the UMPM dataset group. This means that even though there are four and three person sequences as, e.g., "p3 chair 1" (3 persons), motion capture data is only available for two persons and therefore we can retrieve ground truth 2D training and testing poses for the body landmark localizer only for two persons for such sequences.

For the HumanEva dataset there are no sequences where persons are occluded.

V. Different action classes

Different actions are present in the UMPM experiments as walking and sitting down on a chair (01-06), walking around a table and grabbing objects from a table (07-12), two persons playing with a ball (13-14), different "free" poses, e.g., bending down (15-18), arm choreographies (19-24), sitting and laying down on a table (25-30), walking in a triangle (31-36), and meeting another person and handshaking (37-40). The HumanEva experiments (41-64) include poses from two different action classes: walking and boxing. While the walking poses repeat periodically, the boxing poses do not.

Using different actions in the experiments allows to see whether there are differences in the landmark localization performance depending on the action class.

6.3.2. Evaluation measures

A good landmark voting strategy that allows to localize the landmarks reliably should cast the majority of its votes near to the true landmark locations. Further, the vote distributions should be uni-modal and monotonically decreasing to the periphery to allow an optimizer to find the global maximum easily. Instead of relying on only one evaluation measure, we introduce three different evaluation measures (α, β, γ) in order to evaluate to which degree this is fulfilled by the different voting strategies ORIG-VOT, RP-VOT, H-VOT, OW-VOT and COMBI-VOT:

$$\alpha = \frac{1}{W} \sum_{\mathbf{v} \in \mathcal{V}} v_r \delta_r(\|\mathbf{v}_2 - \mathbf{t}\|_2) \text{ with } \delta_r(x) = \begin{cases} 1 & , x \leq r \\ 0 & , x > r \end{cases} \tag{6.2}$$

$$\beta = \frac{1}{W} \sum_{\mathbf{v} \in \mathcal{V}} \frac{v_r}{h} \|\mathbf{v}_2 - \mathbf{t}\|_2 \tag{6.3}$$

$$\gamma(d) = \frac{1}{|X_d|} \sum_{(d,\rho(\mathbf{l})) \in X_d} \rho(\mathbf{l}) \tag{6.4}$$

$$\rho(\mathbf{l}) = \frac{1}{W\lambda(s)} \sum_{\mathbf{v} \in \mathcal{V}} v_r K(\|\mathbf{v}_2 - \mathbf{l}\|_2) \tag{6.5}$$

α: **Ratio of correct votes.** α measures the ratio of correct vs. total votes casted, weighted by the corresponding vote weights. All votes within a circle of radius r around the ground truth location $\mathbf{t}$ are considered as correct. Here we use $r = 0.1h$, where h is the person height measured in pixels. h can be estimated from the stick figure ground truth 2D pose by $h = (L_l + L_r)/2 + S + N$, where L_l and L_r are the lengths of the legs, S is the length of the spine and N is the length from the neck to the head. $W = \sum_{v \in \mathcal{V}} v_r$ is the sum of all vote weights.

β: **Mean distance of votes to landmark.** β measures the mean distance of the votes to the true landmark location, again weighted by the vote weights, such that the distance (to the true location) of a vote with a large weight has a higher impact on the overall measure than a distance of a vote with a small weight. The distance is computed in relative person height units by dividing through h. Note that while for α large values indicate a good landmark localization accuracy, for β small values mean a good landmark localization performance.

γ: Average vote density at different distances. γ measures the average vote density in dependence of the distance to the true landmark location. For this we sample 2D vote space locations $l = (x, y)$ on a regular grid and compute the density of the votes at these locations using a (weighted) kernel density estimator $\rho(l)$, where we use a Gaussian kernel K. For each vote density sample location l, we then compute the distance d of the corresponding 2D vote location v_2 to the true landmark location t in person height units, i.e., $d = \|v_2 - t\|/h$, and add a new sample $x = (d, \rho(l))$ of this distance / vote density example pair to a histogram of 100 distance bins X_d ($d = 0.01n$, $0 \leq n \leq 100$).

Distances are measured explicitly not in pixels for all 3 evaluation measures, but in relative person height units, since pixel distances between votes and true landmark locations will strongly depend on the distance of the person to the camera. E.g., a pixel distance of 10 pixels can be considered as a large error if the person has a height of only 30 pixels display size in the camera image, compared to a display person size of 300 pixels, where a distance of 10 pixels between the vote and the true landmark location can be considered as a smaller error.

Note that the output of the landmark localization step is not a final unique 2D location for each landmark, but a set of votes that are a representation of possible landmark locations based on the corresponding image evidence in the form of words. A final unique 3D and 2D pose, and thereby a single unique 2D location for each landmark as well, is estimated by the pose estimator described in Chapter 7. The uncertainty about the landmark location cannot be resolved during this early step, where votes are generated independently for each landmark location. During the 2D and 3D pose estimation step, the uncertainty about the exact location of each landmark can be resolved much better by considering an overall matching score between a pose hypothesis and all landmark vote distributions.

6.3.3. Quantitative results

All 64 experiments defined in Section 6.3.1 were conducted with each of the five voting strategies independently (resulting in a total of 64x5=320 evaluation experiments conducted).

The results for evaluation measures α and β are shown for the UMPM experiments in and Table 6.4 and for the HumanEva experiments in Table 6.5 and Table 6.6.

Result example

E.g., in exp. 14, where a generic codebook was used to train 15 landmark localization ISMs using 2 training persons showing ball playing poses and where we tested on 2 other persons, only 3.9% of the votes casted by ORIG-VOT were correct, while COMBI-VOT generated 29.2% correct votes. The average (vote weight weighted) distance of the votes to the true landmark location was 48.6% for ORIG-VOT, while it was only 14.5% of the person height for COMBI-VOT. In the last row we show averages for each voting strategy, where we averaged over all 40 UMPM and 24 HumanEva experiments respectively conducted for the corresponding voting strategy.

I. Significantly better landmark localization with new voting strategies

The original voting strategy ORIG-VOT by [Leibe et al., 2008b] generates only 4.6% correct votes (correct according to evaluation measure α) on the UMPM dataset and only 8.2% correct votes on the HumanEva dataset for the task of anatomical landmark localization, i.e., votes that are within a radius of 10% of the person height around the true landmark location. This small percentage shows that the original voting strategy is not appropriate for an accurate localization of anatomical landmarks. All new voting strategies produce more correct votes on both the UMPM and the HumanEva dataset – especially COMBI-VOT, which produces 33.3% correct votes on the UMPM dataset and even 43.3% correct votes on the HumanEva dataset.

Exp No.	Exp code	α				
		ORIG	RP	H	OW	COMBI
01	U-chair-2-1	4.3	14.5	10.0	5.5	28.3
02	G-chair-2-1	4.0	15.0	9.4	5.2	29.6
03	U-chair-4-1	3.9	13.5	8.5	5.1	26.8
04	G-chair-4-1	3.5	14.2	7.9	4.8	27.8
05	U-chair-3-2	4.2	14.6	9.3	5.4	29.9
06	G-chair-3-2	3.6	14.1	8.1	4.9	29.3
07	U-grab-2-1	6.0	18.8	13.2	7.7	38.6
08	G-grab-2-1	6.0	18.8	13.2	7.7	38.6
09	U-grab-4-1	5.4	18.1	11.1	7.1	37.0
10	G-grab-4-1	4.8	18.7	10.1	6.4	37.7
11	U-grab-3-2	4.7	16.9	10.2	6.0	34.1
12	G-grab-3-2	4.2	16.6	9.1	5.4	33.9
13	U-ball-2-2	4.7	15.6	9.5	5.9	29.5
14	G-ball-2-2	3.9	15.2	7.7	5.0	29.2
15	U-free-2-2	4.0	14.1	8.8	5.4	29.6
16	G-free-2-2	3.5	13.8	7.5	4.7	29.2
17	U-free-4-2	4.1	14.3	9.4	5.6	30.8
18	G-free-4-2	3.5	13.9	7.8	4.8	30.0
19	U-ortho-2-1	8.7	23.9	20.1	11.8	48.0
20	G-ortho-2-1	7.2	23.3	16.6	9.8	46.2
21	U-ortho-4-1	8.5	23.9	19.6	11.9	47.2
22	G-ortho-4-1	6.8	23.3	15.5	9.8	45.3
23	U-ortho-3-2	3.2	14.2	8.3	4.4	28.7
24	G-ortho-3-2	2.8	13.6	6.9	3.8	28.0
25	U-table-2-1	3.7	13.2	9.0	4.9	27.9
26	G-table-2-1	3.3	13.0	8.0	4.4	27.6
27	U-table-4-1	3.4	13.1	8.2	4.7	27.5
28	G-table-4-1	2.9	12.8	7.2	4.1	27.4
29	U-table-3-2	3.4	13.7	8.5	4.7	28.5
30	G-table-3-2	3.0	13.7	7.4	4.2	28.0
31	U-tria-2-1	4.7	17.4	9.4	6.3	35.7
32	G-tria-2-1	4.3	17.3	8.2	5.7	34.9
33	U-tria-4-1	4.7	17.3	10.1	6.3	35.6
34	G-tria-4-1	4.3	17.2	8.6	5.8	34.6
35	U-tria-3-2	5.1	17.5	11.0	6.6	35.2
36	G-tria-3-2	4.2	16.8	9.1	5.5	34.2
37	U-meet-2-2	6.2	19.0	13.1	7.7	36.8
38	G-meet-2-2	5.2	18.1	11.0	6.5	35.5
39	U-meet-4-2	6.0	18.2	13.1	7.7	36.3
40	G-meet-4-2	5.1	18.0	10.6	6.6	35.0
∅	**01-40**	**4.6**	**16.5**	**10.3**	**6.1**	**33.3**

Table 6.3.: Results for UMPM landmark localization experiments. For each of the 40 experiments we present how many correct votes were casted (α), specified in %.

Exp No.	Exp code	β				
		ORIG	RP	H	OW	COMBI
01	U-chair-2-1	50.0	27.3	32.8	41.9	16.4
02	G-chair-2-1	52.3	28.0	34.4	43.4	16.0
03	U-chair-4-1	50.1	28.3	34.0	41.4	16.8
04	G-chair-4-1	52.4	28.3	36.0	42.7	16.5
05	U-chair-3-2	45.2	24.4	33.6	37.7	15.6
06	G-chair-3-2	47.7	25.2	35.7	39.6	15.7
07	U-grab-2-1	42.1	20.9	28.6	35.0	11.4
08	G-grab-2-1	42.1	20.9	28.6	35.0	11.4
09	U-grab-4-1	42.9	21.2	30.2	35.2	11.6
10	G-grab-4-1	45.9	20.8	33.1	37.9	11.6
11	U-grab-3-2	43.2	21.6	31.8	36.2	13.4
12	G-grab-3-2	46.3	22.1	34.6	39.0	13.5
13	U-ball-2-2	45.7	23.8	32.5	38.8	14.5
14	G-ball-2-2	48.6	24.3	35.2	41.2	14.5
15	U-free-2-2	46.0	24.4	33.1	36.8	15.0
16	G-free-2-2	48.6	24.8	35.4	39.2	15.1
17	U-free-4-2	45.9	24.1	32.6	36.5	14.5
18	G-free-4-2	48.7	24.8	35.0	39.2	14.7
19	U-ortho-2-1	42.6	21.2	25.1	32.3	11.4
20	G-ortho-2-1	46.0	21.5	28.3	35.9	11.5
21	U-ortho-4-1	44.1	21.1	25.7	31.6	11.4
22	G-ortho-4-1	48.3	21.5	29.2	34.9	11.6
23	U-ortho-3-2	55.6	27.0	36.3	44.3	17.7
24	G-ortho-3-2	59.4	28.4	39.1	47.1	17.9
25	U-table-2-1	55.2	30.8	37.7	46.4	18.1
26	G-table-2-1	57.0	30.9	39.4	48.0	18.0
27	U-table-4-1	56.6	30.3	37.9	46.5	17.8
28	G-table-4-1	59.1	30.3	40.1	48.3	18.1
29	U-table-3-2	51.8	26.3	36.3	42.3	16.7
30	G-table-3-2	54.6	26.4	38.6	44.5	16.9
31	U-tria-2-1	42.4	20.6	31.4	35.2	11.9
32	G-tria-2-1	44.1	20.6	33.4	36.9	12.1
33	U-tria-4-1	44.0	21.2	30.9	35.9	12.1
34	G-tria-4-1	46.1	21.3	33.1	37.7	12.3
35	U-tria-3-2	45.7	22.0	30.8	37.8	12.4
36	G-tria-3-2	49.1	23.1	33.3	40.6	12.5
37	U-meet-2-2	42.1	20.0	29.2	34.0	11.3
38	G-meet-2-2	45.8	21.6	32.0	37.4	11.6
39	U-meet-4-2	41.7	21.0	29.0	34.1	11.7
40	G-meet-4-2	45.2	21.7	31.9	37.5	12.0
∅	01-40	48.0	24.1	33.1	39.1	14.1

Table 6.4.: Results for UMPM landmark localization experiments. For each of the 40 experiments we present the average distance of the votes to the true landmark location (β), specified in %.

Exp No.	Exp code	ORIG	RP	α H	OW	COMBI
41	H-walk-1-1	8.1	26.1	17.5	9.5	46.8
42	G-walk-1-1	6.1	24.6	12.3	7.1	45.2
43	H-walk-2-1	7.5	24.3	16.7	9.2	46.6
44	G-walk-2-1	5.7	22.9	12.2	7.0	44.7
45	H-box-1-1	8.8	26.3	19.2	10.4	46.9
46	G-box-1-1	7.2	26.1	16.8	7.9	45.3
47	H-box-2-1	11.1	25.7	24.1	12.8	51.4
48	G-box-2-1	8.6	24.7	20.0	9.5	48.6
49	H-walk-1-1	8.0	26.1	16.9	9.5	47.5
50	G-walk-1-1	6.6	26.4	13.0	7.9	44.1
51	H-walk-2-1	8.1	26.2	17.5	10.0	46.9
52	G-walk-2-1	6.6	26.1	13.5	8.0	44.0
53	H-box-1-1	10.1	26.6	20.6	11.0	46.6
54	G-box-1-1	7.6	27.5	13.1	8.0	42.5
55	H-box-2-1	10.2	26.6	21.1	11.3	47.9
56	G-box-2-1	6.7	27.8	15.5	7.0	46.4
57	H-walk-1-1	6.7	22.9	12.8	8.0	40.0
58	G-walk-1-1	5.7	22.4	10.0	6.7	37.0
59	H-walk-2-1	7.4	24.3	14.1	9.0	41.1
60	G-walk-2-1	6.2	24.2	10.8	7.5	39.3
61	H-box-1-1	13.7	26.6	19.8	14.8	35.2
62	G-box-1-1	8.9	23.7	14.1	9.6	34.2
63	H-box-2-1	11.6	26.4	20.2	13.7	37.4
64	G-box-2-1	8.8	25.0	14.5	10.0	33.9
∅	41-64	8.2	25.4	16.1	9.4	43.3

Table 6.5.: Results for HumanEva landmark localization experiments.
For each of the 12 experiments we present how many correct votes were casted
(α), specified in %.

The results for the average (vote-strength weighted) distance of the votes
to the true landmark location (evaluation measure β) are consistent with
these results for evaluation measure α: the average weighted distance
of the votes to the true landmark locations is quite high (48.0% of the
person height on UMPM, 40.8% of the person height on HumanEva) for
ORIG-VOT, while this distance can be reduced significantly for all new
voting strategies, especially for COMBI-VOT, which reduces this distance
to 14.1% of the person height on the UMPM dataset and even to 10.8%
on the HumanEva dataset. Although this average distance of the votes
to the true landmark location is still quite high – for a person of 180cm,
10.8% of its height corresponds to 19.44cm – we will see in Chapter 7
that the COMBI-VOT generated vote distributions can be used as input

Exp No.	Exp code	β				
		ORIG	RP	H	OW	COMBI
41	H-walk-1-1	40.2	19.2	25.7	34.1	9.6
42	G-walk-1-1	44.2	19.9	29.8	39.2	10.6
43	H-walk-2-1	43.4	20.0	26.1	35.5	9.7
44	G-walk-2-1	48.1	20.9	29.7	40.8	10.1
45	H-box-1-1	36.7	17.4	23.4	32.6	9.2
46	G-box-1-1	40.8	18.3	29.9	38.7	11.2
47	H-box-2-1	35.9	19.2	20.5	31.8	8.3
48	G-box-2-1	41.5	19.7	28.3	39.3	9.4
49	H-walk-1-1	37.8	18.2	24.5	32.2	9.4
50	G-walk-1-1	41.2	17.8	27.7	35.8	10.1
51	H-walk-2-1	39.8	18.6	24.3	32.8	9.4
52	G-walk-2-1	43.8	18.6	27.7	37.3	10.0
53	H-box-1-1	35.9	17.6	22.2	32.7	10.0
54	G-box-1-1	42.5	19.3	31.0	41.0	17.0
55	H-box-2-1	39.8	16.9	22.6	36.7	9.1
56	G-box-2-1	48.5	17.6	29.7	47.3	11.3
57	H-walk-1-1	40.6	18.3	30.2	35.1	11.3
58	G-walk-1-1	42.8	17.7	33.5	38.2	12.4
59	H-walk-2-1	40.0	18.5	30.2	34.0	11.0
60	G-walk-2-1	43.3	17.8	33.8	38.2	11.7
61	H-box-1-1	32.5	16.4	23.1	29.7	10.4
62	G-box-1-1	42.9	17.9	34.8	40.6	16.0
63	H-box-2-1	35.8	15.7	24.8	30.8	10.1
64	G-box-2-1	42.0	17.0	32.4	37.9	11.0
∅	**41-64**	**40.8**	**18.3**	**27.7**	**36.3**	**10.8**

Table 6.6.: Results for HumanEva landmark localization experiments. For each of the 12 experiments we present the average distance of the votes to the true landmark location (β), specified in %.

for estimating 3D poses using a vote density maximization approach. The reason for this can probably be traced back to the fact that a more important aspect for the 3D pose estimator described in the following chapter is, that while simultaneously a lot of votes can be far away from the true landmark location, the input vote distribution for the 3D pose estimator should at least show a clear peak in the vote density near to the true landmark location, which is better reflected by evaluation measures α and γ, that measure the number of correct votes and the average vote density near to the true landmark location.

Fig. 6.16 shows the results for the evaluation measure γ for the UMPM dataset. For each of the strategies we plot the density as a function of the distance to the true landmark location. We can see that COMBI-VOT

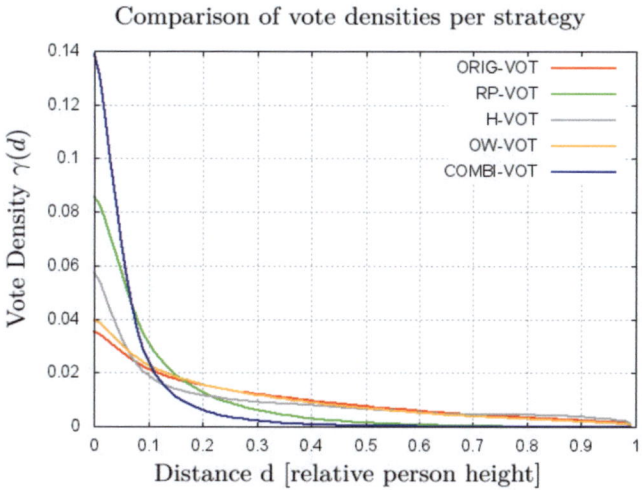

Figure 6.16.: Vote density per strategy. For each of the voting strategies, we plot the average vote density $\gamma(d)$ as a function of the distance d to the true landmark location (distance specified in relative person height units).

shows the steepest vote density gradient when running into the direction of the ground truth landmark location, i.e., this strategy casts significantly more of the vote mass near to the true landmark location. But also RP-VOT, H-VOT, and OW-VOT place more of the vote mass near to the true landmark location compared to ORIG-VOT.

Different localization accuracies for different landmarks

In Fig. 6.17 we show the vote density per strategy again, but now for four individual landmarks: the head, right shoulder, right elbow and the right hand. We can see that for landmarks that are attached to body parts that do not show much variation in their location relative to the person center as the head or the right shoulder, we can much more easily localize the corresponding landmarks compared to landmarks that are attached to body parts as the right elbow or right hand that show more variation in

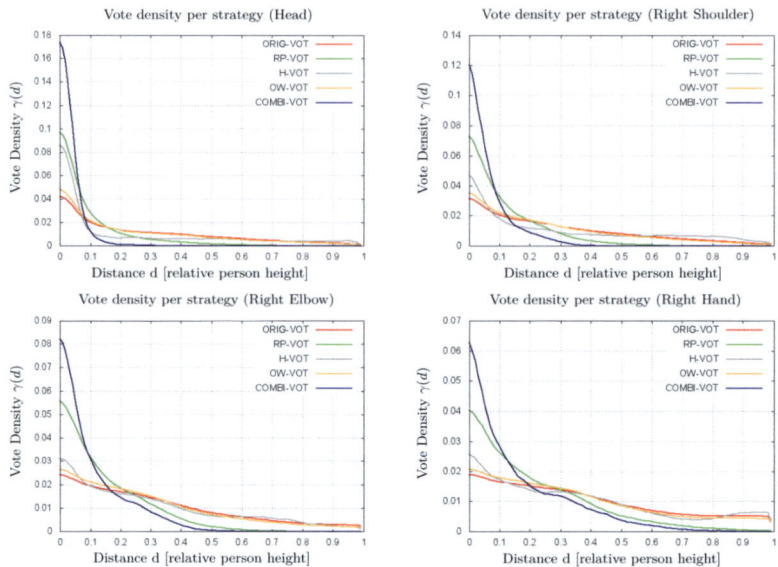

Figure 6.17.: Vote density per strategy and landmark. The more articulation we find for the sub-part of the body an anatomical landmark is assigned to, the less the accuracy for localizing this landmark.

their location relative to the person center. This is reflected by a smaller vote density near to the true landmark location and in addition a flatter vote density gradient. Nevertheless, the relative ranking of the voting strategies concerning the localization accuracy remains the same, even for individual landmarks[12].

II. No large influence of the codebook

The results from Table 6.3 show no large differences between the two codebook scenarios for the UMPM experiments: compare the results of the "U" experiments (e.g., exp. 39 → 36.3% correct votes for COMBI-VOT) where we used the UMPM codebook with the results of the "G"

---

[12]The corresponding vote density plots for the HumanEva experiments are nearly identical. For this we omit these plots here.

experiments (e.g., exp. 40 → 35.0% correct votes for COMBI-VOT) where we used the generic codebook.

In contrast, the difference between the two codebook scenarios is much larger for the HumanEva experiments as Table 6.5 shows: e.g., in exp. 63 where the HumanEva codebook is used 37.4% of the votes are correct, while the usage of the generic codebook in exp. 64 results in only 33.9% correct votes. This difference can be explained by the fact, that while the UMPM codebook was generated on different persons that did not appear in the test videos, the HumanEva codebook contains image structures from the same persons on which we later tested, since this dataset only contains four persons and therefore it was not possible to use different persons for the HumanEva codebook generation that do not appear in the test videos. Nevertheless, in the majority of the HumanEva experiments, the drop in the number of correct votes from the experiments where we used the HumanEva codebook to the experiments where we used the generic codebook is only in the range of 1-3%.

This seems to indicate that even though (i) there are large differences between the image sources used for the generation of the application specific codebooks and the generic codebook and (ii) the number of words contained in each codebook is different (UMPM: 1315 words, HumanEva: 301 words, generic: 843 words), the final generated vote distributions do not differ much.

This is an important result, because it suggests that the codebook seems not to have a large impact on the overall performance. It further suggests that it is possible to train a codebook on different image data (here: ETHZ Pedestrian dataset for generic codebook) compared to the image data for which we later want to localize landmarks (here: UMPM / HumanEva).

III. Small number of persons in the training data is sufficient

Better results were expected for experiments, where we used more training persons (e.g., 2 persons in exps. 31/32 vs. 4 persons in exps. 33/34, or 1 person in exps. 41/42 vs. 2 persons in exps. 43/44). But the resulting landmark localization measures do not show large differences. This means that – at least for learning the landmark localization ISMs for the different action classes used here – examples of word to landmark locations of a single or two training persons are already enough, since using observation vectors additionally from more persons does not result in a better landmark localization as the quantitative results show.

IV. Performance drop for occlusion cases

As expected, the landmark localization accuracy drops in cases of occlusions: while in exps. 19-22, e.g., no occlusions are present (only one test person), in exps. 23-24 occlusions are present (two test persons that often occlude each other). The landmark localization accuracy measured in the ratio of correct votes decreases here significantly with up to approx. 20% (for COMBI-VOT) less correct votes. Nevertheless, as the qualitative results presented in the next section show, landmark localization is often possible in cases of occlusions thanks to the new voting strategies.

V. Large differences for different action classes

The results for the UMPM experiments in Table 6.3 show significant differences for the action classes concerning the landmark localization accuracy. For the "ortho" sequences we can reach up to 48% (COMBI-VOT) correct votes for a single non occluded test person (exps. 19-22), while for the "chair" sequences only up to 29.6% votes (COMBI-VOT) are correct (exps. 01-04). The reason is probably that for different action sequences (i) the number of different poses shown are very different and (ii) poses of some action classes can be better discriminated (especially the "ortho" poses).

6.3.4. Qualitative results

Better landmark localization with new voting strategies

In Fig. 6.18 and Fig. 6.19 we show the resulting vote densities for each of the 5 voting strategies for 10 different input images (from different experiments) from UMPM experiments and in Fig. 6.20 and Fig. 6.21 for

6 different input images from HumanEva experiments. The vote density visualizations confirm the quantitative results from the previous section: the votes are much more focused for the new voting strategies and the vote density peaks often occur at the true landmark location, especially for COMBI-VOT.

In appendix B we show a comparison for the vote locations and vote densities generated for an example frame for each of the 15 landmarks by ORIG-VOT and COMBI-VOT.

Landmark localization in cases of occlusion

As mentioned in Section 6.3.1, the UMPM dataset allows to test for the capability of the approach proposed here to localize landmarks in occlusion cases. The quantitative results from the previous section showed that in occlusion cases, the landmark localization accuracy decreased by up to 20% concerning the number of correct votes (for COMBI-VOT). Nevertheless, Fig. 6.22 shows that even in occlusion cases, the landmark localization can succeed at least for non-occluded landmarks. The examples show, that votes are often generated by ORIG-VOT on image structures belonging to the person in the foreground. But especially COMBI-VOT and RP-VOT, can distinguish between the words of the background person we are interested in and the foreground person by making use of the reference point: words that appear on the foreground person often have a wrong (wrong in terms of not observed during the ISM training phase) location when considering the reference point of the background person.

Landmark localization for foreground persons in case of the presence of a background person

A foreground person that occludes a background person makes it hard to localize the landmarks for the background person, since (i) image structures of the background person are occluded, and (ii) words on the foreground person can act as distractors during the voting procedure leading to wrong votes for landmarks of the background person.

While the image structures of a foreground person are not occluded, words appearing on the background person can act as distractors as well and make it harder to localize the landmarks of the foreground person (see Fig. 6.23).

Fig. 6.24 shows some example images for the landmark localization of a foreground person, where the presence of a background person introduces words that lead to additionally wrong votes. Again, the usage of a reference point can help a lot here, since it allows to discard words that appear at wrong locations relative to the reference point and therefore must belong to the background person.

Examples of failed landmark localization

If there are too few words that vote for the image structure we want to localize, e.g., since the landmark is occluded or there are too few keypoints near to the landmark, it can happen that no or only few votes are generated for the true landmark location, or that the votes for the true landmark location are dominated by the votes for another wrong landmark location. In Fig. 6.25 we show some examples of such failed landmark localization cases.

Input   ORIG-VOT   RP-VOT   H-VOT   OW-VOT   COMBI-VOT

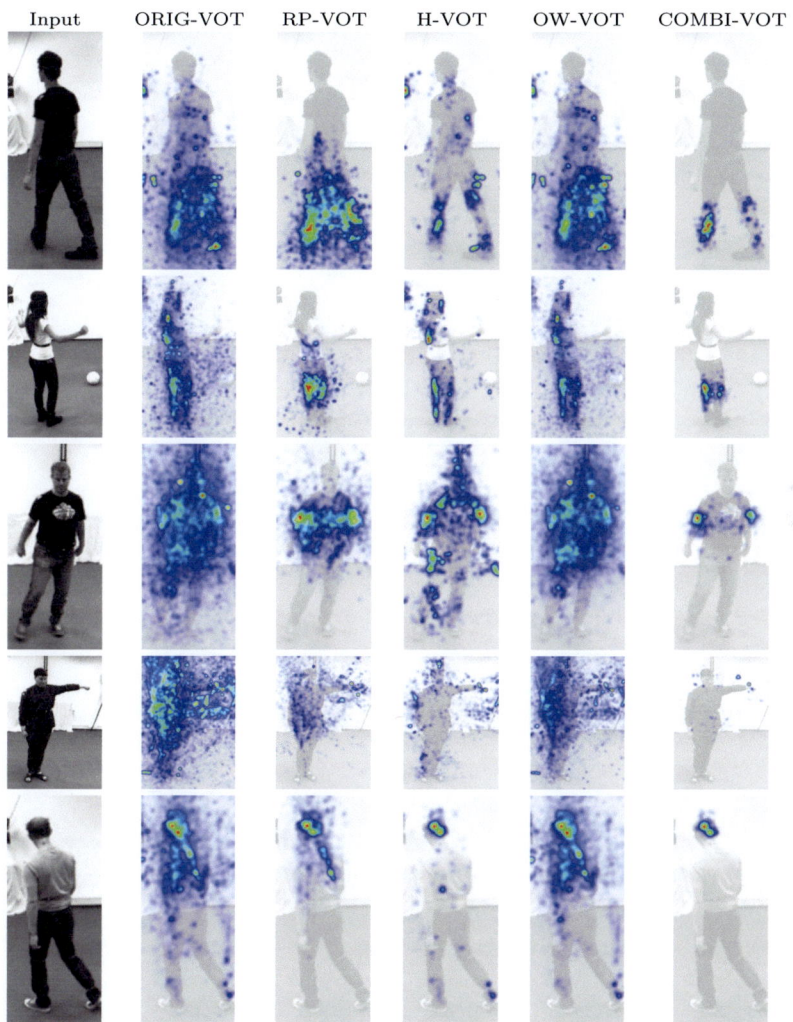

Figure 6.18.: Examples of vote densities for UMPM input images.
For each of the 5 voting strategies we show for some experiments and
landmarks the resulting vote densities. Row 1: left foot, exp01. Row 2:
left knee, exp 13. Row 3: right elbow (exp 18). Row 4: left hand (exp 24).
Row 5: head (exp 39).

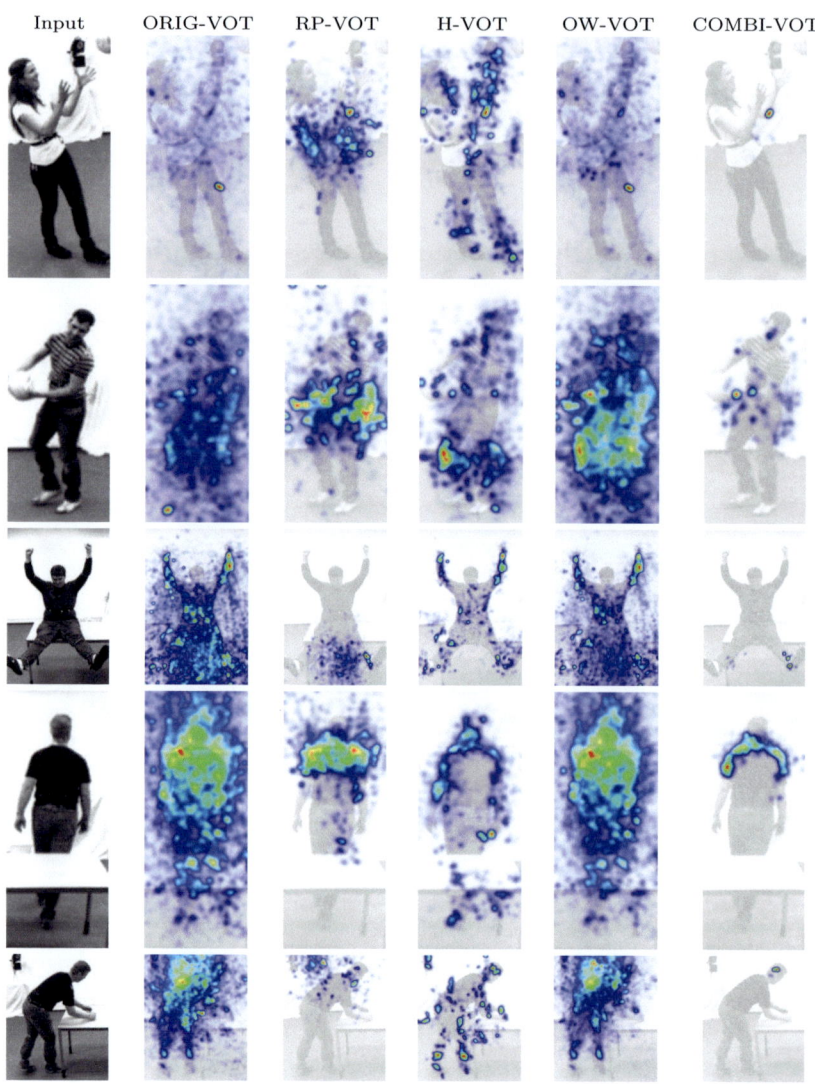

Figure 6.19.: Examples of vote densities for UMPM input images.
Row 1: left elbow (exp 13). Row 2: left hand (exp 13). Row 3: left foot
(exp 29). Row 4: left shoulder (exp 29). Row 5: head (exp 30).

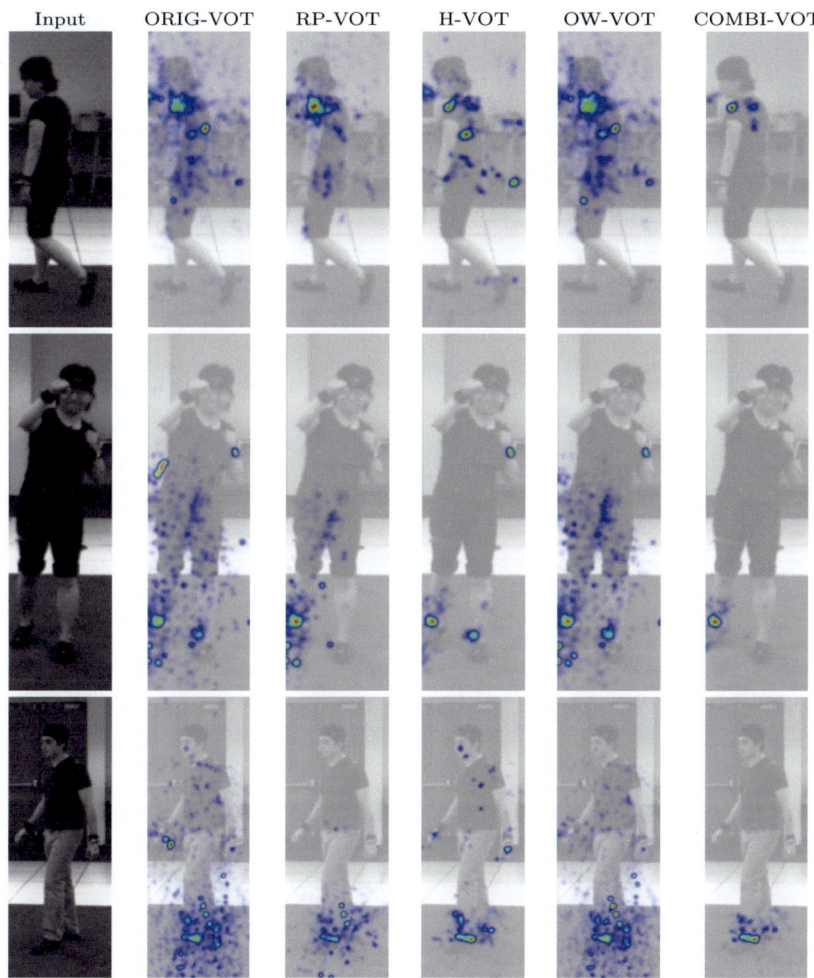

Figure 6.20.: Examples of vote densities for HumanEva input images. Row 1: left shoulder (exp 41). Row 2: right foot (exp 45). Row 3: left foot (exp 49).

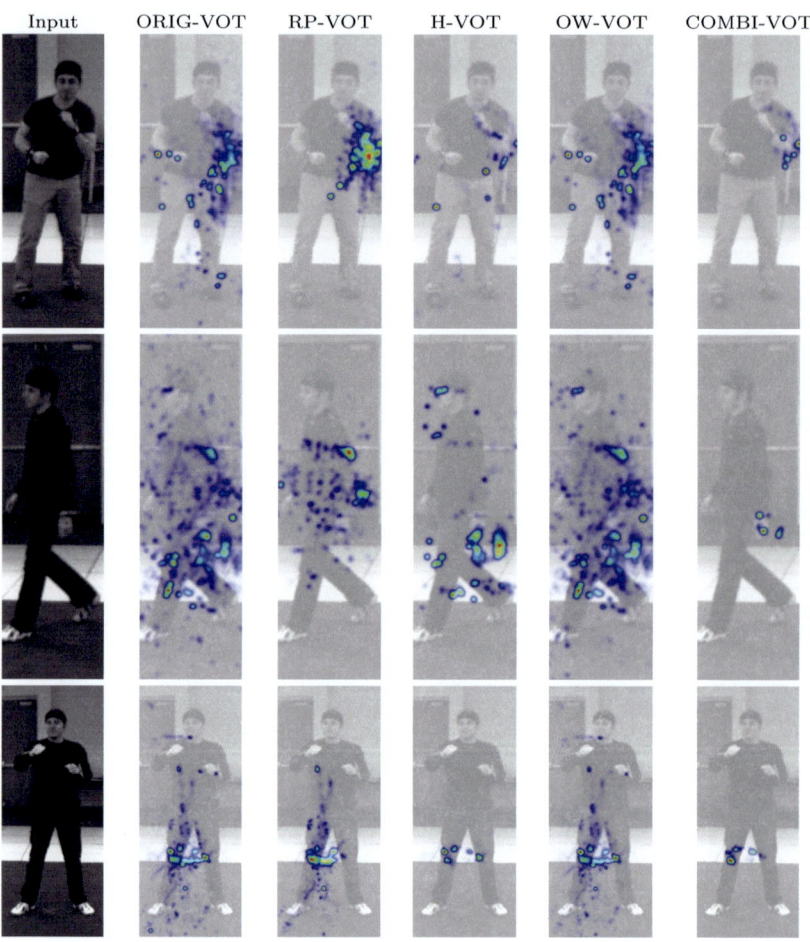

Figure 6.21.: Examples of vote densities for HumanEva input images. Row 1: left elbow (exp 53). Row 2: left hand (exp 57). Row 3: right knee (exp 61).

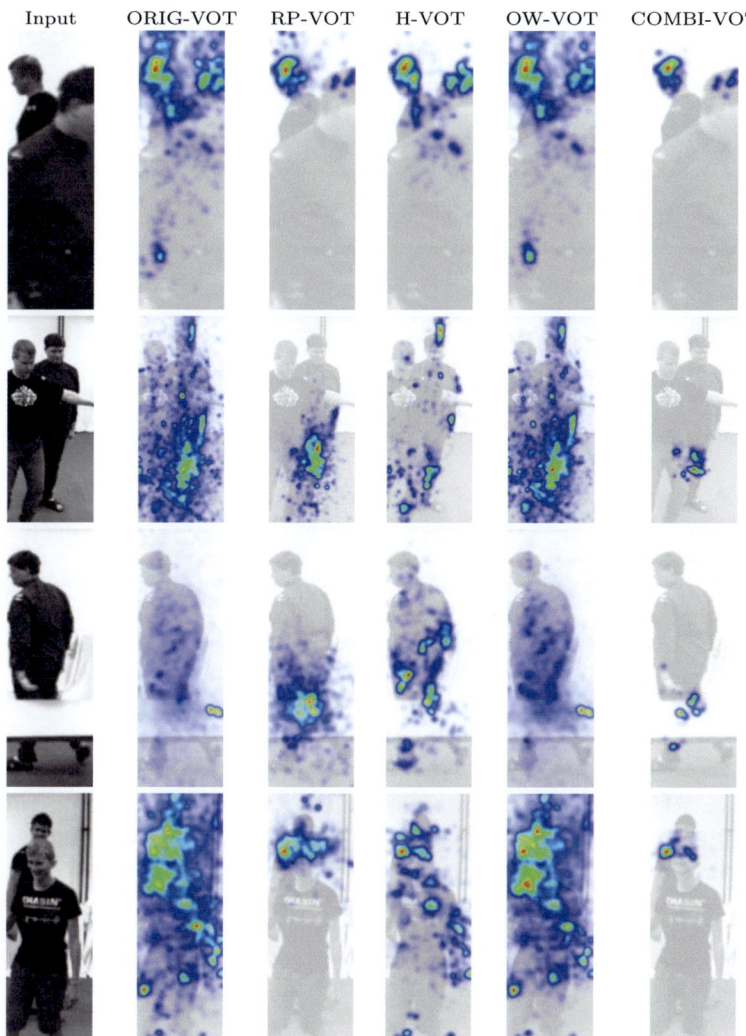

Figure 6.22.: Successful landmark localization for occlusion cases.
Despite large occlusions of image structures of the person in the background – by another person or an object – non-occluded landmarks of the background person can often be localized. Row 1: head (exp 15). Row 2: left knee (exp 23). Row 3: left knee (exp 29). Row 4: right shoulder (exp 40).

Input   ORIG-VOT   RP-VOT   H-VOT   OW-VOT   COMBI-VOT

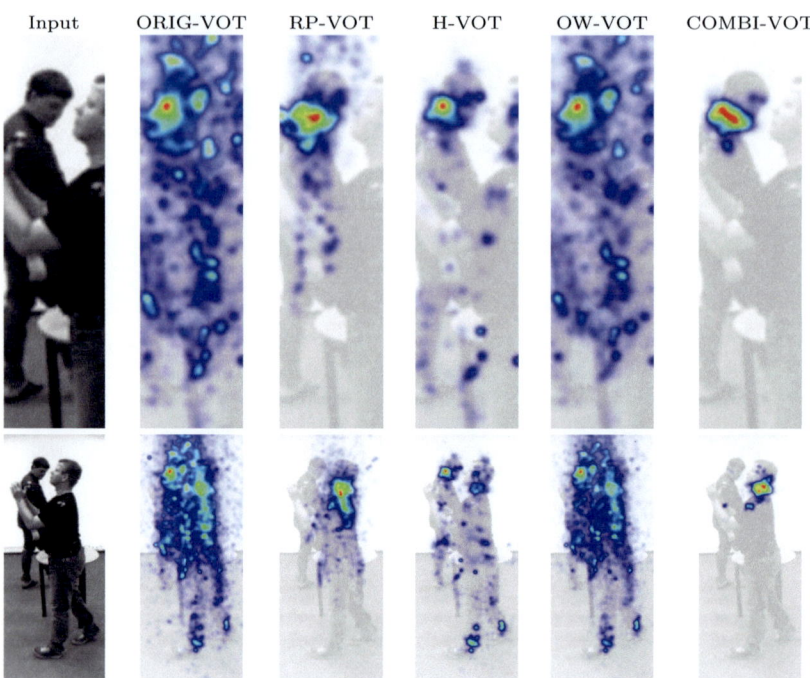

Figure 6.23.: Two types of distractor cases. Top row (occlusion + distractor case): votemaps for upper spine of person in background. Parts of this person are occluded by the person in the foreground. Additionally, words for the person in the foreground can act as distractors during the voting procedure for the landmarks of the background person. Bottom row (no occlusion, but distractor case): votemaps for upper spine of person in the foreground. The image structures of the person in the background act as distractors for the upper spine landmark voting procedure of the person in the foreground. Row 1: upper spine of background person (exp 12). Row 2: upper spine of foreground person (exp 12).

Input   ORIG-VOT   RP-VOT   H-VOT   OW-VOT   COMBI-VOT

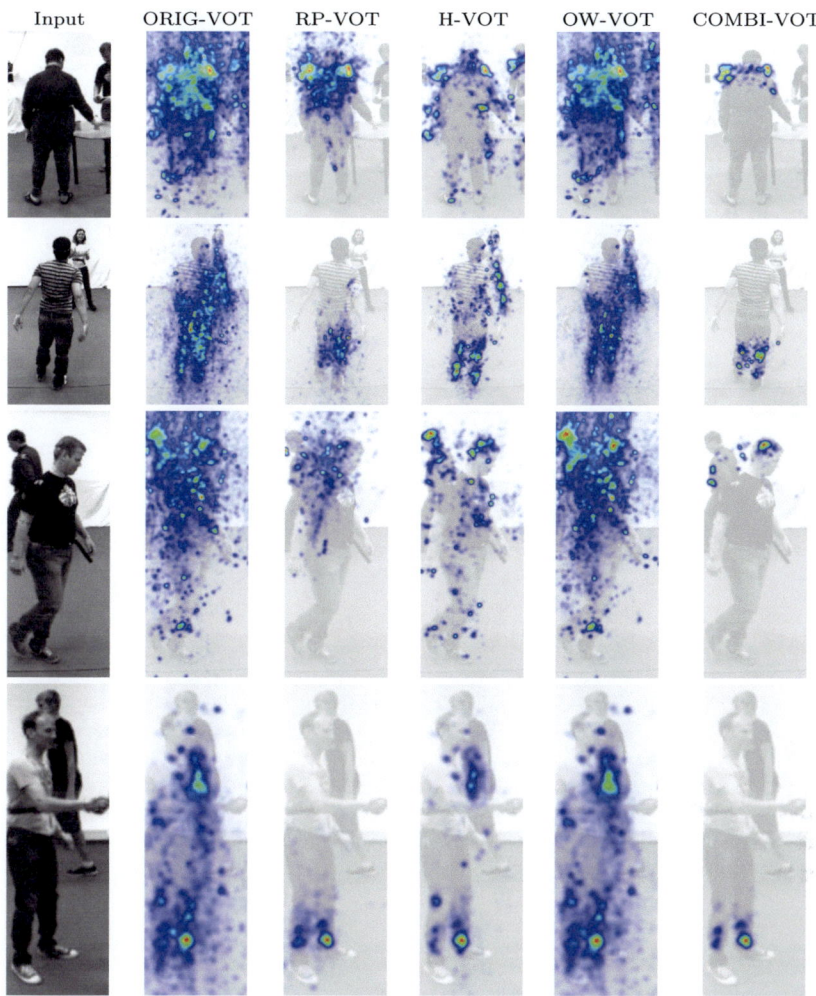

Figure 6.24.: Landmark localization for a foreground person. Image structures belonging to the background person can lead to wrong votes. Nevertheless, COMBI-VOT can often untangle which words belong to which person, resulting in an overall better localization performance for such cases. Row 1: left shoulder (exp 12). Row 2: right knee (exp 13). Row 3: head (exp 15). Row 4: left foot (exp 40).

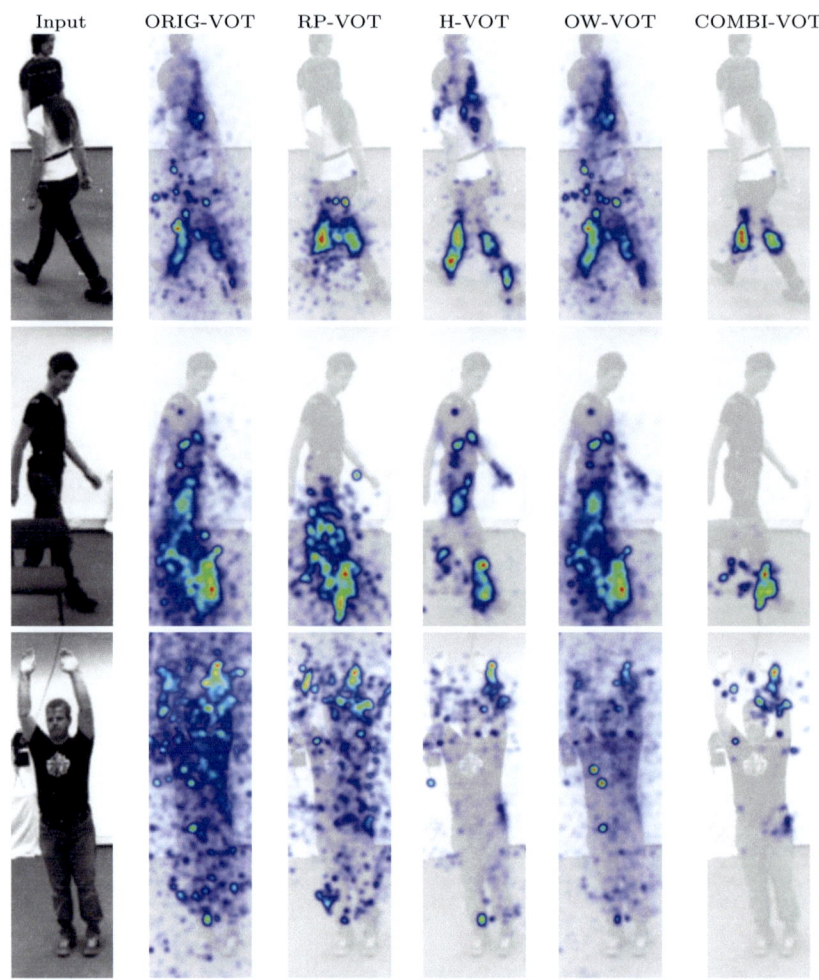

Figure 6.25.: Examples of failed landmark localization. Row 1: left knee (exp 35). Row 2: left foot (exp 01). Row 3: right hand (exp 23).

6.4. Conclusions

In this chapter we showed that the ISM object model can be extended in order to localize anatomical landmarks. For this, a separate ISM is learned for each landmark. The input for each landmark ISM is a set of local features (words). If an ISM based person detector (tracker) is used to detect persons, we can reuse the same features that were used to detect a person, to vote for the landmark localizations. Thereby we can benefit from the figure-ground segmentation during the person detection step in the landmark localization step directly. If no ISM based person detector (tracker) is used but a generic detector that provides person bounding boxes – as in evaluation the experiments conducted here – local features can be sampled within that bounding box. The output of the landmark localization process is a set of discrete votes for each landmark, which can be used to compute a landmark vote density for each image location.

Since the landmark localization accuracy of the original ISM approach does not generate vote distributions that are clearly focused at the true landmark locations, we proposed new voting strategies, which make use of the person center reference point from the person detection step, the information about the presence of a landmark within the descriptor region of the feature, or how good each ISM observation vector – collected during ISM training – is able to predict the landmark locations. Especially the combination of all these ideas in one voting strategy (COMBI-VOT) allows to increase the landmark accuracy significantly as the quantitative and qualitative results from a total of 320 landmark localization experiments on the UMPM and the HumanEva datasets show.

Fortunately, it is possible to use a generic codebook, i.e., there is no need to generate a codebook on similar images. Further, a small number of persons is already sufficient to train the ISMs for landmark localization. The final localization accuracy for the landmarks seems to depend strongly on the type of actions used. For videos containing images of occluded persons, landmark localization performance drops up to approx. 20% (correct votes). Nevertheless, the qualitative examples show that often landmark localization is still possible in such situations for the non-occluded landmarks.

While the new voting strategies presented here are evaluated exclusively for the task of localization of landmarks on persons, for future work it would be interesting to evaluate the benefit of these strategies for the detection of rigid objects and subparts of rigid objects as well.

7. Generative 3D pose estimation with vote distributions

In the previous chapter we showed how to extend the ISM for the task of anatomical landmark localization. In this chapter we present a method that can be used to estimate 3D poses just based on the results of this landmark localization process, i.e., the landmark vote distributions. Although the new voting strategies presented in the previous chapter place more of the votes near to the true landmark locations, a method is needed that is robust to possible errors during this localization process.

Section 7.1 introduces the key idea of this new method: 3D pose hypotheses are projected to the 2D image plane and are compared directly with the vote distributions resulting from the landmark localization process. **Section 7.2.1** formulates the 3D pose estimation task as an optimization process, where we try to find a 3D pose and 3D to 2D projection parameters such that the projected 3D pose maximizes an overall landmark matching score.

The objective function used during optimization is introduced in **Section 7.2.2**. It is a measure of the average landmark vote density near to the projected landmark locations of the hypothesized 3D pose. **Section 7.2.3** discusses the set of projections we consider here and the projection parameters that have to be optimized. **Section 7.2.4** is dedicated to the question which pose candidates we want to consider during the optimization process at all. We propose to use example poses in order to compensate for the possible fuzzy landmark localization results and show how to retrieve a sparse set of example poses from the CMU motion capture database. **Section 7.2.5** then discusses another important issue, namely which optimizer to use. We use Particle Swarm Optimization (PSO) since it is a method that has shown to be able to find good solutions for high dimensional search problems, as it is the case in the context of pose estimation.

Section 7.2.6 proposes an alternative idea for generating 3D pose hypotheses that will be considered during the optimization process. Complete motion sequences are represented by "pose splines", which are a sparse set of supporting point poses, where poses from the original motion sequence can be omitted, since they are linearly interpolated by supporting poses. Pose splines fit perfectly into the proposed optimization approach of Particle Swarm Optimization and introduce only one more search space dimension which encodes the location on the spline.

Section 7.3 evaluates the quality of the estimated 3D poses using example based and pose spline based pose priors. **Section 7.4** presents the conclusions based on the experimental results.

7.1. Introduction

The method proposed in this chapter is a top-down (generative) approach. Top-down HPE approaches project 3D pose hypotheses into the image and compare it with image features extracted from the person image. An important issue for top-down methods is the definition of a matching method, that allows to compare a projected hypothesis with the input image robustly and rapidly.

Image features used for matching

The wish to model the human body as realistic as possible has lead to a preference of volumetric body models used in top-down approaches: [Bregler and Malik, 1998] use ellipsoids, [Roth et al., 2004] use cylinders, and [Sminchisescu and Triggs, 2003] use super-quadrics. [Sigal et al., 2007] use a detailed polymesh based shape model with 25,000 polygons to model the human body. Generated 2D silhouette projections of 3D pose

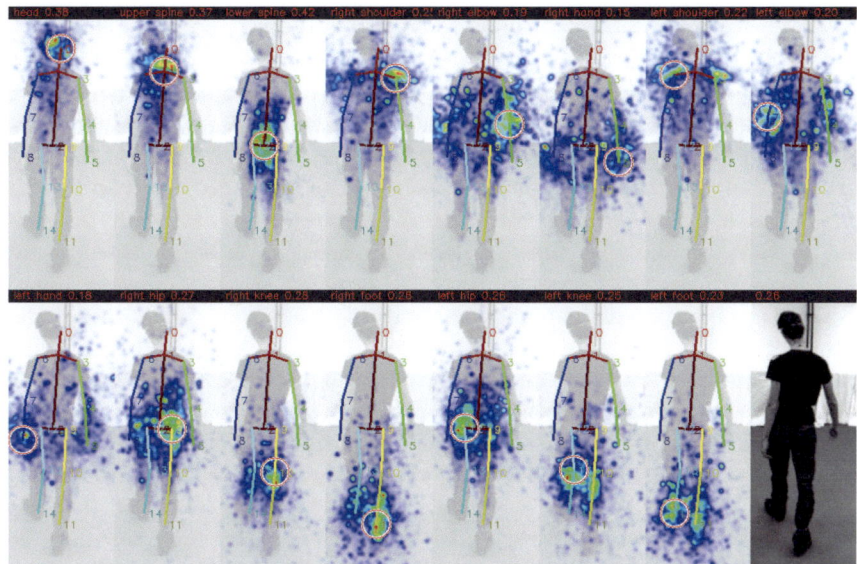

Figure 7.1.: Key idea of pose estimation with vote distributions. Pose hypotheses of a simple 3D stick-figure model are projected into 2D image space and projected landmark coordinates are compared with the vote distributions for the landmarks. The image evidence for a 3D pose hypothesis can be measured by accumulating the vote densities near to the projected landmarks.

hypotheses are compared with the silhouette extracted from the person input image.

While silhouettes are probably most often used to compare the projected model with the input image, edges are used very often as well. [Drummond and Cipolla, 2001] project edges of their 3D body model into the image and searches for real edges into the direction of the projected edge normal. Instead of using fixed geometric primitives for modeling the 3D body model, [Charles and Everingham, 2011] recently proposed a new method, where for each 3D limb used in the body model the 2D shape of its projection to the image is learned. In this publication Microsoft's Kinect was used, which provides an easy way to collect a large amount of example data of 3D poses and projected shapes.

Reasons for high computational costs of top-down approaches

Compared to bottom-up approaches, top-down approaches are claimed to be computationally demanding. This has mainly three reasons: First, a lot of 3D pose hypotheses have to be generated to test for a wide range of 3D poses. Second, each 3D pose hypothesis has to be projected to the 2D image space which can be costly. Third, the projection of each hypothesis has to be compared with the real person image using silhouettes, edges, or other image features. Using a complex 3D human body model to model the appearance of a person as realistic as possible leads to high computational costs for projecting the hypotheses to the 2D image space and comparing the projections with the input image. Such high computational costs can result in a computational bottleneck which can mean that the number of pose candidates that can be considered during optimization has to be reduced to a small set. Due to the high computational costs when considering many 3D pose hypotheses, some top-down approaches rely on an initial known 3D pose which is tracked in successive frames in order to limit the hypotheses search space (e.g., [Bregler and Malik, 1998], [Sminchisescu and Triggs, 2003], [Drummond and Cipolla, 2001]). This means that the person for which we want to estimate its poses has to start with a pre-defined initial 3D pose or the starting 3D pose to be tracked in the following has to be manually provided, e.g., by labeling. Both approaches strongly limit the range of applications.

Avoiding high computational costs

Instead of using the image space for a comparison, we use the 2D vote space for comparing projected 3D pose hypotheses with the image evidence. We replace the low-level image evidence (edges, silhouettes, etc.) widely used with a representation that on the one hand still captures the landmark location ambiguity inherent in the 2D domain, but on the other hand allows to use a simple body model. We use a simple 3D stick-figure model with 15 3D landmarks to represent the human body. This allows to project a 3D pose rapidly onto the 2D image plane, since only 15 3D coordinates have to be projected. For each projected landmark location we compute a measure of the image evidence that the observed 2D landmark is really at that location based on the 2D vote distribution computed for this landmark during the landmark localization process. The individual image evidences are then combined to an overall measure of how good the projected 3D pose hypothesis matches to the 15 landmark vote distributions.

Visualization of the key idea

Fig. 7.1 shows a visualization of the matching process, where we display the (i) vote density maps computed (by RP-VOT) for each of the 15 anatomical landmarks and the input image, and (ii) the projection of a single 3D pose hypothesis onto these vote density maps. In each landmark votemap the red/white circle center marks the projected landmark location. For computing a matching score between such a projected hypothesis and the image evidence given by these vote density maps, for each landmark we first compute the sum of the vote density within the area around the projected landmark location, visualized by the red/white circle. A final matching score is then computed by the average matching score of all individual landmark matching scores (in this case: 0.26, where 0 is the minimal possible score, and 1 the maximum possible score).

The pose hypothesis shown here is the hypothesis that maximizes this matching score, i.e., all other hypothesis had smaller scores. Note, that despite the very ambiguous landmark localization results (see, e.g., the vote distributions for the left shoulder / left foot) and wrong peaks in individual landmark votemaps (e.g., the highest vote density for the right hand is at the left of the bounding box), the final pose hypothesis is roughly correct, because individual landmark localization errors and ambiguous localization results can be compensated by searching for a pose hypothesis that maximizes the overall score.

Similar approach

[Andriluka et al., 2010]) (see Section 2.1.7) shares a similar approach idea – namely lifting the low-level image evidence to some intermediate level and comparing the image evidence with projected 3D pose hypotheses at this intermediate level – but with some important differences. In their approach short sequences of 2D poses ("tracklets") using the pictorial structures model are estimated first and are used as input for the 3D pose estimation. The most important difference to the approach presented in this thesis is that in their method an early decision about the 2D pose is made, since for each frame a single unique 2D pose is estimated using a 2D kinematic model, which means that 2D projection ambiguities have to be solved very early in the processing pipeline in 2D space. In contrast, we do not use any 2D kinematic model and do not even try to estimate an unique 2D pose since we believe that landmark ambiguities that appear in the 2D image can better be resolved in the 3D world. Here, the projection ambiguity is captured by the 2D landmark vote distributions which is used as input for a 3D pose estimation process.

7.2. Method

7.2.1. Pose estimation as an optimization process

We formulate the 3D pose estimation as an optimization problem where we want to find the 3D pose $\mathbf{q}^*$ and the 3D to 2D projection $\mathbf{t}^*$ that maximizes a projection vs. vote distribution matching score S:

$$(\mathbf{q}^*, \mathbf{t}^*) = \underset{\mathbf{q} \in Q, \mathbf{t} \in T}{\arg\max} S(\mathbf{t}(\mathbf{q})) = \underset{\mathbf{q} \in Q, \mathbf{t} \in T, \mathbf{q}' = \mathbf{t}(\mathbf{q})}{\arg\max} S(\mathbf{q}') \qquad (7.1)$$

where Q is the set of 3D pose candidates that we consider, T a set of 3D to 2D projections, $\mathbf{t}$ is a projection that maps a 3D pose $\mathbf{q}$ to a 2D pose $\mathbf{q}'$, $\mathbf{q} = \{\mathbf{m}_i = (x_i, y_i, z_i) : 1 \leq i \leq J\}$ is the representation of a single 3D pose by J 3D landmark coordinates $\mathbf{m}_i$, and $\mathbf{q}' = \mathbf{t}(\mathbf{q}) = \{\mathbf{m}'_i = (x'_i, y'_i) : 1 \leq i \leq J\}$ is the corresponding 2D pose under projection $\mathbf{t}$.

While $\mathbf{q}^*$ is the resulting estimated 3D pose, the method yields a 2D pose estimate $(\mathbf{q}^*)'$ as well, since the projection of the 3D pose $\mathbf{q}^*$ to 2D with the best projection $\mathbf{t}^* \in T$ found during the optimization process for projecting $\mathbf{q}^*$ onto the vote distributions is the best matching 2D pose:

$$(\mathbf{q}^*)' = \mathbf{t}^*(\mathbf{q}^*) \tag{7.2}$$

$$\mathbf{t}^* = \underset{\mathbf{t}\in T}{\arg\max}\, S(\mathbf{t}(\mathbf{q}^*)) \tag{7.3}$$

There are four things that have to be specified within such an approach:

- We have to define the matching score function S that maps a 2D pose to a score value (see Section 7.2.2)

- We need to specify the set of projections T allowed during the optimization process (see Section 7.2.3)

- We have to specify the set of 3D poses Q that will be considered (see Section 7.2.4)

- We need to choose an optimization strategy that realizes the search on the set of pose candidates Q and projections T (see Section 7.2.5)

7.2.2. Matching score function

Definition of a pose & landmark matching score

As described in the previous section, the main idea for the definition of the matching score $S(\mathbf{q}')$ is to accumulate the vote density near to the projected landmark coordinates for each landmark individually and to use the average landmark matching score as an overall 2D pose matching score:

$$S(\mathbf{q}') = \frac{1}{J}\sum_{i=1}^{J} L(\mathbf{m}'_i) \tag{7.4}$$

where $L(\mathbf{m}'_i)$ is the landmark matching score for a single landmark $\mathbf{m}'_i$ and can be defined by:

$$L(\mathbf{m}_i') \;=\; \frac{1}{W} \sum_{k=1}^{|\mathcal{V}_i|} v_r^k K(\|\mathbf{v}_2^k - \mathbf{m}_i'\|_2) \tag{7.5}$$

$$W \;=\; \sum_{k=1}^{|\mathcal{V}_i|} v_r^k \tag{7.6}$$

where $\mathcal{V}_i$ is the set of all votes for the 2D location of landmark i, v_r^k is the weight of the k-th vote $\mathbf{v}^k$, $\mathbf{v}_2^k$ is the 2D vote location of the k-th vote $\mathbf{v}^k$, W is the sum of all vote weights, and K is a kernel (vote weighting) function.

In words: we estimate the vote density at the projected landmark location $\mathbf{m}_i$ for each landmark (represented by $L(\mathbf{m}_i')$) and use the average of these landmark vote densities as a matching score $S(\mathbf{q}')$ for a single pose hypothesis.

Kernels for vote density estimation

Different kernel functions K can be used. For a flat kernel K:

$$K(x) = \begin{cases} 1 & , x \le r \\ 0 & , x > r \end{cases} \tag{7.7}$$

with radius r, $L(\mathbf{m}_i')$ "counts" how many votes are within a range of r around the projected landmark location $\mathbf{m}_i'$ (weighted by the corresponding vote weights). We can consider all votes within a radius of r around the projected landmark location $\mathbf{m}_i'$ as evidence that the landmark is located at the 2D location $\mathbf{m}_i'$.

While such a kernel does not consider votes that are further away than r, a Gaussian kernel K will consider all votes, weighted by their Euclidean distance to $\mathbf{m}_i'$:

$$K(x) = \frac{1}{\sigma\sqrt{2\pi}} e^{-\frac{1}{2}\left(\frac{x}{\sigma}\right)^2} \tag{7.8}$$

Votes that are near to the projected landmark location $\mathbf{m}'_i$ ($\rightarrow$ small x) will increase $L(\mathbf{m}'_i)$ more compared to votes that are far away from the projected landmark location $\mathbf{m}'_i$ ($\rightarrow$ large x).

In [Brauer et al., 2012] we experimented with different kernels K and observed that the flat kernel yields better 3D pose estimation results compared to the Gaussian kernel. This is probably due to the fact that votes that are far away from the true landmark location can be considered as outliers and should have no influence on the landmark matching score, which is true for the flat Kernel, but not for the Gaussian kernel. Further, there is a large difference concerning the computation time. Since we want to be able to test a large set of 3D pose candidates, and for each pose candidate $\mathbf{q}$ we have to compute the matching score $S(\mathbf{q}')$, it is crucial, that we can compute $S(\mathbf{q}')$ as fast as possible. Since the use of a Gaussian kernel involves the evaluation of an exponential function the resulting matching score for kernel 7.8 is much more costly than using the flat kernel 7.7. For these two reasons we use a flat kernel in the following.

Fast landmark matching score

Nevertheless, even with a flat kernel, the landmark matching score function defined in eqn. (7.5), has one drawback. The computation time is linear in the number of votes $|\mathcal{V}_i|$ and using large training data sets will result in landmark localization ISMs after the ISM training phase where a large number of observation vectors are stored for each word, resulting in a large number of generated votes. This will make the evaluation of the landmark matching score a computational bottleneck.

Therefore, it is desirable to define a landmark matching score function, with a computation time constant in the number of votes. This can be realized by precomputing a vote density map ρ_i for each landmark before we start the optimization process and (ii) making use of the "integral image trick" presented in [Viola and Jones, 2001] to compute the vote density within a rectangular region around the projected landmark $\mathbf{m}'_i$ rapidly. I.e., we use a rectangular area – corresponding to a flat rectangular kernel – for the vote density accumulation in the following. More precisely, for each landmark we first compute a vote density map ρ_i, where for each image location (x, y) we store pre-computed vote density values:

$$\rho_i(x,y) = \frac{1}{W} \sum_{k=1}^{|\mathcal{V}_i|} v_r^k K(\|\mathbf{v}_2^k - (\mathbf{x},\mathbf{y})^T\|_2) \qquad (7.9)$$

where the size of the kernel K (radius for a flat kernel, or variance σ for a Gaussian kernel) should be set proportional to the height of the person hypothesis (e.g., person bounding box height).

For each vote density map ρ_i a corresponding integral image Ω_i is computed as well before the optimization process is initiated:

$$\Omega_i(x,y) = \sum_{x'\leq x} \sum_{y'\leq y} \rho_i(x',y') \qquad (7.10)$$

The integral image value $\Omega_i(x,y)$ corresponds to the sum of all vote density values above and left to (x,y) for landmark i.

For a projected landmark coordinate $\mathbf{m}_i' = (x_i',y_i')$ the vote density within a radius r in a rectangular region with top left corner $(x_i' - r, y_i' - r)$ and bottom right corner $(x_i' + r, y_i' + r)$ can then be computed by just four additions with the help of the integral image, since:

$$
\begin{aligned}
L(\mathbf{m}_i') &= \sum_{x_i'-r\leq x\leq x_i'+r} \sum_{y_i'-r\leq y\leq y_i'+r} \rho_i(x,y) \\
&= \overbrace{\Omega_i(x_i'+r, y_i'+r)}^{D} - \overbrace{\Omega_i(x_i'-r, y_i'+r)}^{B} - \\
&\quad \underbrace{\Omega_i(x_i'+r, y_i'-r)}_{C} + \underbrace{\Omega_i(x_i'-r, y_i'-r)}_{A} \qquad (7.11)
\end{aligned}
$$

This allows us to evaluate the vote density near to a hypothesized landmark location of a pose hypothesis within some rectangular region – that depends on the 2D pose hypothesis size – very quickly using just four look-ups in the integral image Ω_i and four additions (see Fig. 7.2). With this we avoid the need to re-compute the vote density near to each hypothesized

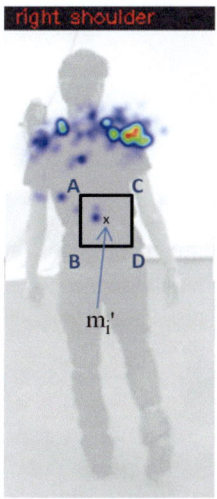

Figure 7.2.: Integral image trick for fast vote density integration. With four integral image matrix look-ups and four additions it is possible to compute the sum of vote density values within a rectangular region (where the size of this region depends on the 2D height of the current pose hypothesis) around a projected landmark $\mathbf{m}'_i$.

landmark location using the kernel density estimator from eqn. (7.5) again and again[1].

As we will see later in experiments Section 7.3 of this chapter, this definition for the landmark matching score function allows to test several millions of 3D pose candidates per second on a standard PC.

---

[1]Note, that the kernel size used for estimating the vote density nearby a hypothesized landmark location depends on the 2D size of the current pose hypothesis and therefore for each hypothesis the kernel size has to be adapted, which prohibits to pre-compute vote density values once with a fixed kernel size and use these vote density values.

Size of vote density accumulation area

The size r of the vote density accumulation area depends on the size h' of the projected pose hypothesis, i.e., we set $r \propto h'$, since we want to accumulate the vote density nearby the projected landmark locations. But "nearby" depends on the projected size of the pose hypothesis: for a person far away from the camera (having a projected size of, e.g., 100 pixels) the integration area should be small (e.g., $r = 10$), while for a person near to the camera (having a projected size of e.g., 500 pixels) the integration area should be correspondingly larger (e.g., $r = 50$)[2].

Further there is a tradeoff for the choice of r between hypothesis localization accuracy and providing gradients for the matching score function S to be made. On the one hand, r should be made small, such that the final projected landmark locations are located at the peaks of the vote density distributions in the corresponding landmark voting maps. On the other hand, a too small r could mean that an optimizer that searches for a good projection of a pose hypothesis onto the votemaps and that is guided by the form of the energy landscape induced by the score function S, can not find any gradients that guide the search into the right direction (e.g., if the vote density accumulation areas are such small that temporarily no vote density is contained within the areas).

7.2.3. Projections considered

The set of allowed projections T should correspond to the camera and its mapping properties used during application of the 3D pose estimator, i.e., if we expect, e.g., strong perspective foreshortening effects in the camera images (as in the experiments in Section 8.3), we have to use a perspective projection model and have to perform the optimization (see eqn. (7.1)) over the set of all perspective camera parameters. In the case of camera images that resemble orthographic projections, we can use a

---

[2] We could say that due to the usage of a simple stick-figure body model, landmarks are represented only as points in 3D and 2D, while they actually have some extension in reality. For this we have to accumulate the vote density in an area near to the projected landmark location $\mathbf{m}'_i$ proportional to the size (here: height in pixels) of the current 2D pose hypothesis considered for evaluation.

scaled orthographic projection model. The number of the projection model parameters is important, since the more parameters the projection model has, the larger will be the search space and the computation times.

For the experiments in this thesis we use the perspective projection model since it is the more generic model compared to the scaled orthographic projection model. For a given 3D pose candidate $\mathbf{q}$ represented by direction vectors between the 3D landmarks, we first generate a rotated and tilted version (rotation angle α, tilt angle β). Since we further do not know the size of the person, we also rescale the direction vectors by scaling factor s and shift the resulting 3D pose to a location (g_x, g_y, g_z) specified in global camera-centric coordinates. A 3D landmark (x, y, z) of this final 3D pose is then projected to a 2D pose $\mathbf{q}'$ using a perspective projection:

$$x' = -f\frac{x}{z} + c_x \qquad (7.12)$$
$$y' = -f\frac{y}{z} + c_y \qquad (7.13)$$

where f is the focal length, and (c_x, c_y) is the principal point, for which we use the image center here as an approximation. The resulting pose and projection parameters to be optimized are therefore $(\alpha, \beta, s, g_x, g_y, g_z, f)$, i.e., for each pose candidate we consider, there is a 7-dimensional parameter search space.

7.2.4. Pose candidates considered

7.2.4.1. Pose priors

One key issue in the optimization approach presented here is the definition of Q, which represents the set of all possible 3D poses that are considered during the optimization process.

A first approach is to allow for all possible pose candidates, that can be generated with the body model used (see Chapter 4). In the top row in Fig. 7.3 we generated 100 example poses where each of the 24 joint angles was drawn randomly from $[-\pi, \pi]$, i.e., here the poses were

45° viewpoint   120° viewpoint

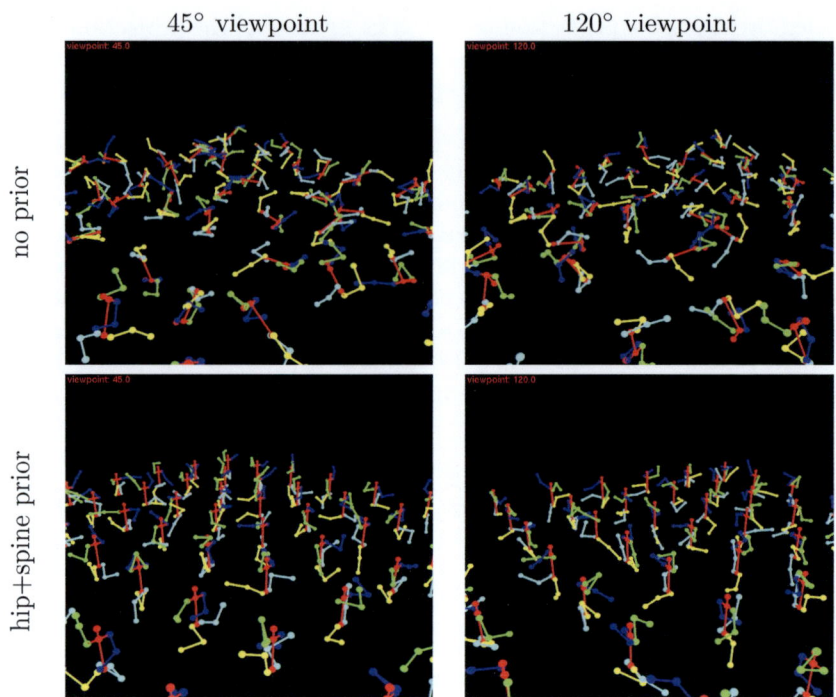

Figure 7.3.: Example poses drawn from different priors. 1st row: no prior, free deformation of the body model. 2nd row: hip parallel to floor, spine orthogonal to hip.

freely deformable. The set of sampled poses shows a lot of invalid body configurations concerning kinematic joint constraints. Even for a perfect landmark localization, where all the votes are casted at exactly the ground-truth locations of the landmark, a 3D pose $\mathbf{q}^*$ from this set of poses Q that maximizes S can be invalid, since its projection $\mathbf{q}'$ could perfectly project onto the true landmark locations, but violating joint constraints at the same time.

Further, the restricted monocular camera information leads to an inherent ambiguity in landmark localization as shown in chapter 6 (see e.g., Figs. 6.18, 6.19, B.4). In addition, landmark localization is often erroneous,

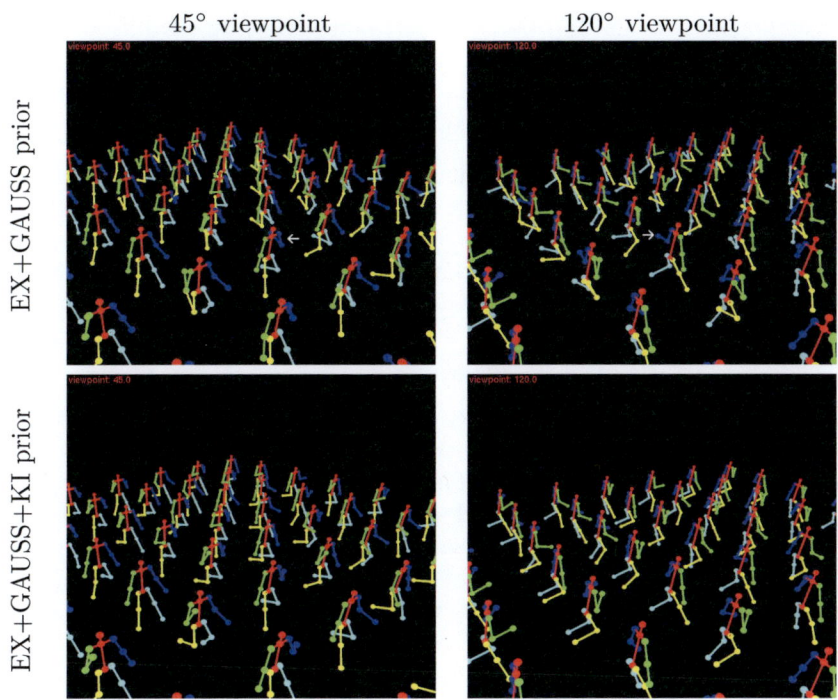

Figure 7.4.: Further examples of pose priors. 1st row: Gaussian-deformed example poses. 2nd row: Gaussian-deformed example poses with kinematic constraints.

due to many possible different sources of errors in the landmark localization pipeline: unstable keypoints, features declared to be a part of the person, while actually being a part of a background structure, etc.

Therefore, it is a natural idea to make use of information about typical human poses in the form of pose priors in order to compensate for missing, erroneous, or ambiguous information about the locations of the landmarks.

In the second row of Fig. 7.3 we used a first simple pose prior, where we restricted the hip plate to be parallel to the floor and the spine to be orthogonal to the hip plate, which is a valid assumption for many applications, where persons stand upright. Nevertheless, this pose prior is still inappropriate: many of the poses are invalid in the sense of impossible joint states compared to human joint restrictions.

In the first row of Fig. 7.4 we randomly draw a pose from the CMU motion capture database poses and generated 100 modified versions from it by changing each joint angle ϕ_i in the elbows and knees by some random offset joint angle α drawn from a Gaussian: i.e., $\phi_i' = \phi_i + \alpha$ and $\alpha \propto \mathcal{N}(0, \sigma^2)$. But by this procedure, impossible joint angles in the knees and elbows can result. As an example see the left elbow joint angle of the pose marked by the small white arrow in the image.

In the second row of Fig. 7.4 we show another pose prior. Here, we used the CMU motion capture database to first compute valid ranges for each joint angle of our body model (see appendix C). For each DOF of a joint all angles were considered as valid, which were observed at least once in the motion capture database and invalid else. Then we used the same mechanism as for drawing pose samples in the first row of Fig. 7.4, but discarded all 3D poses where we observed invalid joint angles. The resulting body configurations are now all valid variants of a given single example pose.

Using examples of real human poses has two main advantages. First, we can easily make sure that no invalid poses will result from the estimation step, since all example poses are valid 3D poses. Second, we can select the 3D example poses in advance such that the poses correspond to the poses that we expect in the pose estimation application and that we want to discriminate.

7.2.4.2. Example based pose prior

As motivated in the previous section, example poses can be used as prior knowledge about human poses to compensate for missing, erroneous, and ambiguous information provided by the landmark localization step. Here we consider the question how to map motion capture data to 3D poses such that it fits to our body model and how to retrieve a sparse set of example poses from the set of all 3D poses.

CMU motion capture database

Currently, the CMU motion capture database[3] is the largest publicly available motion capture database. It provides motion capture data for 144 different subjects, performing a large spectrum of different movements, including everyday movements as walking, running, sitting down, two persons shaking-hands, bending down and picking something up, etc. as well as sport movements as climbing, dancing, basketball, football, martial arts, gymnastics etc. Motions are recorded using a Vicon motion capture system that records the poses with 120 Hz, i.e., providing the poses with a high temporal resolution. The data is provided in the .c3d format, a common format used in bio-mechanics, gait analysis, and animation. For each landmark attached to the human body 3D coordinates are provided for each motion capture frame.

Landmark locations differing from used body model

When using motion capture data in order to learn, e.g., typical joint angles, or to generate a set of example poses, one has to make sure that the landmark locations used in the motion capture data are comparable to the landmark locations used in the body model. Fig. 7.5 shows the names and locations used for the CMU motion capture sequences.

We can see that the left hip landmarks are placed at lower locations compared to our body model. Further, the left and right hip landmarks are positioned at different heights which allows for a better distinction between both landmarks in the Vicon motion capture system, but is different to our body model where both hip landmarks are positioned at the same height. For this, there is a need to adapt the landmark locations slightly in order to make them consistent with our body model, i.e., here we have to shift the left and right hip landmark upwards on the direction vector from the knee to the hip landmark and to correct for the height difference between the left and right hip landmark.

---

[3]http://mocap.cs.cmu.edu

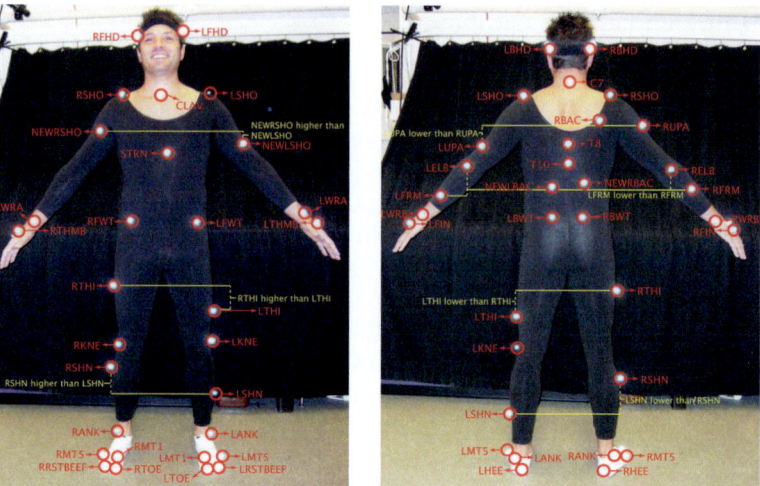

Figure 7.5.: Landmark locations used for CMU database. Locations and names of all landmarks recorded for the CMU motion capture sequences. Note, that the right hip and left hip landmarks are attached at different heights onto the legs.

Missing landmarks

Further, some landmarks of our body model are not present at all in the motion capture data. There is no corresponding lower spine landmark in the CMU motion capture landmark set. Since this landmark is located in our body model between the left and right hip, we compute this lower spine landmark location by $\mathbf{m}_2 = \mathbf{m}_9 + 0.5(\mathbf{m}_{12} - \mathbf{m}_9)$. There is also no corresponding head center landmark, but two landmarks ("RFHD" = right forehead, "LFHD" = left forehead) attached to the left and right side of the forehead (see Fig. 7.5 left). The location of the head center landmark in our body model is therefore approximated by the mean of the locations $\mathbf{m}_{RFHD}$ and $\mathbf{m}_{LFHD}$ of these two landmarks: $\mathbf{m}_0 = 0.5(\mathbf{m}_{RFHD} + \mathbf{m}_{LFHD})$.

Fig. 7.6 shows a comparison between an example of an original motion capture data sequence (top row) with the motion capture data adapted to our body model (bottom row). In the top row we only show the landmarks

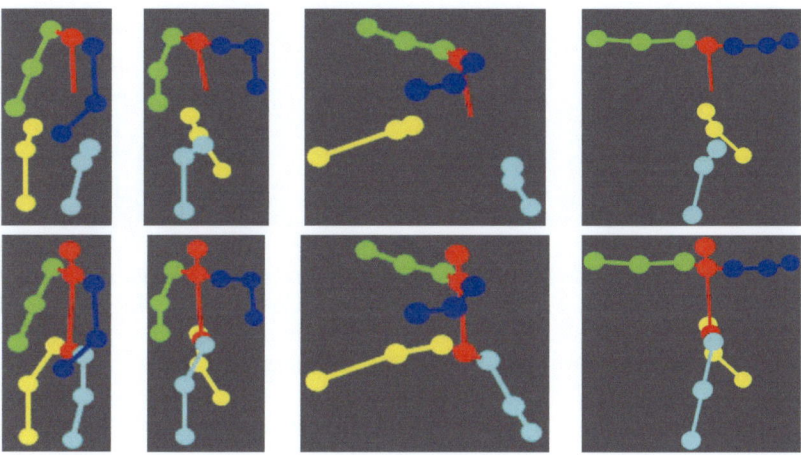

Figure 7.6.: Mapping motion capture data to the body model. Top row: original CMU motion capture data. Bottom row: motion capture data adapted to our body model.

from the CMU landmark set that directly correspond to our body model: the head, and lower spine landmarks are missing. Further, left and right hip landmarks are at different heights (compare yellow and blue leg).

Motion capture data vs. ground truth data

Marker-based motion capture data as the CMU motion capture data is often considered as ground truth data in the context of HPE. Nevertheless, sometimes even the marker-based capturing process fails and some landmark locations are wrong. We observed that this is especially the case for the head landmark in the CMU motion capture sequences. Since for a wrong landmark location, the relative limb length of a limb typically changes dramatically compared to the standard relative limb lengths, we check for each 3D pose generated from the CMU motion capture data whether the relative limb lengths are plausible, i.e., correspond to Table 4.1 (b) with some small tolerance. If this is not the case, we discard the 3D pose.

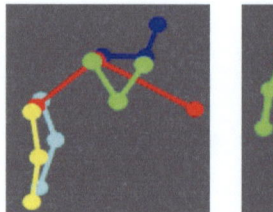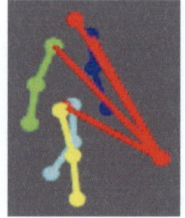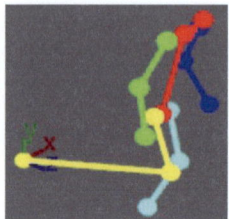

Figure 7.7.: Wrong CMU motion capture landmark locations. For some motion capture frames, the landmark-based motion capture process fails. We detect such wrong 3D poses by checking the relative limb lengths for plausibility which allows to filter for wrong 3D poses automatically.

Selection of example poses

The CMU motion capture database consist of approximately 2.7 million (valid) example 3D poses. This number is far too large to use all these 3D poses as examples for an example based pose estimation, since for each example 3D pose we have to find the optimal projection parameters, to project the example pose onto the vote distribution.

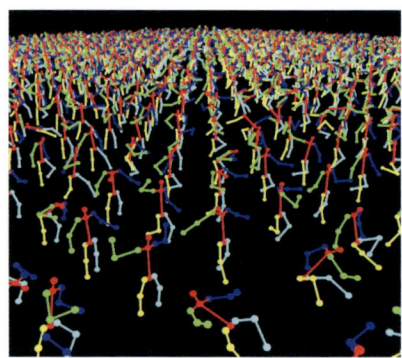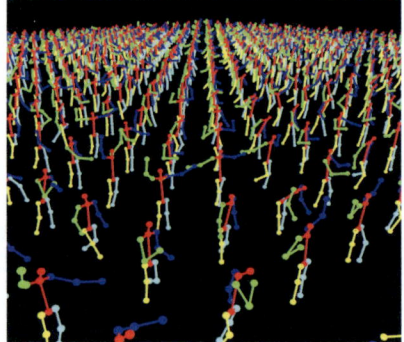

Figure 7.8.: Example poses retrieved from CMU and UMPM database. Left: 4270 example poses retrieved from CMU motion capture database. Right: 2284 example poses retrieved from UMPM database.

Therefore we reduce the motion capture dataset to a much smaller number of example poses by traversing the whole database pose by pose and adding only such poses to a growing set of example poses Q_0 that are significantly different to the example poses collected so far. A pose $\mathbf{q}_1$ is considered as *significantly different*, if we can find no pose $\mathbf{q}_2 \in Q_0$, such that the difference between all articulation angles is less than Θ (here: $\Theta = \pi/4$), i.e.

$$\min(|\phi_i^{q_1} - \phi_i^{q_2}|, 2\pi - |\phi_i^{q_1} - \phi_i^{q_2}|) < \Theta \qquad (7.14)$$

The CMU motion capture database consists of 2395 sequences (.c3d files), but 276 were unreadable, so only 2119 sequences could be used. From these we analyzed 2.779.646 valid 3D poses, while 564.376 were discarded as invalid, since one of the 14 limb lengths was detected to be abnormal. Using the procedure explained above to select example poses, we collected 4270 poses (see Fig. 7.8 left).

The UMPM motion capture database consists of 69 sequences (.c3d files). 684.346 poses were valid, 21.932 invalid. The resulting example set contains 2284 example poses (see Fig. 7.8 right). The 6 sequences used from the HumanEva dataset contain 2495 different 3D poses. The generated example set contains 1300 of these poses.

In Fig. 7.9 we plot the growth of the example set Q_0, while traversing the motion capture database. In both cases, for some of the motion capture sequences the number of example poses added to Q_0 is large which results in a fast growth of $|Q_0|$, since significant new poses are contained in the corresponding sequences. In contrast, some sequences do only show a small number of new 3D poses compared to the example poses collected so far, resulting only in a minor increase of $|Q_0|$.

For each single example pose $\mathbf{r} = (\mathbf{n}_0, ..., \mathbf{n}_J) \in Q_0$ consisting of J 3D landmark locations $\mathbf{n}_i$ ($0 \leq i \leq J$, here: $J{=}14$) we have to consider tilted (by angle α) and rotated (by angle β) versions $\mathbf{q} = (\mathbf{m}_0, ..., \mathbf{m}_J)$ during the optimization process, since we want to project the 3D pose onto the landmarks but do not know the orientation of the overall pose relative to the camera. The set Q of 3D pose candidates considered during optimization can therefore be written as:

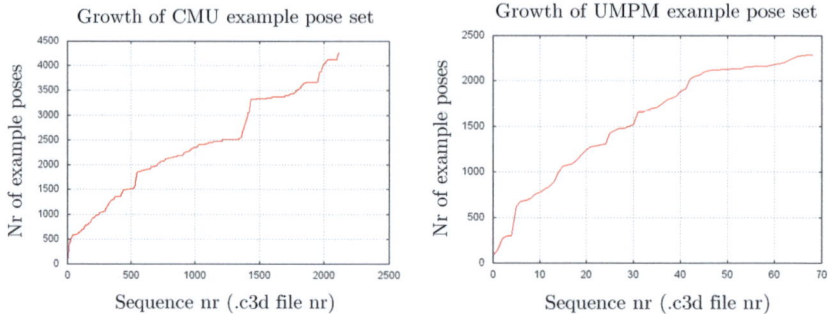

Figure 7.9.: Growth of example pose set while traversing the CMU and UMPM motion capture database. While the motion capture database is traversed sequence by sequence and example poses are collected, we plot the size $|Q_0|$ of the set of example poses Q_0 to visualize its growth. Left: for CMU, Right: for UMPM.

$$Q = \{\mathbf{q} = (\mathbf{m}_0, ..., \mathbf{m}_J) : \mathbf{r} = (\mathbf{n}_0, ..., \mathbf{n}_J) \in Q_0,$$
$$\alpha, \beta \in \mathbb{R}, \mathbf{m}_i = R_x(\alpha)R_y(\beta)\mathbf{n}_i, 1 \le i \le J\} \quad (7.15)$$

where R_x and R_y are 3x3 rotation matrices that rotate a 3D point around the x- or y-axis (see Section 4.3).

7.2.5. Optimization strategy

The number of projection and pose parameters that can be modified during the optimization process for finding a good 3D pose and projection pair, can result in a high number of search space dimensions. Even for a small number of projection / pose parameters and a discrete sampling step width for each parameter it is usually not possible to try out all parameter combinations due to the combinatorial explosion of the number of parameter combinations. For this, it is important to choose an optimization strategy that is suitable for large search space dimensions.

Particle based methods, as e.g., particle filters, are often used for generative approaches to human pose estimation, e.g. [Feldmann, 2012]. Here we propose to use Particle Swarm Optimization (PSO) which was originally introduced in [Kennedy and Eberhart, 1995]. Evaluations on benchmarks with high dimensional test functions have shown that PSO is appropriate to work even for search problems in high dimensional search spaces (e.g., finding the maximum of test functions with dimension 30, [Bratton and Kennedy, 2007]). [Poli et al., 2007] provides an excellent introduction and overview on variants of the PSO approach family.

There are only 3 other publications that used PSO in the context of HPE, but none of them for monocular HPE. [Ivekovič et al., 2008] uses silhouettes, [John et al., 2010] uses edges and silhouettes, and [Zhang et al., 2011] uses the visual hull for comparing the model with the image evidence. All three approaches are multiple view approaches, i.e., input images from more than just one camera are needed, while the approach presented here works with the much more limited monocular camera information.

7.2.5.1. Particle Swarm Optimization

The basic idea of PSO is to use a set $P = \{\mathbf{l}_i = (\mathbf{x}_i, \mathbf{v}_i, \mathbf{b}_i, \mu_i) : 1 \leq i \leq R\}$ (the population / the swarm) of R particles that move through the search space of dimension D and evaluate each search space location visited. Since not all search space locations can be visited, a strategy is needed that controls how the particles move around. For this, each particle does not only store its location $\mathbf{x}_i \in \mathbb{R}^D$ in the search space, but also has a velocity vector $\mathbf{v}_i \in \mathbb{R}^D$.

The velocity vector update formula for a particle $\mathbf{l}_i$ is controlled by two forces: it is pulled into the direction of its so called "personal best" location $\mathbf{b}_i \in \mathbb{R}^D$ (where the score function evaluates to μ_i) – found so far in the search space traversal history of the particle – and into the direction of the so called "global best" location $\mathbf{g}^* \in \mathbb{R}^D$ (where the score function evaluates to μ^*), which corresponds to the best location found by all the particles since the search started. At each iteration of the optimization, a new velocity vector is computed for each particle and used to update the location of the particle. The $d-th$ components ($1 \leq d \leq D$) of the D-dimensional velocity and location vectors of a particle are updated by:

$$v_i^d \leftarrow \xi \left(v_i^d + r_1(b_i^d - x_i^d) + r_2(g^d - x_i^d)\right) \tag{7.16}$$

$$x_i^d \leftarrow x_i^d + v_i^d \tag{7.17}$$

where $r_1 \in \mathcal{U}(0, \phi_1)$ and $r_2 \in \mathcal{U}(0, \phi_2)$ are random numbers, uniformly drawn from the intervals $[0, \phi_1]$, and $[0, \phi_2]$ respectively, i.e., PSO is a Monte-Carlo approach, since the strength of the force with which the velocity is updated into the direction of the personal and global best is computed randomly. By this particle location update procedure the particles switch randomly between a local search ($r_1 > r_2$) and moving towards the best global maximum found so far ($r_2 > r_1$). ξ is called "constriction coefficient" since it can be chosen such that the convergence of the particles can be ensured, if

$$\phi = \phi_1 + \phi_2 > 4 \tag{7.18}$$

$$\xi = \frac{2}{\phi - 2 + \sqrt{\phi^2 - 4\phi}} \tag{7.19}$$

The convergence proof for this parameter selection was first presented in [Clerc and Kennedy, 2002]. The particles are initialized at random start locations $\mathbf{x}_i$ with random velocity vectors $\mathbf{v}_i$. Locations and velocities are updated according to eqn. (7.16) and eqn. (7.17) until all particles or C% of the particles have converged, i.e., the velocity vector of C% of the particles is near to the null vector. In our experiments we used C=90%. Finding the global maximum cannot be guaranteed by the PSO algorithm, but an advantage of this search method is that it is not gradient based, i.e., the objective (evaluation) function needs not to be differentiable.

While this is the standard PSO algorithm, a lot of PSO variants have been proposed in literature. Some works explored different communication topologies (including even dynamic topologies) between the particles for communicating their personal best location. Variants of the velocity update formula (7.16) have been explored as well. Instead of using the personal best and global best direction vector only, e.g., a variant is to use the probabilistic sum of the direction vectors to the personal best locations of all particles, which is called "Fully Informed PSO" [Kennedy, 2002]:

$$v_i^d \quad \leftarrow \quad \xi(v_i^d + \frac{1}{R} \sum_{i=1}^{R} r_i(b_i^d - x_i^d)) \tag{7.20}$$

with $r_i \in \mathcal{U}(0, \phi)$.

7.2.5.2. PSO for optimizing pose and projection parameters

As mentioned in Section 7.2.3 there are 7 parameters to be optimized by the particle swarm optimizer: $(\alpha, \beta, s, g_x, g_y, g_z, f)$.

Algorithm 3 shows the pseudo code for 3D pose estimation using a PSO optimizer. In line 12 within the ESTIMATE function a separate PSO optimization is initiated for each 3D example pose $\mathbf{r}$. Since the optimizations for the example poses are independent of each other, this loop can be processed in parallel (using e.g., OpenMP). For each example pose $\mathbf{r}$ an own swarm P is generated in lines 13-19, and particles are updated till convergence in lines 19-31. The objective function evaluations for an example pose / particle location $\mathbf{x}_i$ pair takes place in the EVALUATE function, which first generates a rotated and tilted version $\mathbf{q}$ of the example pose $\mathbf{r}$, scales all of the segments of the resulting 3D pose by s, moves this 3D pose to the global camera-centric coordinates (g_x, g_y, g_z), and uses a perspective projection to project it to the 2D image in order to compute a matching score value $S(\mathbf{q}')$.

Algorithm 3 PSO based 3D Pose Estimation Pseudo Code
input:
(c_x, c_y): image center
Q_0: set of example 3D poses
ρ_l: vote density map for each landmark $(1 \leq l \leq J)$
N: number of particles to use
C: convergence threshold
output:
$(\mathbf{g}^*, \mathbf{r}^*)$: best matching 3D pose $\mathbf{r}^*$ with pose and projection parameters $\mathbf{g}^*$ found

---

1: **function** evaluate($\mathbf{r} = (\mathbf{n}_0, ..., \mathbf{n}_J), \mathbf{x}_i = (\alpha, \beta, s, g_x, g_y, g_z, f)$)
2:     $\mathbf{q} = (\mathbf{m}_0, ..., \mathbf{m}_i)$ with $\mathbf{m}_i = R_x(\alpha)R_y(\beta)\mathbf{n}_i$ $(1 \leq i \leq J)$ ▷ rotate/tilt pose
3:     $\mathbf{q} = \mathbf{q}.\text{scale}(s)$ ▷ rescale direction vectors to adopt for person size
4:     $\mathbf{q} = \mathbf{q}.\text{translate}(g_x, g_y, g_z)$ ▷ move to 3D global camera coordinates
5:     $\mathbf{q}' = (\mathbf{m}'_0, ..., \mathbf{m}'_J)$ with $\mathbf{m}'_i = (-f\frac{x}{z} + c_x, -f\frac{y}{z} + c_y : \mathbf{m}_i = (x, y, z))$ ▷ project
6:     compute $S(\mathbf{q}')$ according to eqn. (7.4) using vote density maps ρ_l
7:     **return** matching score $S(\mathbf{q}')$
8: **end function**
9:
10: **function** estimate($(p_x, p_y), Q_0, \{\rho_l : 1 \leq l \leq J\}, N, C$)
11:     $\mu^{**} \leftarrow -\infty$ ▷ init best score found for all example poses
12:     **for all** $\mathbf{r} \in Q_0$ **do**   ▷ for all example poses
13:         $\mu^* \leftarrow -\infty$ ▷ init best score found for current example pose
14:         $P \leftarrow \varnothing$
15:         **for** i=1 to N **do**   ▷ generate particle population
16:             generate random start location $\mathbf{x}_i = (\alpha, \beta, s, g_x, g_y, g_z, f)$, velocity $\mathbf{v}_i$
17:             $\mathbf{b}_i \leftarrow \mathbf{0}, \mu_i \leftarrow -\infty$
18:             $P \leftarrow P \cup \{l_i = (\mathbf{x}_i, \mathbf{v}_i, \mathbf{b}_i, \mu_i)\}$ ▷ add new particle to population
19:         **end for**
20:         **repeat**
21:             **for** i=1 to N **do**   ▷ evaluate & update each particle
22:                 score = evaluate($\mathbf{r}, \mathbf{x}_i$)
23:                 **if** score $> \mu_i$ **then**   ▷ new personal best found?
24:                     $\mu_i \leftarrow score, \mathbf{b}_i \leftarrow \mathbf{x}_i$ ▷ store new personal best score & location
25:                     **if** $\mu_i > \mu^*$ **then**   ▷ new global best found?
26:                         $\mu^* \leftarrow \mu_i, \mathbf{g} \leftarrow \mathbf{b}_i$ ▷ store new global best score & location
27:                     **end if**
28:                 **end if**
29:                 update $\mathbf{v}_i, \mathbf{x}_i$ according to eqn. (7.16),eqn. (7.17)
30:             **end for**
31:         **until** $>$ C% of particles converged
32:         **if** $\mu^* > \mu^{**}$ **then**   ▷ found better matching example pose?
33:             $\mu^{**} \leftarrow \mu^*, \mathbf{g}^* \leftarrow \mathbf{g}, \mathbf{r}^* \leftarrow \mathbf{r}$
34:         **end if**
35:     **end for**
36:     **return** $(\mathbf{g}^*, \mathbf{r}^*)$
37: **end function**

7.2.6. Pose splines

7.2.6.1. Softening the example based prior

The example based pose prior from Section 7.2.4.2 is a "hard" prior: we only consider rotated and tilted versions of example 3D poses as pose hypotheses. All other 3D poses are not considered. The idea presented here is to increase the set of allowed poses by allowing for linearly interpolated versions of two example 3D poses as well. For two randomly selected example poses, we can not guarantee that the linear interpolated pose will be a valid pose in terms of kinematic joint constraints. But for two 3D poses that appear shortly after each other within a motion sequence, we can linearly interpolate between both and the resulting interpolated 3D pose will be valid with a very high probability if the poses are not too different. By using interpolated poses as pose candidates as well, we do not only increase the number of pose candidates, but we can also try to compress motion sequences significantly by representing a whole motion sequence by a sparse set of supporting point 3D poses and generate the omitted poses – that were present in the original motion sequence, but are not selected as a supporting pose – by linear interpolation. Here we call this resulting sparse representation of a motion sequence by means of supporting poses a "pose spline". It can be considered as an alternative to the example based pose prior.

7.2.6.2. Interpolating 3D poses

An important issue is how to interpolate between two 3D poses. The Euler joint angle representation of a 3D pose is not appropriate, since Euler rotations consist of 3 successive rotations where each rotation is executed about the coordinate axis of the resulting rotated coordinate system. This corresponds mathematically to the product of 3 basic rotation matrices. Since the order of matrices is important in the product, Euler rotations are not commutative.

Instead of interpolating between Euler angles for computing an interpolated 3D pose, we linearly interpolate between the bone direction vectors of two example 3D poses $\mathbf{r}_1$ and $\mathbf{r}_2$. This is one of many approaches used in computer graphics for generating new motions (e.g., [Wiley and Hahn, 1997]). The bone (limb, segment) unit direction vector $\mathbf{b}_{k}^{ij}$ from landmark i to landmark j for the example pose $\mathbf{r}_k$ (k=1,2) can be computed by

$$\mathbf{b}_{k}^{ij} = (\mathbf{m}_{j}^{k} - \mathbf{m}_{i}^{k})/\|\mathbf{m}_{j}^{k} - \mathbf{m}_{i}^{k}\| \qquad (7.21)$$

where $\mathbf{m}_{i}^{k}$ is the i-th 3D landmark coordinate from example 3D pose $\mathbf{r}_k$.

For an interpolated 3D pose $\mathbf{q}$, the bone $\mathbf{b}^{ij}$ unit direction vector of $\mathbf{q}$ can then be computed by

$$\mathbf{b}^{ij} = \tau \mathbf{b}_{1}^{ij} + (1 - \tau)\mathbf{b}_{2}^{ij} \qquad (7.22)$$

The 3D coordinates of the interpolated 3D pose can then be computed by iteratively reconstructing the landmark coordinates along the hierarchy of the kinematic tree. If we already have the parent landmark coordinate $\mathbf{m}_i$ computed, we can reconstruct the child landmark $\mathbf{m}_j$ coordinate by

$$\mathbf{m}_j = \mathbf{m}_i + r_{ij}\mathbf{b}^{ij} \qquad (7.23)$$

where r_{ij} is the typical relative bone/segment length form landmark i to landmark j, see Table 4.1 (b).

Fig. 7.10 shows two interpolation experiment examples, where we varied τ from 0 to 1 for two randomly selected 3D poses and observed the interpolation results. The figures show the interpolated 3D pose $\mathbf{q}$ (denoted by [ip] = [interpolated pose] in Fig. 7.10) for $\tau \in \{0.75, 0.5, 0.25\}$.

The resulting interpolated poses shown in Fig. 7.10 are valid 3D poses. Nevertheless, this interpolation strategy does not guarantee that $\mathbf{q}$ will be a valid 3D pose in terms of possible human joint states. While the example 3D poses $\mathbf{r}_1, \mathbf{r}_2$ used in Fig. 7.10 are very different, since randomly selected from different motion sequences and random motion capture frame numbers, for a motion sequence successive 3D poses are much more similar and the probability that the interpolated 3D pose is invalid is therefore much smaller.

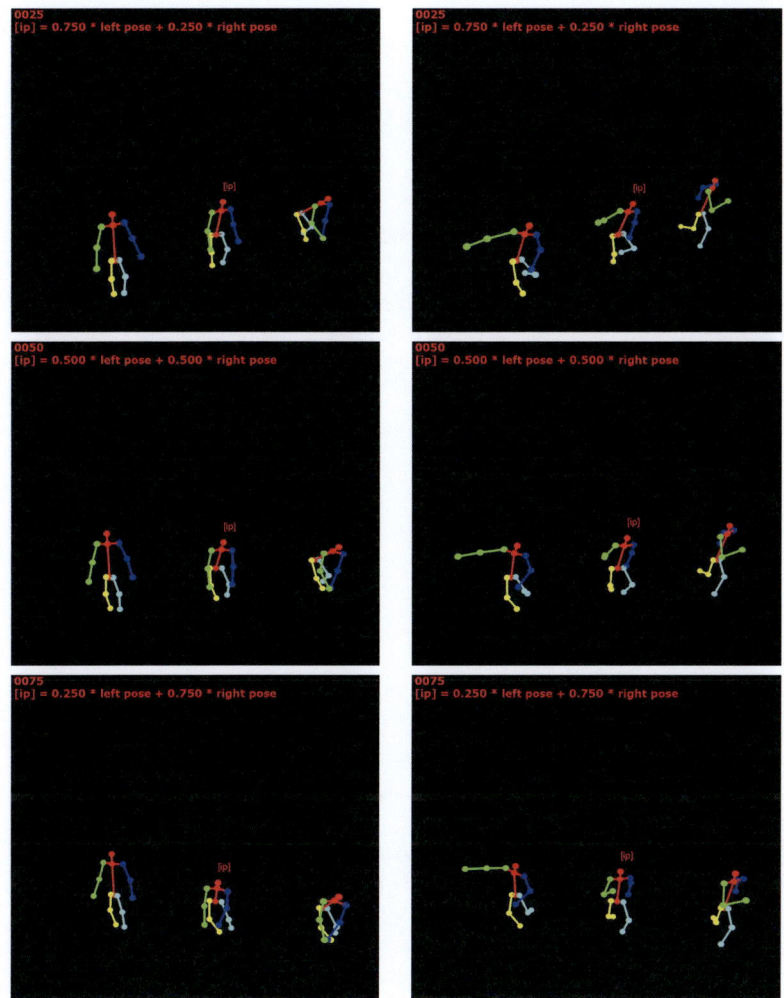

Figure 7.10.: Examples of linearly interpolated 3D poses. 1st column: examples of 3D pose interpolation results for a (i) standing and (ii) volleyball pose. 2nd column: examples of 3D pose interpolation results for two different running poses.

7.2.6.3. Generating pose splines

A linear spline is a piecewise linear function f, specified by a set of supporting points, where the function values between two supporting points are linearly interpolated.

We represent a whole motion sequence of length N, consisting of example poses $\mathcal{S}_0 = \{\mathbf{r}_1, ..., \mathbf{r}_N\}$ by the linear spline idea, i.e., select a sparse set of supporting points (poses) $\mathcal{S} \subseteq \mathcal{S}_0$ such that omitted 3D poses $\mathbf{r}$ $(\mathbf{r} \in \mathcal{S}_0 \wedge \mathbf{r} \notin \mathcal{S})$ can be linearly interpolated with two successive supporting poses $\mathbf{r}_1, \mathbf{r}_2$, i.e., we can find a $\tau \in [0,1]$ such that $\circledast(\tau, \mathbf{r}_1, \mathbf{r}_2) \approx \mathbf{r}$, where $\circledast$ is the pose interpolation operator (method) described in previous Section 7.2.6.2.

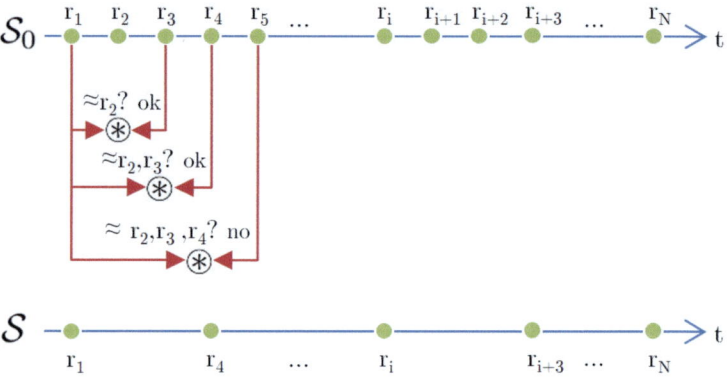

Figure 7.11.: Pose spline generation. For a given motion sequence, we determine a sparse set of supporting 3D poses, such that omitted 3D poses can linearly be interpolated using the non omitted poses.

For the generation of a pose spline $\mathcal{S}$ representation of a motion sequence $\mathcal{S}_0$, we want to "compress" the motion sequence as much as possible, i.e., to omit as many poses as possible. For this, we start by adding the first 3D pose $\mathbf{r}_1 \in \mathcal{S}_0$ to $\mathcal{S}$ and then test whether $\mathbf{r}_2$ can be linearly interpolated by $\mathbf{r}_1$ and $\mathbf{r}_3$. If this is not the case, $\mathbf{r}_2$ is added to $\mathcal{S}$ as well. If it is the case, we try whether we can interpolate $\mathbf{r}_2$ and $\mathbf{r}_3$ with the help of $\mathbf{r}_1$ and $\mathbf{r}_4$. If this is not the case, we add $\mathbf{r}_3$ to $\mathcal{S}$. If it is the case, we proceed in the same way, always trying to push the next supporting pose as far (temporarily) as possible from the last supporting pose to omit as many intermediate poses from the original motion sequence as possible (see Fig. 7.11).

For the above pose spline generation procedure we need a test method that checks whether for two given supporting point candidate poses $\mathbf{r}_i, \mathbf{r}_j$, a third pose $\mathbf{r}$ can be linearly interpolated by both. For this, we compute the set

$$\mathcal{I}(\mathbf{r}_i, \mathbf{r}_j) = \{\mathbf{r}' = \circledast(\tau, \mathbf{r}_i, \mathbf{r}_j) : \tau = n0.001, 1 \leq n \leq 1000\} \tag{7.24}$$

of interpolated variants and search for an interpolated 3D pose $\mathbf{r}'$ that is similar to $\mathbf{r}$. Here, $\mathbf{r}'$ is considered as similar to $\mathbf{r}$ if none of the joint angles is more different than $10°$. If we find at least one similar pose, we say that $\mathbf{r}$ can be linearly interpolated by $\mathbf{r}_i$ and $\mathbf{r}_j$.

7.2.6.4. Optimization with pose splines

An advantage of pose splines is not only that we can represent a whole motion sequence by a sparse set of supporting point poses, but also that we can move continuously along the motion sequence by a single parameter $\lambda \in [0, 1]$, where 0 represents the starting point and 1 the end point of the sequence.

For a given $\lambda \in [0, 1)$ we compute the corresponding 3D pose $\mathbf{q}$ given a pose spline $S = \{\mathbf{r}_1, ..., \mathbf{r}_N\}$ as follows:

$$i = \left\lfloor \frac{\lambda}{N} \right\rfloor \tag{7.25}$$

$$\lambda' = \lambda - i \tag{7.26}$$

$$\mathbf{q} = \circledast(1 - \lambda', \mathbf{r}_i, \mathbf{r}_{i+1}) \tag{7.27}$$

Here i represents the next supporting point to the left from λ, λ' is the fraction with which we have to go from supporting point pose $\mathbf{r}_i$ into the direction of $\mathbf{r}_{i+1}$ on the interpolation line. For $\lambda = 1$, we use the last supporting point pose of the spline / motion sequence, i.e., $\mathbf{q} = \mathbf{r}_N$.

Adapting the PSO optimization approach to work with pose splines is straightforward. Instead of traversing all example poses, we traverse over all pose splines (see algorithm 3, line 12). Additionally, we introduce a new search space dimension, namely the location λ on the pose spline, i.e., augment the PSO particle state vectors by one further dimension to $\mathbf{x}_i = (\alpha, \beta, s, g_x, g_y, g_z, f, \lambda)$. For the evaluation of a particle location, we have to generate the example pose first according to eqn. (7.27) using the pose spline generation (i.e., in algorithm 3 before line 2), before rotating and tilting it.

7.3. Evaluation

7.3.1. Experiments conducted

Evaluation datasets

From the list of publicly available evaluation datasets in Chapter 3 we choose the UMPM dataset for evaluation. Persons appear natural and the dataset allows to define a large set of experiments since it is by far the largest of all human pose evaluation datasets. Another important reason to choose this dataset is the possibility to test the 3D pose estimation accuracy in cases of occlusion as well, in contrast to all other publicly available datasets. For the UMPM dataset, we use the same set of experiments conducted for landmark localization accuracy evaluation defined in Table 6.1. Unfortunately, there are no other works that report 3D pose estimation performance on this dataset since the dataset is available only since November 2011. For this, we conduct another set of experiments on the HumanEva dataset – which is the most widely used evaluation dataset in the context of HPE and available since 2006 – as well, to make the performance of the method presented here better comparable to other works.

Pose priors used

For the evaluation of the generative pose estimation approach presented here, we used 6 variants of pose estimators. EX-UMPM, EX-HE, and EX-CMU are example-based pose estimators, that use the 2284 UMPM, 1300 HumanEva and 4270 CMU example poses retrieved from the corresponding motion capture databases, as described in details in Section 7.2.4.2.

PS-UMPM, PS-HE, and PS-CMU are pose spline based pose estimators. For PS-CMU we used 2119 .c3d motion capture sequences (276 others were unreadable) of the CMU motion capture database. From the 2779646 valid poses 94926 were kept as supporting poses for the pose splines, i.e., the database representation was compressed to 3.41% of the original number of 3D poses.

For PS-HE we used all 6 motion capture sequences available. From the 2495 poses, 252 3D poses were used as supporting point poses for the pose splines, i.e., the sequences were represented by 10% of the original number of 3D poses.

For PS-UMPM all .c3d sequences were used except the sequences that were later used for testing, resulting in 127 pose splines. 667349 poses were valid, 7209 were automatically detected as invalid (see Section 7.2.4.2) due to abnormal limb lengths when reading the motion sequences. The total number of supporting points needed for all 127 pose splines was 16494, i.e., the 127 motion sequences could be compressed using the pose splines idea to 2.47% of the original number of 3D poses.

Input/output for each experiment

For estimating the 3D pose of a person in each experiment we use as input the set of all local features that have their keypoint location within the ground truth bounding box of a person image. These local features vote for the location of each of the 15 anatomical landmarks using COMBI-VOT as described in Chapter 6. Then the actual 3D pose estimation process starts using pose candidates from the set of example poses (EX) or sampled from pose splines (PS). The output for each test frame and person hypothesis is the 3D pose $\mathbf{q}^*$ that maximizes the overall matching score S according to Particle Swarm Optimization (see eqn. (7.1)).

7.3.2. Quantitative results

In Table 7.1 we present the 3D landmark location error – μ_{seq} (see eqn. (3.3)) – per 3D pose estimator and experiment and for each pose estimator averaged over all experiments (last line in table) for the UMPM experiments and in Table 7.2 the corresponding results for the HumanEva experiments.

I. Similar 3D pose errors for example based (EX) and pose spline (PS) based pose priors

The example based and pose spline based pose estimators do not show large differences in the resulting errors: e.g., in exp. 41 for EX-HE the average landmark localization error is about 9.9cm, while it is for PS-HE 9.5cm. This means that the pose spline representation based estimators yield 3D pose estimates of similar quality as the example based 3D pose estimators.

II. Large influence of the pose prior

When searching for a 3D pose that fits good to the observed landmark vote distributions, it is important that there is a similar 3D pose in the set of possible pose candidates compared to the one that is currently visible in the image. This is shown clearly by the quantitative results. For example EX-HE uses 3D poses from the HumanEva motion capture database, while EX-CMU uses example poses retrieved from the CMU motion capture database that do not directly contain boxing 3D poses and therefore needs to approximate the actual visible boxing pose by a similar 3D pose contained in the database. This explains why the average 3D pose error is only 16.2cm for EX-HE, while it is 24.6cm for EX-CMU. A similar difference in the resulting error can be observed for PS-HE and PS-CMU as well.

III. No large influence of the codebook

Similar to the results for the landmark localization accuracy in Section 6.3.3, there is no large difference regarding the 3D landmark localization error between the experiments where the UMPM or HumanEva codebook is used and the experiments where the generic codebook is used (compare results of experiments with odd number with results of experiments with even number). E.g., in exp. 59 where we used the HumanEva codebook (15 landmark ISMs are trained on HumanEva codebook) the average 3D localization error is 12.1cm for EX-HE, while in exp. 60 where we used the generic codebook (15 landmark ISMs are trained on the generic codebook) the average error is 12.9cm.

IV. Large differences for different action classes

There are large differences between the experiments regarding the absolute pose estimation errors. These differences can often be traced back to the differences in the ISM based landmark localization step. In experiments where the landmark localization was better, the 3D pose estimation results are often better as well. E.g., for experiments 01-06 less votes were correct compared to experiments 07-14 (for COMBI-VOT, see Table 6.3). Correspondingly, the 3D landmark localization error in experiments 01-06 is significantly larger compared to experiments 07-14 (for EX-UMPM).

V. Spline based pose estimators converge faster to a solution than example based variants

In Table 7.3 we present computation times needed for each of the 6 different 3D pose estimator variants (averaged over all persons, frames and experiments 01-40 for UMPM and 41-64 for HumanEva respectively), evaluated on a standard desktop PC (Intel Xeon W3690 64bit processor, 3.47 GHz, 6 cores).

In the first column we present the absolute computation time needed by the implementation[4] of the author for each of the methods to return a single 3D pose estimate. PS-HE is by far the fastest method with 50 poses / sec. But these numbers can not be directly used to rank the methods regarding their computation times, since the number of example poses (EX-HE: 1300, EX-UMPM: 2284, EX-CMU: 4270) and pose splines (PS-HE: 6, PS-UMPM: 127, PS-CMU: 2119) used as basis for retrieving 3D pose hypotheses are very different. The difference in the absolute computation times are therefore mainly due to the different numbers of example poses or motion sequences used as pose priors.

Nevertheless, since each of the EX and PS variant is trained on the same database and the resulting 3D pose errors are nearly the same as shown

---

[4]Algorithms implemented in C++ code.

above, it is interesting to compare the number of 3D pose evaluations[5] needed by the EX pose estimator and its corresponding PS variant till the PSO based optimization procedure converges and stops[6]. Here we see a clear difference: all the PS based 3D pose estimators need fewer evaluations compared to their EX analogue. E.g., EX-UMPM has to evaluate 9.84 million 3D poses till convergence, while PS-UMPM only needs 0.79 million evaluations.

The reason why the pose spline based 3D pose estimators converge faster to a solution compared to the example based pose estimators might be traced back to the fact that while an example based pose estimator will always have to consider all 3D pose candidates in its example set, the spline based pose estimators can treat the pose candidates on each spline as a dimension where they can freely move along in order to find a good 3D pose candidate and thereby are not forced to test always all possible 3D pose candidates.

Both, the example based and pose spline based 3D pose estimators evaluate a huge set of 3D pose candidates per second. While the example-based 3D pose estimator can evaluate approx. 10 million 3D poses per second, the spline based 3D pose estimator evaluate approx. 3 million 3D poses per second. The number of evaluations per second is smaller for the spline based pose estimators since these have to generate a 3D example pose from for a given spline location λ first before it can be projected to the 2D image, while the 3D example based pose estimator variants directly store example poses as a set of 15 3D landmark locations.

---

[5]EVALUATE() function calls in Algorithm 3

[6]Using the same PSO stop criterion: 75% of the N=100 particles have to converge.

Exp #	Exp code	3D landmark localization error [cm]			
		EX-UMPM	EX-CMU	PS-UMPM	PS-CMU
01	U-chair-2-1	27.5	33.1	28.9	30.5
02	G-chair-2-1	28.2	32.4	27.2	30.5
03	U-chair-4-1	30.1	35.5	31.3	33.5
04	G-chair-4-1	28.4	33.6	29.9	32.6
05	U-chair-3-2	23.2	26.6	22.9	25.5
06	G-chair-3-2	23.8	27.5	23.5	26.1
07	U-grab-2-1	16.6	21.9	17.1	20.2
08	G-grab-2-1	16.6	21.9	17.1	20.2
09	U-grab-4-1	17.2	22.3	16.3	20.8
10	G-grab-4-1	15.9	20.3	17.0	18.5
11	U-grab-3-2	21.9	24.5	22.0	24.0
12	G-grab-3-2	23.2	24.6	23.3	24.9
13	U-ball-2-2	22.7	24.4	22.3	23.9
14	G-ball-2-2	22.3	24.1	22.7	24.1
15	U-free-2-2	28.3	29.4	25.9	28.7
16	G-free-2-2	27.7	29.6	26.6	28.3
17	U-free-4-2	23.0	26.5	21.7	25.0
18	G-free-4-2	23.6	26.3	22.0	25.0
19	U-ortho-2-1	32.7	33.6	32.8	33.7
20	G-ortho-2-1	32.6	33.6	32.5	33.5
21	U-ortho-4-1	32.0	33.5	31.9	33.4
22	G-ortho-4-1	32.4	32.9	31.9	32.9
23	U-ortho-3-2	27.8	29.7	26.4	29.3
24	G-ortho-3-2	29.6	30.6	28.4	31.1
25	U-table-2-1	30.5	34.3	29.6	33.8
26	G-table-2-1	28.9	34.8	28.7	34.3
27	U-table-4-1	28.1	33.7	29.2	32.6
28	G-table-4-1	28.4	33.7	28.8	33.0
29	U-table-3-2	26.4	28.8	25.2	27.3
30	G-table-3-2	26.0	28.5	23.2	25.5
31	U-tria-2-1	20.1	24.3	19.5	23.3
32	G-tria-2-1	21.2	25.2	20.9	24.4
33	U-tria-4-1	20.8	25.9	20.8	24.0
34	G-tria-4-1	22.0	27.6	21.7	24.5
35	U-tria-3-2	19.5	20.7	18.5	19.0
36	G-tria-3-2	18.6	20.5	18.2	20.5
37	U-meet-2-2	21.9	24.4	21.9	25.6
38	G-meet-2-2	21.3	23.6	22.0	25.1
39	U-meet-4-2	21.6	24.1	21.9	24.9
40	G-meet-4-2	20.6	23.5	20.9	24.4
∅	**01-40**	**24.6**	**27.8**	**24.3**	**27.0**

Table 7.1.: 3D landmark localization errors for UMPM experiments.
For each of the 40 experiments we present the average 3D landmark localization
error for the example based and the pose splines based 3D pose estimators, using
example poses / pose splines generated from the CMU, or the UMPM motion
capture databases respectively.

| Exp # | Exp code | 3D landmark localization error [cm] | | | |
		EX-HE	EX-CMU	PS-HE	PS-CMU
41	H-walk-1-1	9.9	12.7	9.5	11.7
42	G-walk-1-1	11.3	14.1	10.6	13.9
43	H-walk-2-1	10.0	13.4	9.2	12.6
44	G-walk-2-1	11.7	13.4	10.3	13.1
45	H-box-1-1	17.3	16.1	10.7	14.2
46	G-box-1-1	17.0	16.2	12.1	15.9
47	H-box-2-1	14.3	15.2	12.5	16.5
48	G-box-2-1	15.2	16.0	12.5	18.2
49	H-walk-1-1	15.4	39.5	16.6	34.5
50	G-walk-1-1	16.2	45.5	17.4	45.1
51	H-walk-2-1	14.5	36.0	15.5	34.2
52	G-walk-2-1	17.2	40.0	17.5	36.3
53	H-box-1-1	24.7	39.0	23.6	41.8
54	G-box-1-1	25.9	38.8	25.7	42.2
55	H-box-2-1	22.1	43.0	21.8	43.9
56	G-box-2-1	24.5	46.0	23.4	43.9
57	H-walk-1-1	13.3	17.8	13.8	15.5
58	G-walk-1-1	14.1	17.8	15.0	17.2
59	H-walk-2-1	12.1	15.7	12.7	14.8
60	G-walk-2-1	12.9	16.4	14.0	14.9
61	H-box-1-1	17.3	21.1	16.0	19.2
62	G-box-1-1	17.1	19.4	16.9	18.5
63	H-box-2-1	17.3	18.3	15.4	16.3
64	G-box-2-1	16.6	18.3	15.4	16.5
∅	**41-64**	**16.2**	**24.6**	**15.3**	**23.8**

Table 7.2.: 3D landmark localization errors for HumanEva experiments.
For each of the 24 experiments we present the average 3D landmark localization
error for the example based and the pose splines based 3D pose estimators, using
example poses / pose splines generated from the CMU, or the HumanEva motion
capture databases respectively.

Estimator	Speed [s]	Pose evaluations needed [mio]
EX-HE	0.66	6.62
EX-UMPM	0.98	9.84
EX-CMU	1.89	18.92
PS-HE	0.02	0.06
PS-UMPM	0.24	0.79
PS-CMU	3.39	11.31

Table 7.3.: 3D pose estimator computation speeds. For each of the four
pose estimator variants used we show the (i) time needed to return a final pose
estimate, (ii) the average number of poses evaluated until the optimization
converged (specified in million poses).

7.3.3. Qualitative results

Examples of estimated 3D poses

In Fig. 7.12 we show some resulting 3D pose estimates for different persons from different experiments on the UMPM and the HumanEva dataset[7].

Standing up sequence

Fig. 7.13 shows the ground truth and the final estimated 3D pose for 4 frames of a short sequence where the test person stands up from a chair. The estimation results are from experiment 01 / EX-UMPM.

Occlusion cases

In Section 6.3.3 we showed that the landmark localization accuracy drops significantly when parts of a person are occluded. Nevertheless, in Fig. 6.22 we showed that sometimes at least the landmarks that are still visible can be localized. Accordingly, sometimes the 3D pose estimation succeeds as well. Fig. 7.14 shows some examples of such cases where parts of the persons are occluded (by a small or large table, a chair, or another person), but the overall estimated poses are approximately correct.

Examples of wrongly estimated poses

In Fig. 7.15 we show some examples where pose estimation failed. In 1) the left leg of the estimated 3D pose is stretched, while it is not stretched for the ground truth pose. In 2) the estimated 3D pose bends forward, but the ground truth pose not. 3) shows a typical example where the ambiguity in landmark vote distributions leads to a confusion of left-right body parts. 4)-5) shows two examples where the articulation is estimated (roughly) correctly (lying on a table, sitting down), but the estimated relative orientation of the person to the camera is wrong. 6) shows an

---

[7]For image 1) 3D poses are only estimated for 2 persons, since ground truth 3D poses for evaluation are only available for 2 persons as well.

example where both, the articulation and the relative orientation to the camera of the estimated pose is wrong.

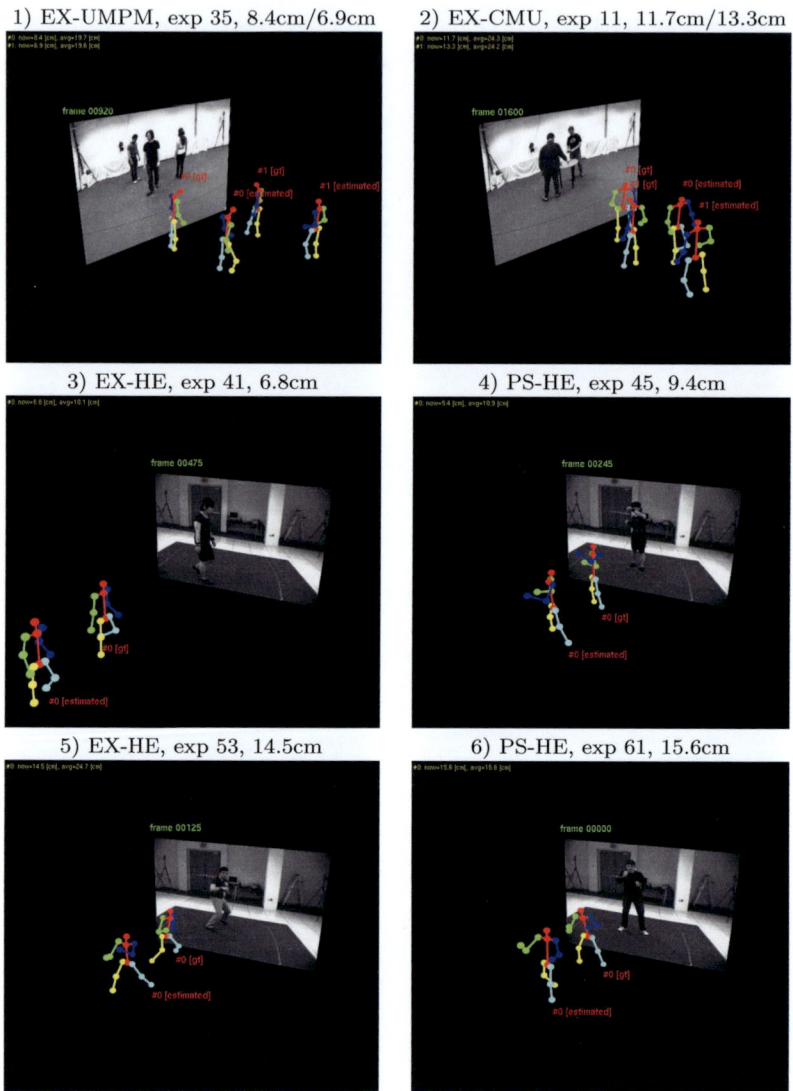

Figure 7.12.: Examples of estimated 3D poses. [gt] = ground truth 3D pose, [estimated] = estimated 3D pose. Poses: 1) walking, multiple persons 2) grabbing objects from a table, multiple persons 3) walking 4)-6) boxing

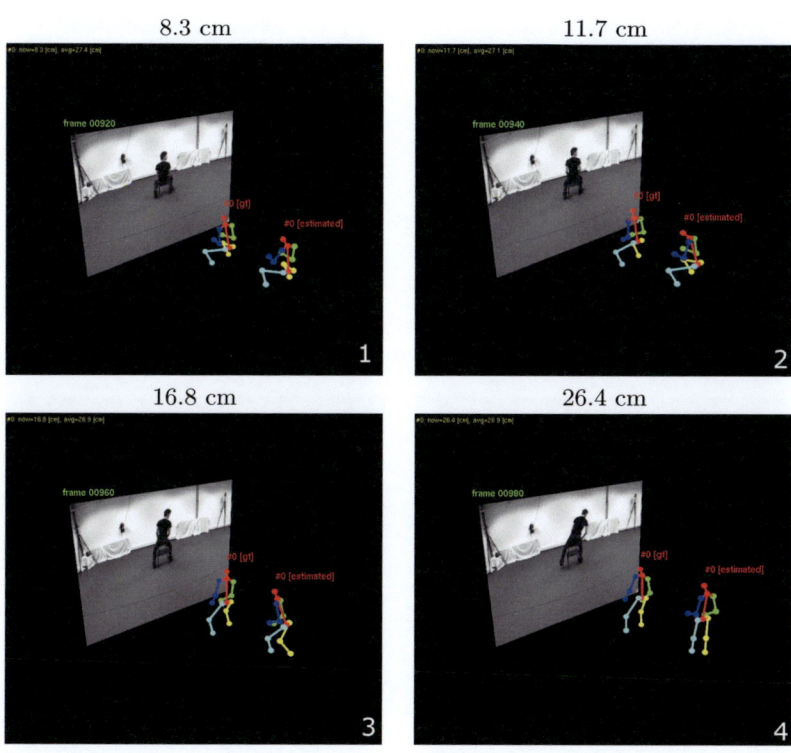

Figure 7.13.: Estimated 3D poses for a standing up from a chair sequence. For four frames at frame 920, 940, 960, and 980 the estimated and ground truth 3D pose are shown. Even though the errors of the estimated 3D poses range between 8.3-26.4cm the overall action (standing-up from a sitting pose) can be recognized.

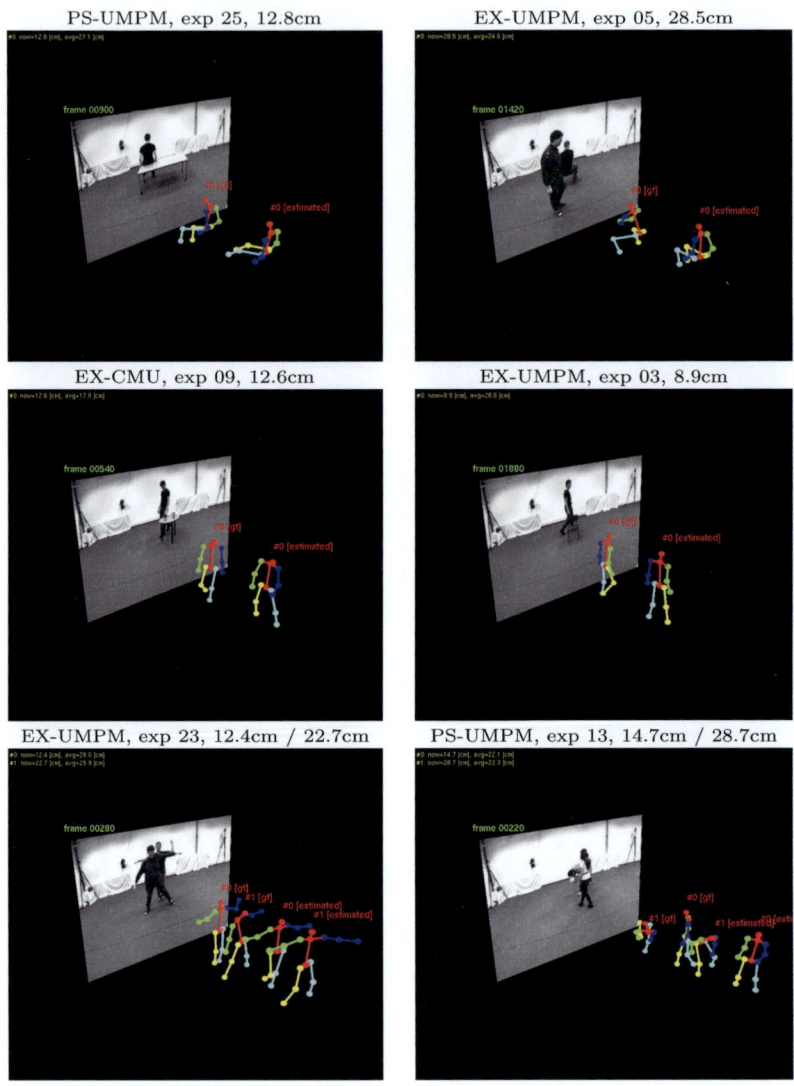

Figure 7.14.: Examples of estimated 3D poses for occlusion cases.
Despite partial occlusions of persons by objects or other persons and resulting missing image evidence for some of the 15 landmarks, the overall 3D pose found by the optimization procedure is similar to the ground truth 3D pose.

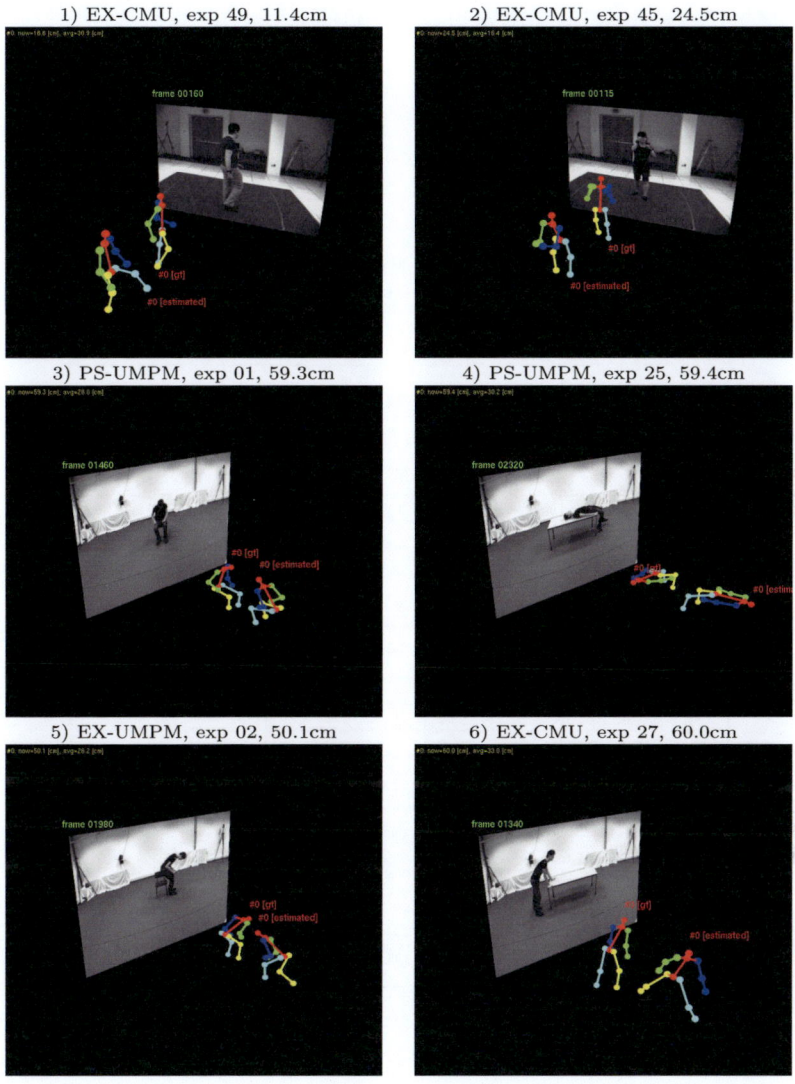

Figure 7.15.: Examples of wrongly estimated 3D poses. Error (of estimated 3D pose): 1) left leg stretched 2) person bend forward 3)-5) overall pose correct, but relative orientation to camera wrong 6) orientation to camera wrong; arms and legs stretched too wide

7.3.4. Comparison with state-of-the-art

For a fair comparison of the experimental results with state-of-the-art results reported in literature we first have to assess the level of difficulty of our experiments which depends on the chosen evaluation dataset and the experiment settings.

	I Evaluation on UMPM	II Evaluation on HumanEva
dataset(s)	UMPM	HumanEva
pose vector dimension	45	45
DATASET CHALLENGES		
1. cross evaluation	−	−
2. public	+	+
3. occlusions	+	−
4. non frontal poses	+	+
5. low resolution	−	−
6. background clutter	+	+
EXPERIMENTS CHALLENGES		
7. test persons new	+	+
8. test poses new	−	−
9. large pose variety	−	−
10. single images	+	+
11. small training sets	+	+
12. large evaluation	+	−
Overall difficulty	**8 of 12**	**6 of 12**
Error [cm]	**26cm**	**19cm**
Computation time [sec]	**0.24-3.39**	**0.02-3.39**

Table 7.4.: Assessment of the level of difficulty of our experiments. For a better comparison with state-of-the-art results, we assess the difficulty of our experiments independently for both the evaluation on the UMPM and the HumanEva dataset.

Table 7.4 summarizes our results and experiment settings and can be compared with the state-of-the-art experiment settings and results listed in Table 3.2. Since experiments 01-40 were conducted on the UMPM dataset containing, e.g., sequences with occlusions, while experiments

41-64 did not contain sequences with occlusions, we split the results into two parts.

UMPM results

In column I we show the experiment settings and results for experiments 01-40, i.e., for a single dataset (1). The UMPM dataset is public (2). Train and test sequences were used where people occlude each other (3), showing frontal and non frontal poses (4). The persons appear at high resolution (5), while the background in the person bounding boxes changes (6), since persons move around in the room and the background is not homogeneously. Persons used for training the codebook and the landmark ISMs were different from the persons in the test sequences (7), but poses shown by the training persons are similar to the ones in the test phase (8). Compared to works that evaluate 3D pose estimation on the CMU video sequences, we cannot say, that there is a large pose variety (9), even though there are 9 different action classes used. We estimate on a per-frame-basis (10), using small training sets from 1-2 videos (11). Compared to other evaluations listed in Section 3.3, the 40 experiments conducted on the UMPM benchmark can be ranked as a large evaluation (12).

Comparing the average error of about 26cm (average of EX-UMPM, PS-UMPM, EX-CMU, PS-CMU for experiments 01-40) with Table 3.2) we can therefore say that the error is at the top end of the 19-25cm error spectrum reported in [Andriluka and Sigal, 2012] while the difficulty of the experiments here is significantly higher (4 of 12 for [Andriluka and Sigal, 2012] compared to 8 of 12 here).

HumanEva results

In column II we show the experiment settings and results for experiments 41-64, i.e., again for a single dataset (2). The HumanEva dataset is public (1). Persons are never occluded (2), but non-frontal poses are included (3). Persons are recorded at high resolution (4), while background clutter is present in the person bounding boxes (6), since persons move around during the recordings and background clutter is present. Training and test persons are always different (7)[8]. Only two different actions are used, i.e., there is no large pose variety (9). 3D poses are estimated on a per-frame basis (10). For training the landmark localizer ISMs only 1 or 2 videos were used (11). Even though 24 experiments were conducted, we rank it not as a large evaluation, since as in [Daubney et al., 2009] the evaluation results are computed only for 3 different persons[9].

Comparing the average error of about 19cm (average of EX-HE, PS-HE, EX-CMU, PS-CMU for experiments 41-64) again with the works listed in Table 3.2) the error is slightly higher than the 17.5cm reported by [Tian et al., 2010], but at the lower end of the 19-25cm error spectrum reported by [Andriluka and Sigal, 2012], where the overall experiment settings had a lower level of difficulty (4 of 12 for [Andriluka and Sigal, 2012] compared to 6 of 12 here).

Overall we can say that the results are similar to state-of-the-art errors reported by works that used experiments with a relative high difficulty. Nevertheless, comparing the difficulty of our experiments with the difficulty of experiments in Table 3.2 shows that our experiments show a higher level of difficulty.

Temporal information has not been exploited so far in the 3D pose estimation process by the method presented here, in contrast to [Andriluka and Sigal, 2012], which is supposed to help to decrease the average landmark localization error even further.

---

[8]For the experiments where we used the HumanEva codebook some of the test persons were also used to generate the codebook.

[9]Evaluation results for HumanEva can maximally be reported for up to 4 different persons since there are only 4 different persons in the HumanEva dataset.

7.4. Conclusions

In this chapter we introduced a method for 2D and 3D human pose estimation based on the landmark vote distributions generated by ISM based landmark localizers. 3D pose hypotheses are retrieved from a set of example poses, or generated from pose splines – a compact representation of motion sequences using a sparse set of supporting poses – and projected to 2D, in order to measure the vote density near to the projected landmark coordinates. The search for a good pose estimate and projection parameters is formulated as an optimization problem which is solved using Particle Swarm Optimization.

An important aspect of the top-down method presented in this chapter is that pose hypotheses are compared with vote distributions and not with low level image features as, e.g., edges or silhouettes. This allows to use a simple stick-figure body model which can be projected to 2D with negligible computational costs. Due to the fact that the projected pose hypotheses and the image evidence are compared in the vote space and not in the image space and due to a careful design of the projected hypothesis vs. image evidence (i.e., vote distributions) matching function, we are able to generate and evaluate millions of different 3D pose hypotheses per second on a standard PC (approximately 10 millions for the example based methods, and approximately 3 millions for the pose spline based methods).

The experimental results show that example based and pose spline based 3D pose priors yield similar 3D pose estimation errors, while the pose spline based prior representation has the advantage that the number of evaluations needed till convergence of the PSO based optimization process is significantly smaller. Using similar poses in the pose prior helps to reduce the error. While the codebook has no large influence on the overall results as for the landmark localization step, we have to expect large differences concerning the pose estimation error depending on the type of actions present in the test data. The pose estimation errors are comparable to state-of-the-art results of works using a relative high level of difficulty for their experiments, while our experiment settings are at a higher level of difficulty.

For future work on the basis of the method presented here it will be interesting to see how much the 3D landmark localization error can further be reduced by exploiting temporal information.

8. Geometric reconstruction of 3D poses

Assuming we already have estimated a 2D pose, this chapter addresses the question how to map such a 2D pose estimate to a 3D pose estimate.

In **Section 8.1** we describe a simple geometrical working principle to reconstruct a set of possible 3D pose candidates given a 2D pose. **Section 8.2.1** underlines three important drawbacks of the original work on geometric reconstruction of 3D poses: the limited camera projection model, the non-uniqueness of the 3D reconstructions, and the unknown projection parameters. Nevertheless, in the following sections we present solutions for these three problems.

Section 8.2.2 shows that the basic working principle can be adopted to the standard perspective projection camera model as well. **Section 8.2.3** deals with the question how to automatically select an unique 3D pose estimate from the large set of 3D pose candidates. In **Section 8.2.4** we describe an approach to select the parameters needed by the reconstruction algorithm based on the average probability of the geometrically reconstructed 3D pose candidates for different parameter choices.

Section 8.3 presents qualitative and quantitative results for the geometric reconstruction experiments conducted. Finally, **Section 8.4** summarizes and discusses the results from this chapter.

8.1. Introduction

In [Taylor, 2000] the idea to reconstruct a 3D pose given a 2D pose using the working principle of geometric reconstruction was published. The approach combines knowledge about the 3D to 2D projection process together with limb foreshortening information, i.e., the information how long a projected 3D limb appears in the 2D image in order to reconstruct the missing depth information that does not come with a 2D pose.

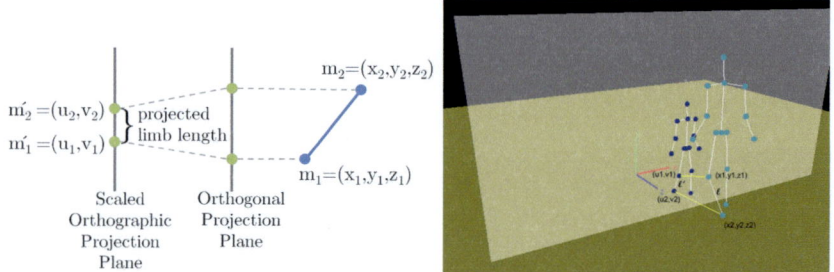

Figure 8.1.: Scaled orthographic projection. A 3D point $\mathbf{m} = (x, y, z)$ is first projected orthogonally to the x-y plane, i.e., to (x, y), followed by a scaling of the projected coordinates (x, y) to $\mathbf{m}' = (sx, sy) = (u, v)$.

Camera model

Taylor assumed that the 2D pose is the result of a scaled orthographic projection of the 3D pose (see Fig. 8.1): a 3D point or landmark $\mathbf{m} = (x, y, z)$ is mapped to a 2D point $\mathbf{m}' = (u, v)$ by scaling the x- and y-coordinates with scale parameter s:

$$u = s \cdot x, \quad v = s \cdot y \tag{8.1}$$

which corresponds to an orthogonal projection to the x-y plane, followed by a scaling.

The chosen scaled orthographic camera projection model means that the z-coordinate of the 3D landmark $\mathbf{m}$ has no influence on the resulting projection coordinates (u, v) which means that the distance of the object to the camera has no importance concerning the size of the projected image. Of course, this is an oversimplification for real cameras, where an object that is far away results in a smaller projected image compared to an object that is nearer to the camera. Nevertheless, this camera model was chosen by Taylor for two reasons. First, it allows a simple reconstruction of the relative z-coordinates between limb start and end points. Second, if the limb depth differences are small compared to the distance between the person and the camera, the scaled orthographic projection model is a good approximation since in such a case it is similar to a perspective projection: the small distance differences in the z-direction between the limbs are then negligible compared to the distance of the person to the camera.

Reconstruction working principle

If we already have a 2D pose estimate, we know the projected coordinates of each limb start $\mathbf{m}_1' = (u_1, v_1)$ and limb end point $\mathbf{m}_2' = (u_2, v_2)$. If we further have estimates for each 3D limb length l and knowledge about the scale parameter s for the scaled orthographic projection model, we can reconstruct the displacement $\Delta_z := (z_1 - z_2)$ of the limb in z-direction between the two 3D landmarks $\mathbf{m}_1 = (x_1, y_1, z_1)$ and $\mathbf{m}_2 = (x_2, y_2, z_2)$. For solving for Δ_z a simple reformulation of the Euclidean equation is used. Since $\mathbf{m}_1$ and $\mathbf{m}_2$ are projected to points (u_1, v_1) and (u_2, v_2) respectively by a scaled orthographic projection, we have:

$$u_1 - u_2 = s(x_1 - x_2) \tag{8.2}$$
$$v_1 - v_2 = s(y_1 - y_2) \tag{8.3}$$

Together with the Euclidean equation we get:

$$l^2 = (x_1 - x_2)^2 + (y_1 - y_2)^2 + (z_1 - z_2)^2 \tag{8.4}$$
$$\Leftrightarrow (z1 - z2) = \pm\sqrt{l^2 - (x_1 - x_2)^2 - (y_1 - y_2)^2} \tag{8.5}$$
$$\Leftrightarrow \Delta_z = \pm\sqrt{l^2 - \frac{(u_1 - u_2)^2 + (v_1 - v_2)^2}{s^2}} \tag{8.6}$$

Thus we can reconstruct the limb displacement Δ_z between the landmarks $\mathbf{m}_1$ and $\mathbf{m}_2$ using the projected points (u_1, v_1), (u_2, v_2), the knowledge about the limb length l and the scale s up to a sign ($\pm$) ambiguity. The sign ambiguity stems from the fact that we cannot say whether $\mathbf{m}_1$ or $\mathbf{m}_2$ is nearer to the camera just based on the 2D pose (see Fig. 8.1).

8.2. Method

8.2.1. Drawbacks of the original approach

In this section we underline three major disadvantages of the approach presented in [Taylor, 2000].

8.2.1.1. Unrealistic camera model

As mentioned before the scaled orthographic projection is a bad approximation for the projection process of real cameras which are better modeled by perspective projections.

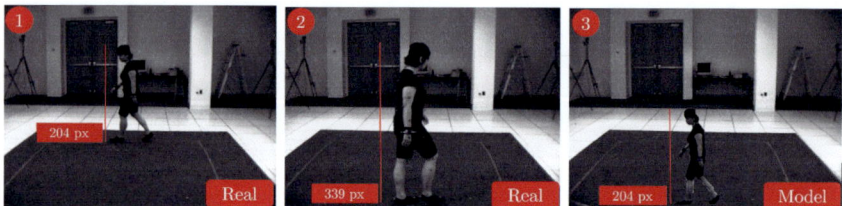

Figure 8.2.: Unrealistic camera model. (1)+(2): real images with different projected person sizes due to different person to camera distances. (3): predicted size of the person from image (1) according to the scaled orthographic camera model if the person is observed at a distance similar to image (2). Obviously the predicted size is too small.

Wrong projected object size

First, for real cameras, the projected size of a person depends on the distance of the person to the camera. But this is not true for the scaled orthographic camera model. In Fig. 8.2 we visualized this drawback. Image 1 and 2 show images recorded by a real camera. The projected size of the person in image 2 is larger compared to the projected size in image 1, since the person is nearer to the camera. Image 3 shows the size of the person as observed in image 1 which we would expect – according to the scaled orthographic projection camera model – if the person is standing as near to the camera as in image 2. Obviously the projected size of the person in image 3 is too small.

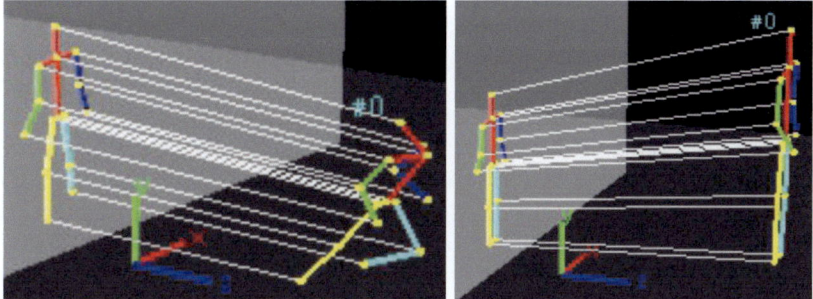

Figure 8.3.: Results when over- or underestimating the scale. Example results for a 3D pose when overestimating (left) or underestimating (right) the scale parameter s. Source: [Brauer and Arens, 2011].

No good scaling parameter for whole video sequence

Second, if there are no strong perspective effects, we might be able to choose a good projection scale parameter s for one image. But for a sequence of images where the distance of the person to the camera changes dramatically, we cannot choose a single s such that all projections can be explained. Using a single s will therefore result in an over- or underestimation of the absolute value of the depth displacement Δ_z: if we overestimate s the fraction in eqn. (8.6) will be too small, and thus the term below the square root will be too large, resulting in a too large absolute value of Δ_z. Fig. 8.3 shows two resulting 3D pose reconstruction candidates when over- or underestimating the scale. The resulting reconstructed poses appear exaggerated when the scale is overestimated (resulting in too large assumed limb displacements) or too flat when the depth is underestimated (resulting in too small assumed limb displacements).

Perspective effects cannot be explained

Third, for images showing strong perspective effects – as shown, e.g., in Fig. 8.10 left – the scaled orthographic model has to explain observed limb foreshortenings, which are actually the result of a strong perspective viewpoint, by limb displacements in the depth direction which will result in wrongly estimated 3D poses.

[Parameswaran and Chellappa, 2004] is the only known work which tried to exchange the scaled orthographic camera model by a perspective camera model. Unfortunately, their approach makes a lot of assumptions which are hard to guarantee (torso twist has to be small, four landmarks on the head have to be provided). For details see Chapter 2, Section 2.1.6.

8.2.1.2. Non-uniqueness of reconstruction

Unfortunately, the sign ambiguity in eqn. (8.6) leads to a combinatorial explosion of possible 3D pose candidates. Since we have two possibilities for reconstructing the relative depth between m_1 and m_2 this results in $2^{14} = 16384$ possible pose reconstructions for our body model with 14 limbs.

In [Taylor, 2000] the uniqueness of the final 3D pose estimate was achieved by letting the user choose for each limb whether the start or end point of the limb is closer to the camera, i.e., in this form the approach was only a semi-automatic 3D pose reconstruction algorithm, which strongly limits the range of application scenarios.

The related work survey in Chapter 2, Section 2.1.6 presents two approaches ([Mori and Malik, 2006], [Jiang, 2010]) that followed Taylor's work and tried to provide unique 3D poses, but the work either relied on large manually labeled training data ([Mori and Malik, 2006]) or limited the 3D pose candidates to a set of example poses ([Jiang, 2010]).

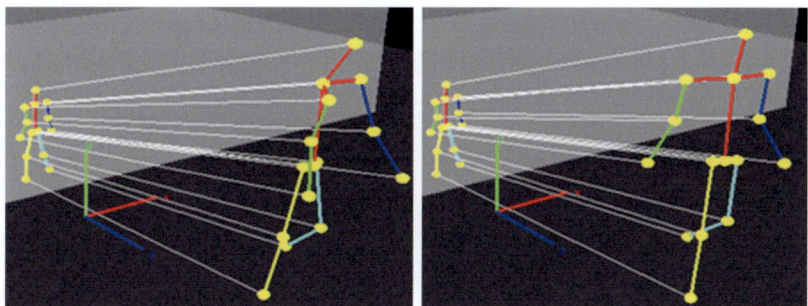

Figure 8.4.: Non-uniqueness of reconstructed 3D poses. Two different 3D poses which project to the same 2D pose. Source: [Brauer and Arens, 2011].

8.2.1.3. Unknown projection parameters

The original approach in [Taylor, 2000] does not provide any idea how to come to an estimate for the scale parameter s even for a single frame. But the scale parameter s is one of the three ingredients we need to reconstruct the set of 3D pose candidates beside the 2D input pose and the knowledge about 3D limb lengths.

In Chapter 2, Section 2.1.6 we reviewed the work presented in [Wei and Chai, 2009] which tried to tackle the problem of the unknown projection parameter. Using additional projection constraints, the reconstruction and the estimation of s is formulated as an optimization problem, but the authors could not guarantee that the additional constraints are sufficient to resolve the ambiguity in all cases and sometimes feedback of the user is needed, resulting in a semi-automatic approach again.

8.2.2. Reconstruction for perspective projections

In this section we show that we can use the working principle used for the geometric reconstruction of 3D poses not only with a scaled orthographic camera model but also with a perspective camera model.

Within a perspective projection model a 3D point $\mathbf{m}_i = (x_i, y_i, z_i)$ is projected to a 2D point $\mathbf{m}_i' = (u_i, v_i)$ by

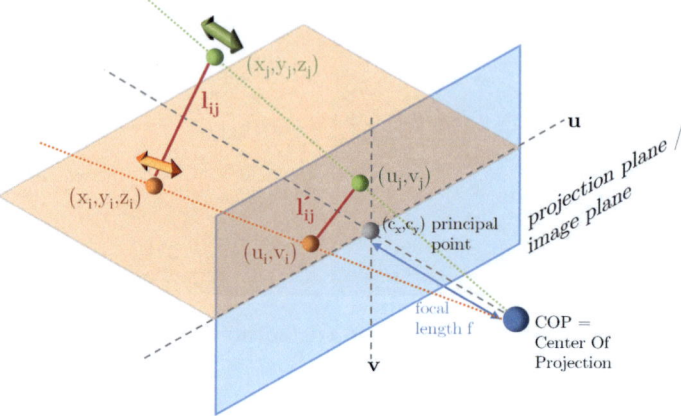

Figure 8.5.: Perspective projection. 3D landmarks (x, y, z) are projected to 2D points (u, v) under a perspective projection. The 3D pose is reconstructed by an iterative procedure. Starting with an already reconstructed parent landmark with coordinates (x_0, y_0, z_0) we reconstruct the child landmark coordinates (x_1, y_1, z_1) by using knowledge about the perspective projection and the fore-shortened projected limb length l'_{ij} in the image that can be compared with knowledge about the 3D limb length l_{ij}.

$$u_i = -f\frac{x_i}{z_i} + c_x \tag{8.7}$$

$$v_i = -f\frac{y_i}{z_i} + c_y \tag{8.8}$$

where f is the focal length and (c_x, c_y) is the origin of the projection plane (called "principal point") (see Fig.8.5). In contrast to the scaled orthographic projection model, the distance z_i of the point to the image plane has an influence on the resulting projection coordinates (u_i, v_i) within the perspective projection model.

The principal point (c_x, c_y) is just a 2D translation after scaling the x_i and y_i coordinates by the z_i coordinates and the focal length $-f$, see eqn. (8.7) and eqn. (8.8). For reconstructing the 3D coordinates (x_i, y_i, z_i)

based on a 2D pose estimate we can therefore start with inverting the 2D translation step and work with principal point normalized 2D coordinates, i.e., $u_i' = u_i - c_x$ and $v_i' = v_i - c_y$. For reasons of simplicity of presentation, we assume that this translation has been done when writing (u_i, v_i) in the following.

The pinhole camera model produces an image of the world that is upside-down, thus the minus sign before the focal length f in eqn. (8.7) and eqn. (8.8). In a code implementation this would mean that we have to rotate the produced 2D image by $180°$ to view the image. To avoid this we can simply work with f instead of $-f$.

Assume we had an estimate for z_i. Then x_i, y_i could be reconstructed given u_i, v_i, f:

$$x_i = \frac{z_i u_i}{f} \tag{8.9}$$

$$y_i = \frac{z_i v_i}{f} \tag{8.10}$$

This means, for each 3D landmark $\mathbf{m}_i$ to be reconstructed we have one unknown z_i. Since all $\mathbf{m}_i = (x_i, y_i, z_i)$ that lie on the perspective projection ray through the point (u_i, v_i) into the direction of the center of projection (COP) are possible candidates for z_i (see green and orange line in Fig. 8.5), we have infinite many possible solutions for z_i if we consider each landmark $\mathbf{m}_i$ in our body model independently, i.e., considering the 3D points isolated does not help to find the z_i coordinates. We can think of the points $\mathbf{m}_i$ as pearls that can be moved along strings (the perspective projection rays). If we move one of these pearls $\mathbf{m}_i$ along its corresponding projection line, the corresponding projected point $\mathbf{m}_i'$ does not change. But since some of these pearls are interconnected and the lengths of these connections are known (limb lengths) we can impose further constraints on the relative positions of the pearls. If the body is modeled as a kinematic tree with a root landmark $\mathbf{m}_r$ and l_{ij} denotes the (relative) length of the limb connecting a child landmark $\mathbf{m}_i$ with its parent landmark $\mathbf{m}_j$, the length l_{ij} can be expressed as the Euclidean distance between points $\mathbf{m}_i$ and $\mathbf{m}_j$:

$$l_{ij} = \sqrt{(x_i - x_j)^2 + (y_i - y_j)^2 + (z_i - z_j)^2} \qquad (8.11)$$

We can reformulate the Euclidian equation as follows, if we replace x_i, x_j, y_i, y_j in eqn. (8.11) by eqn. (8.9) and eqn. (8.10). Using the following sequence of equivalence transformations, we can then come up with a quadratic equation (8.17) and a corresponding p-q formula solution (8.19):

$$
\begin{aligned}
l_{ij}^2 &= (\frac{z_i u_i}{f} - \frac{z_j u_j}{f})^2 + (\frac{z_i v_i}{f} - \frac{z_j v_j}{f})^2 + (z_i - z_j)^2 &(8.12)\\
\Leftrightarrow l_{ij}^2 &= \frac{1}{f^2}[(z_i u_i - z_j u_j)^2 + (z_i v_i - z_j v_j)^2] + (z_i - z_j)^2 &(8.13)\\
\Leftrightarrow f^2 l_{ij}^2 &= (z_i u_i)^2 - 2z_i z_j u_i u_j + (z_j u_j)^2 + (z_i v_i)^2 - \\
& \quad 2z_i z_j v_i v_j + (z_j v_j)^2 + f^2(z_i^2 - 2z_i z_j + z_j^2) &(8.14)\\
\Leftrightarrow f^2 l_{ij}^2 &= z_i^2 \underbrace{(u_i^2 + v_i^2 + f^2)}_{=:A} + z_j^2 \underbrace{(u_j^2 + v_j^2 + f^2)}_{=:B} - \\
& \quad z_i z_j \underbrace{2(u_i u_j + v_i v_j + f^2)}_{=:C} &(8.15)\\
\Leftrightarrow 0 &= z_i^2 + \frac{B}{A}z_j^2 - \frac{C}{A}z_i z_j - \frac{f^2 l_{ij}^2}{A} &(8.16)\\
\Leftrightarrow 0 &= z_i^2 + \underbrace{\left(-\frac{Cz_j}{A}\right)}_{=:p} z_i + \underbrace{\left(\frac{B}{A}z_j^2 - \frac{f^2 l_{ij}^2}{A}\right)}_{=:q} &(8.17)\\
\Leftrightarrow z_{i_{1/2}} &= -\frac{p}{2} \pm \sqrt{(\frac{p}{2})^2 - q} &(8.18)\\
\Leftrightarrow z_{i_{1/2}} &= \frac{Cz_j}{2A} \pm \sqrt{\left(\frac{Cz_j}{2A}\right)^2 - \left(\frac{B}{A}z_j^2 - \frac{f^2 l_{ij}^2}{A}\right)} &(8.19)
\end{aligned}
$$

For reconstructing the landmark z_i coordinates using eqn. (8.19) we need the following input:

- depth information z_r of the root landmark $\mathbf{m}_r$ of the body model

- 3D limb lengths l_{ij}

- focal length f

- a 2D pose, i.e., projected point coordinates $\mathbf{m}'_i = (u_i, v_i)$ $(1 \leq i \leq J)$

An intuitive interpretation for eqn. (8.19) is, that for an already reconstructed parent landmark $\mathbf{m}_j$ coordinate, the sign ambiguity before the root corresponds to the fact that we have two possibilities for positioning the child landmark $\mathbf{m}_i$ on its corresponding perspective projection ray such that the length of the projected line between $\mathbf{m}_j$ and $\mathbf{m}_i$ fits to the actual measured line between $\mathbf{m}'_j = (u_j, v_j)$ and $\mathbf{m}'_i = (u_i, v_i)$ (see Fig. 8.5).

The pseudo code for the geometric reconstruction assuming the perspective camera model is presented in algorithm 4.

The algorithm has to be started with:

$$\texttt{Reconstruct}(\varnothing, \text{root-landmark-id}, z_r, \{l_{km}\}, f, \mathbf{q}')$$

First, the 3D coordinates $\mathbf{m}_r = (x_r, y_r, z_r)$ for the root landmark are reconstructed and added to the list of landmarks $\mathcal{M}$ that have been reconstructed so far during the recursive reconstruction procedure of a single 3D pose candidate. In line 22 the reconstruction of all child landmarks of a current reconstructed landmark is initiated. By this procedure the algorithm steps down the kinematic tree of the body model till all J landmarks are reconstructed, i.e., a new 3D pose candidate $\mathbf{q}$ is reconstructed, which is added to the set $\mathcal{Q}$ of all possible 3D candidates that project to the 2D pose $\mathbf{q}'$.

While for the scaled orthographic projection the z-coordinate can be reconstructed independently for each landmark, since in eqn. (8.6) the displacement Δ_z can be reconstructed for each landmark independently, the usage of a perspective camera model results in an recursive reconstruction algorithm where we start with the z-coordinate of the root landmark and then reconstruct the z-coordinates of the child landmarks while stepping down the kinematic tree. This difference is due to the perspective projection, where the possible solutions for the z-coordinate of a child

---

Algorithm 4 Geometric Reconstruction Pseudo Code: computes a set of 3D pose candidates

---

input:

l: next landmark id to reconstruct

set of 3D landmark coordinates reconstructed so far: $\mathcal{M} = \{m_i = (x_i, y_i, z_i)\}$

z_r: estimate for the distance of the person (root landmark) to the camera

3D limb lengths $\{l_{km}\}$

focal length f

estimated 2D pose $\mathbf{q}' = (\mathbf{m}'_0, ..., \mathbf{m}'_J)$ with $\mathbf{m}'_i = (u_i, v_i)$, $1 \leq i \leq J$

kinematic tree model $\mathcal{T}$, with $(l, l') \in \mathcal{T}$ if l is parent landmark and l' is child landmark

output:

set of 3D pose candidates $\mathcal{Q} = \{\mathbf{q} = (\mathbf{m}_0, ..., \mathbf{m}_J) : \mathbf{m}_i = (x_i, y_i, z_i), \; 1 \leq i \leq J\}$

1: static global $\mathcal{Q} = \varnothing$ ▷ initialize set of possible 3D pose candidates

2:

3: **function** Reconstruct($\mathcal{M}, l, z_r, \{l_{km}\}, f, \mathbf{q}'$)

4: $\quad \mathcal{Z} \leftarrow \varnothing$ ▷ init. set of possible solutions for z-coord of landmark l

5: $\quad$ **if** $l =$ root-landmark **then**

6: $\quad\quad \mathcal{Z} \leftarrow \{z_r\}$

7: $\quad$ **else**

8: $\quad\quad$ compute $z_{i_{1/2}}$ according to eqn. (8.19)

9: $\quad\quad \mathcal{Z} \leftarrow \mathcal{Z} \cup \{z_{i_1}, z_{i_2}\}$

10: $\quad$ **end if**

11: $\quad$ **for** a=1 to $|\mathcal{Z}|$ **do** ▷ consider all possible solutions for z_i

12: $\quad\quad x_i = \frac{z_{i_a} u_i}{f}$ ▷ reconstruct x_i and y_i given z_{i_a}

13: $\quad\quad y_i = \frac{z_{i_a} v_i}{f}$

14: $\quad\quad \mathbf{m}_i \leftarrow (x_i, y_i, z_{i_a})$ ▷ set 3D landmark $\mathbf{m}_i$ of 3D pose reconstructed so far

15: $\quad\quad \mathcal{M} \leftarrow \mathcal{M} \cup \{\mathbf{m}_i\}$

16:

17: $\quad\quad$ **if** $|\mathcal{M}| = J$ **then** ▷ all J landmarks of a 3D pose candidate reconstructed?

18: $\quad\quad\quad \mathcal{Q} \leftarrow \mathcal{Q} \cup \{\mathbf{q} = (\mathbf{m}_0, ..., \mathbf{m}_J)\}$ ▷ add 3D pose candidate to $\mathcal{Q}$

19: $\quad\quad\quad$ **return** ▷ at a leaf of the reconstruction tree $\rightarrow$ stop recursion here

20: $\quad\quad$ **end if**

21:

22: $\quad\quad$ **for all** child landmarks l' **do** ▷ go one step deeper in the kinematic tree

23: $\quad\quad\quad$ Reconstruct($\mathcal{M}, l', z_r, \{l_{km}\}, f, \mathbf{q}'$) ▷ recursive call

24: $\quad\quad$ **end for**

25: $\quad$ **end for**

26: **end function**

---

landmark depend on the previously selected solution for the z-coordinate of the parent landmark, see eqn. (8.19).

8.2.3. Automatic selection of pose candidates

Algorithm 4 will always reconstruct exactly $|\mathcal{Q}| = 2^l$ 3D pose candidates where l is the number of limbs, since for each limb end landmark point $\mathbf{m}_i$ two possibilities for z_i are considered. From a purely mathematical viewpoint all these 3D pose candidates are correct. But the majority of these 3D poses represent impossible 3D poses, because human joint constraints are not respected (as an example see Fig. 8.6).

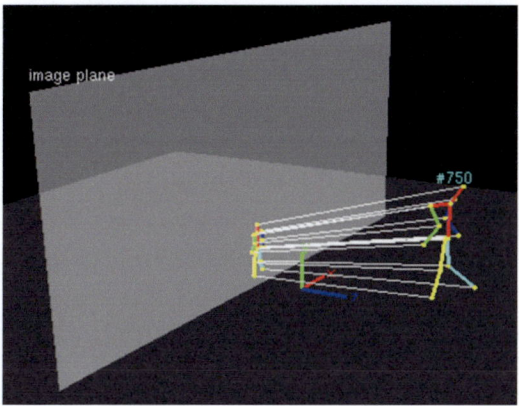

Figure 8.6.: Invalid reconstructed 3D pose. Example of a reconstructed 3D pose that is mathematically valid but violates human joint constraints.

Detecting invalid poses while reconstructing

It is a good idea to filter for such invalid 3D poses already during the generation of the pose candidates since this allows to prune the reconstruction tree and save computation time. While we could check for each 3D candidate whether to add it or not to $\mathcal{Q}$ in line 17 when all J landmark coordinates are reconstructed, it is possible to save a lot of computation time by checking already earlier whether joint angles violate kinematic joint constraints. During the generation of each 3D pose candidate – directly after the reconstruction of the 3D coordinates for landmark $\mathbf{m}_i$ in line 14 – we can check the joint that connects the parent landmark with this landmark for violations and stop the recursion eventually already here. This results in a pruning of the 3D pose reconstruction tree and saves a lot of computation time especially if the pruning happens at an early level of the reconstruction tree.

Ranking of remaining 3D pose candidates

Nevertheless, even with joint violations filtering typically some hundreds of 3D pose candidates remain. For determining a final 3D pose candidate from this remaining set of pose candidates, we compute a probability $P(\mathbf{q})$ for each 3D pose candidate $\mathbf{q}$ based on the joint angle probabilities. From motion capture data we can learn the joint probability to observe a certain joint configuration $(\mathbf{r}_1, ..., \mathbf{r}_J)$ by its occurrence frequency and could define $P(\mathbf{q})$ by the joint probability of the joint states:

$$P(\mathbf{q}) = P(\mathbf{r}_1, ..., \mathbf{r}_J) \qquad (8.20)$$

where $\mathbf{r}_j$ $(1 \leq j \leq J)$ represents the j-th joint state, represented by Euler angles. But such a definition has one main drawback: it will assign a probability near to 0 to poses not contained in the joint state observation training data. For this, instead of using the joint probability of joint states definition for defining the probability of a 3D pose, we prefer the following definition based on the product of the individual joint state probabilities:

$$P(\mathbf{q}) = \prod_{j=1}^{J} P(\mathbf{r}_j) \qquad (8.21)$$

where we assume that the joint states $\mathbf{r}_j$ $(1 \leq j \leq J)$ are independent of each other with the argumentation that humans can move their limbs independently from each other. The advantage of the definition eqn. (8.21) compared to definition eqn. (8.20) is that it does not impose such a strong prior to poses contained in the training data. Consider, e.g., a motion capture database that contains poses of 1.) persons sitting on a chair with arms lowered and 2.) persons standing and raising their hands, but containing no examples of 3.) persons sitting on a chair and simultaneously raising their hands. While definition (8.20) will assign a probability near to 0 to poses similar to 3.) (since the whole joint configuration has not been observed before), definition (8.21) will not, since the joint states are considered isolated and the leg and arm joint state configurations of 3.) have been observed by examples in 1.) and 2.) before.

8.2.4. Automatic estimation of parameters

The geometric reconstruction algorithm 4 expects an estimate for the distance of the person to the camera, which corresponds to the depth z_r coordinate of the root landmark. In our experiments we first tried to estimate z_r using the scale of the local features associated with the person hypothesis, similar to the estimation of the person height as described in Section 6.2.1.4. While this is in principle possible, it demands a previous learning step for which we have to provide (word id, feature scale, distance camera $\leftrightarrow$ person) training data vectors.

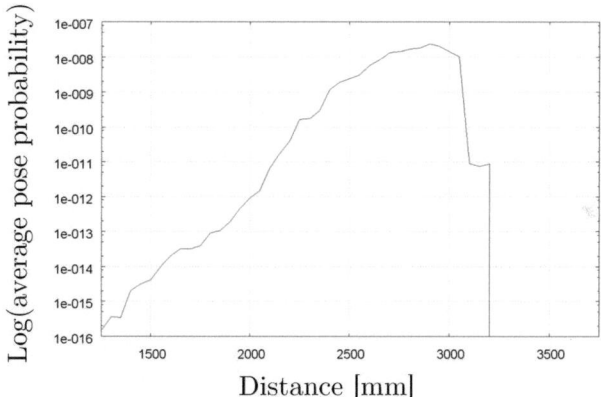

Figure 8.7.: Automatic estimation of distance parameter. For each distance candidate we compute the average probability of reconstructed 3D poses.

Here we propose another idea, which results in a much more simpler estimation of z_r. First, the set of all possible 3D pose candidates $\mathcal{Q}_d$ is computed for different test distances $d = z_r$. Then, the average probability

$\tilde{P}(\mathcal{Q}_d)$ of the reconstructed poses contained in $\mathcal{Q}_d$ at each distance d is computed:

$$\tilde{P}(\mathcal{Q}_d) = \frac{1}{|\mathcal{Q}_d|} \sum_{\mathbf{q} \in \mathcal{Q}_d} P(\mathbf{q}) \qquad (8.22)$$

Finally, we choose the person to camera distance $z_r = d$ at which we can find the largest value $\tilde{P}(\mathcal{Q}_d)$:

$$z_r = d = \arg \max_{d} \tilde{P}(\mathcal{Q}_d) \qquad (8.23)$$

Fig. 8.7 shows such a distance / average pose probability plot for a sample frame. The ground truth distance is at approx. 2900 mm where the average pose probability for the set of all reconstructed poses indeed reaches a maximum. This can easily be explained by the fact that for distances different from the ground truth distance, the reconstructed poses often can still be squeezed into the perspective rays bundle but the resulting poses will be degenerated in the sense that the resulting joint angles are unlikely which in return results in poses with low probabilities. In contrast, using a too large distance d can mean that only a few (3D poses that are stretched out widely) or no 3D poses fit into the perspective ray bundle (the 3D limb lengths are then too small to connect the 3D landmarks on the perspective rays).

We can go even further and choose not only the distance estimate but also the focal length estimate automatically by considering the average probability of the reconstructed poses. This was done, e.g., for the geometric reconstruction of the 3D pose in image Fig. 8.10 right where no focal length estimate was available due to missing camera calibration data for the digital camera used. Further, we can also estimate the scale parameter s for the case of a scaled orthographic projection using the same idea. Fig. 8.8 shows a corresponding example plot for a single frame. The average probability of the reconstructed poses $P(\mathcal{Q}_d)$ reaches it maximum at approximately $s = 0.078$ which can be used in this case as the estimate for s for this frame.

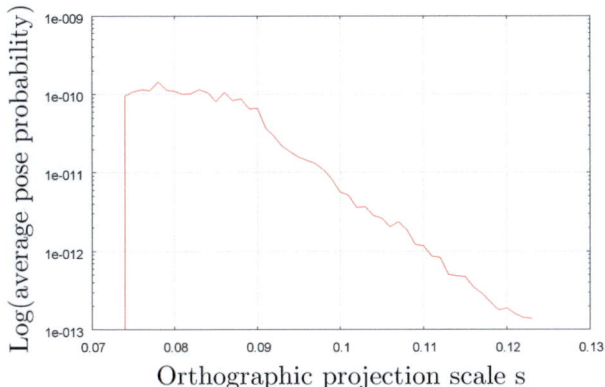

Figure 8.8.: Automatic estimation of scale parameter. For each scale candidate we compute the average probability of reconstructed 3D poses.

8.3. Evaluation

8.3.1. Experiments conducted

Evaluation datasets

In the previous sections we showed how to augment the idea of geometric reconstruction of 3D poses to a perspective camera model. In contrast, the original geometric reconstruction method could only be used with a very limited (scaled orthographic projection) camera model. In order to evaluate this new method it is therefore important to use a human pose evaluation dataset showing images with perspective effects to see whether the method is able to reconstruct the 3D poses in such cases.

In Section 3.2 we present an overview on publicly available HPE evaluation datasets that provide 3D motion capture data with synchronized video data. To the best of our knowledge there is only one evaluation dataset where the video frames show strong perspective effects, namely the TUM kitchen dataset. Since the four cameras used for recording this dataset are mounted in the top four corners of a kitchen environment, the limbs of, e.g., the

Figure 8.9.: TUM kitchen video frames examples. Two example frames from the TUM kitchen dataset. Since the cameras are mounted in the top corners of the room the resulting frames show strong perspective foreshortening effects, which is ideal for the evaluation of the geometric reconstruction method for perspective projections proposed here.

legs of the recorded persons show strong perspective foreshortenings which is ideal to test the new method proposed in this chapter (see Fig. 8.9).

We further choose the HumanEva dataset as a second dataset for evaluation, since it is the most widely used evaluation dataset for HPE. Results on 3D pose estimation errors of the geometric reconstruction method presented here make it therefore easier to compare this method with other approaches.

8.3.2. Input data for the reconstruction algorithm

Root landmark depth coordinate

For estimating the distance of the root landmark to the camera (z_r coordinate) we use the new approach introduced in Section 8.2.4, i.e., reconstruct 3D pose candidates for different distances $\mathcal{Q}_d$, compute the average pose probability for these pose candidate sets, and choose the distance $d = z_r$ where the poses have the highest average probability $\tilde{P}(\mathcal{Q}_d)$.

Limb lengths

The limb lengths l_{km} are set to fixed values of an average person. For this, we use the relative limb lengths r_{km} computed from motion capture data as shown in Table 4.1 (b) and assume a person with average height h (average US person size, averaged over both genders) of 1695mm to compute the absolute limb lengths l_{km}.

Focal length & Principal Point

The TUM kitchen dataset provides extrinsic and intrinsic camera parameters for each of the four cameras. We use the focal length f from this camera calibration data. We could use, the principal point (c_x, c_y) from the calibration data as well, but in the experiments it is always set to the image center, since this is often a good approximation for the principal point and we want to keep the number of input parameters that need to be provided to the reconstruction algorithm as small as possible.

2D input poses

For the experiments we used three different types of input poses for the 3D pose reconstruction algorithm: (i) ground truth 2D input poses, generated by using the camera calibration parameters to project the 3D motion capture data to 2D, (ii) estimated 2D input poses by using the ISM based landmark localization step to generate a vote distribution for each landmark and taking the location with the highest vote density as the final landmark location, and (iii) noisy 2D input poses by adding noise to ground truth 2D input poses.

Exp No.	Test Video	No. of test frames	Per-spec-tive effects	Person size est. error [mm]	Our appr. error [mm]	Ext. Taylor error [mm]	Error cmp
1	0-0 cam0	439	strong	100	131.5	152.4	-14%
2	0-0 cam1	439	strong	100	142.4	160.7	-11%
3	0-9 cam0	587	strong	50	94.9	134.2	-29%
4	0-9 cam1	587	strong	50	98.3	139.9	-29%
5	0-0 cam2	439	weak	100	158.5	150.4	+5%
6	0-0 cam3	439	weak	100	151.1	157.7	-4%
7	0-9 cam2	587	weak	50	124.2	129.7	-4%
8	0-9 cam3	587	weak	50	111.1	131.5	-16%
∅ 1-8					**126.6**	**144.6**	**-13%**

Table 8.1.: Reconstruction results using ground truth 2D input poses.
In these experiments – showing strong or weak perspective effects – we used
ground truth 2D input poses and evaluated the error of the geometrically
reconstructed 3D pose estimates.

8.3.3. Quantitative results

I. Results for ground truth 2D input poses

Table 8.1 shows the experiment definitions and results from [Brauer and
Arens, 2011] conducted to evaluate the proposed method using ground
truth 2D input poses. In experiment 1, e.g., we estimate 3D poses for
person in the TUM kitchen sequence named "0-0" (camera 1) which
consists of 439 frames. Here, the perspective effects are strong (compare
videos from camera 0/1 with videos from camera 2/3). The test person
had a size that was 10cm smaller/larger than the assumed standard person
size of 169.9cm.

Since the original geometric reconstruction approach with a scaled orthographic projection camera model [Taylor, 2000] does not provide a
scale estimate and does not result in a single unique 3D pose estimate, we
estimate the scale parameter s automatically using the approach described
in Section 8.2.4 and determine a final 3D pose candidate as described
in Section 8.2.3. We call this approach "extended Taylor", since it is an
extension that allows to estimate 3D poses now fully automatically without

input needed from the user for (i) an estimate for s and (ii) a labeling whether the bone end or start point is nearer to the camera for each limb, as it is the case for the semi-automatic approach presented in [Taylor, 2000].

In the last line of Table 8.1 we show the errors, averaged over all 8 experiments. The average error for our approach is 126.6mm. In contrast, assuming a scaled orthographic projection yields a larger error of 144.6mm. A benefit of the better perspective camera model can be observed especially in cases of strong perspective effects (experiments 1-4).

II. Results using noisy 2D input poses

In [Gong et al., 2011] we also explored for two test sequences how the error of the reconstructed 3D poses increases if we add more and more noise to the ground truth 2D input poses and compared the result also with an alternative approach, namely using Gaussian Process Regression [Rasmussen and Williams, 2005] to map 2D input poses to 3D poses.

Exp No.	Test Sequence	2%	4%	6%	8%	10%
1	TUM-0-0-cam2	149.19	160.43	175.17	191.87	205.82
2	HE, walk-cam2, S1	159.03	168.07	177.59	189.02	198.49

Table 8.2.: Reconstruction results using noisy 2D input poses. For each frame of the test sequence we added noise of different levels to the corresponding ground truth 2D pose, used the resulting noisy 2D pose as input for the geometric reconstruction of a 3D pose and compared the reconstructed 3D pose with the ground truth 3D pose.

We used noise at levels between $r = 0.02$ and $r = 0.1$, where a noise level of r means that for each 2D landmark location we added a random translation vector (Δ_x, Δ_y) – uniformly drawn from the interval $[-rh, rh] \times [-rh, rh]$ where h is the 2D height of the person (measured in pixels) in the current frame. The evaluations showed, that for a 10% noise level the resulting average landmark localization error is approximately 20.2cm. Therefore, the error rapidly increases if noisy 2D input poses are used, compared e.g., to Gaussian Process Regression method which is less sensitive to noise (for details about this comparison see [Gong et al., 2011]).

III. Results using estimated 2D input poses

Table 8.3 shows the results of the experiments we conducted in [Gong et al., 2011] to evaluate the 3D pose estimation method using estimated 2D input poses.

Exp No.	Train Sequence	Test Sequence	Change of	Error [mm]
1	TUM 0-0-cam3 S1	TUM 0-0-cam2 S1	viewpoint (weak)	230.7
2	HE walk-cam1 S1	HE walk-cam2 S1	viewpoint (weak)	187.6
3	TUM 0-0-cam1 S1	TUM 0-2-cam3 S1	viewpoint (strong)	194.4
4	HE box-cam1 S1	HE box-cam2 S1	viewpoint (strong)	189.3
5	TUM 0-0-cam3 S1	TUM 0-3-cam3 S2	person	198.0
6	HE walk-cam1 S1	HE walk-cam1 S2	person	195.0
7	HE walk-cam1 S2	HE box-cam1 S2	action	202.4
8	HE box-cam1 S2	HE walk-cam1 S2	action	197.3
9	HE walk-cam2 S1	TUM 0-2-cam3 S2	dataset	214.4
10	TUM 0-2-cam3 S2	HE walk-cam2 S1	dataset	188.3
⌀ 1-10				**199.7**

Table 8.3.: Reconstruction results using estimated 2D input poses. In each experiment, we trained landmark ISMs using the train sequence, then estimated a 2D pose for each frame of the test sequence and reconstructed a 3D pose based on this 2D pose estimate.

In experiment 5, e.g., we used the sequence "TUM, 0-0-cam3" showing person "S1" to train an ISM for each of the 15 landmarks using the method described in Chapter 6. Using these landmark ISMs we then generated vote distributions for each landmark on the sequence "TUM, 0-3-cam3" showing another person "S2". For computing a 2D pose estimate needed by the 3D pose estimation method here, for each landmark a final 2D location was estimated by taking the location where the vote density for the corresponding landmark vote distribution reached a global maximum. For each 2D input pose estimate, the corresponding 3D pose was reconstructed for all video frames, resulting in an average reconstruction error of 198mm, where we averaged over all landmarks and video frames.

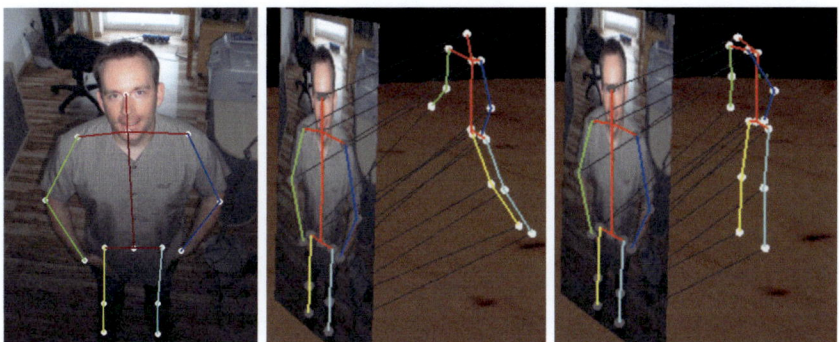

Figure 8.10.: Reconstruction example for a strong perspective. Left: input image with strong foreshortening effects of the legs due to the strong perspective. Middle: reconstruction result using a scaled orthographic projection model. Right: reconstruction result using a perspective projection model. Source: [Brauer and Arens, 2011].

The average 3D pose estimation error for experiments 1-10 is 199.7mm, which is – as expected – larger compared to 126.6mm in the case of ground truth 2D input poses. Averaging just over the HumanEva sequences yields an average error of 197.7mm. Compared to the state-of-the-art results on the HumanEva sequence reported in [Andriluka et al., 2010] of 101mm-107mm (see Chapter 3, and "related work" Section 2.1.7) these results are worse. Nevertheless, while [Andriluka et al., 2010] uses temporal information, here no temporal information is used so far. Further, the average pose estimation error was evaluated in [Andriluka et al., 2010] on basis of two HumanEva sequences only containing similar camera viewpoints, actions and the same person as in training, while here we evaluated on basis of six HumanEva sequences containing camera viewpoint, action, and person changes between training and testing.

8.3.4. Qualitative results

Fig. 8.10 shows a qualitative example that demonstrates the differences in the resulting 3D poses in dependence on the camera model used. While the image in the middle shows the final 3D pose estimate for a scaled orthographic projection camera model, the image right is for the case of a perspective projection camera model.

For the scaled orthographic projection model the observed foreshortening of the legs has to be explained by a (wrong) displacement of the limbs in the depth direction, since it cannot be explained by this simple camera model. In contrast, for the perspective camera model the foreshortening of the legs does not have to be explained by limb displacements, since it can be explained by the properties of the perspective projection.

Fig. 8.11 and Fig. 8.12 show four example 3D pose estimates for different frames of one of the test videos. Despite the strong perspective foreshortening effects present in the input 2D poses, the resulting estimated 3D poses capture the overall articulation of the person very well.

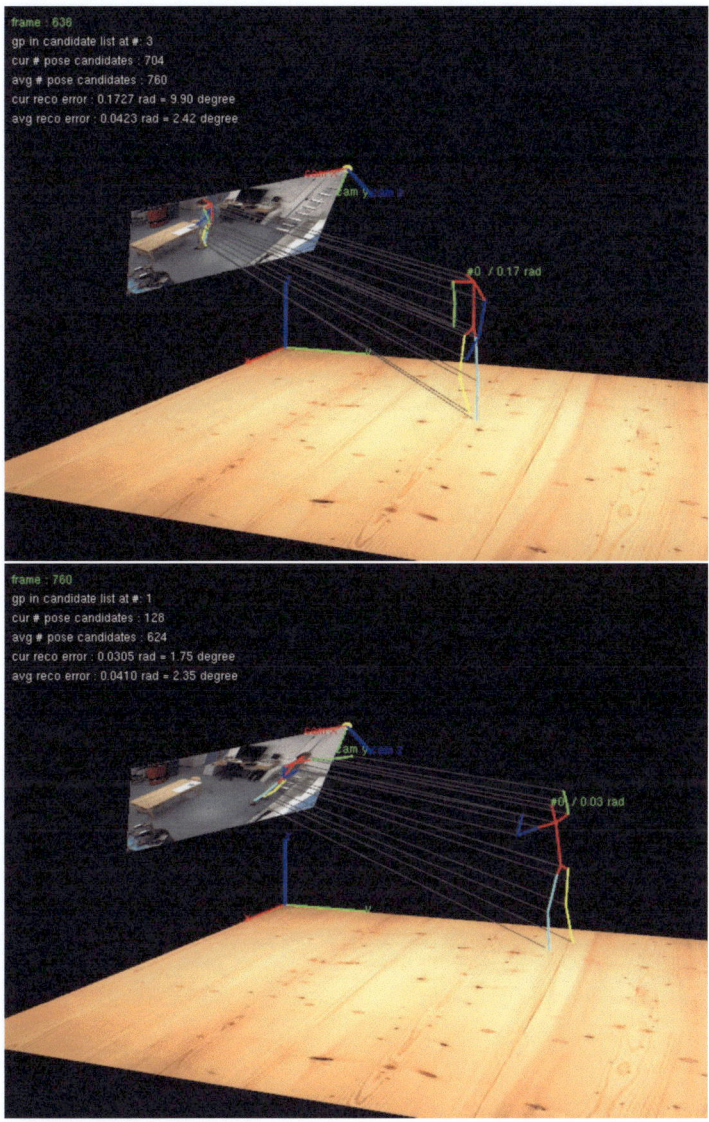

Figure 8.11.: Examples of reconstructed 3D pose estimates. Each image shows the top 3D pose candidate #0 from the list of pose candidates ordered by decreasing probability, i.e., the 3D pose estimate with the highest probability.

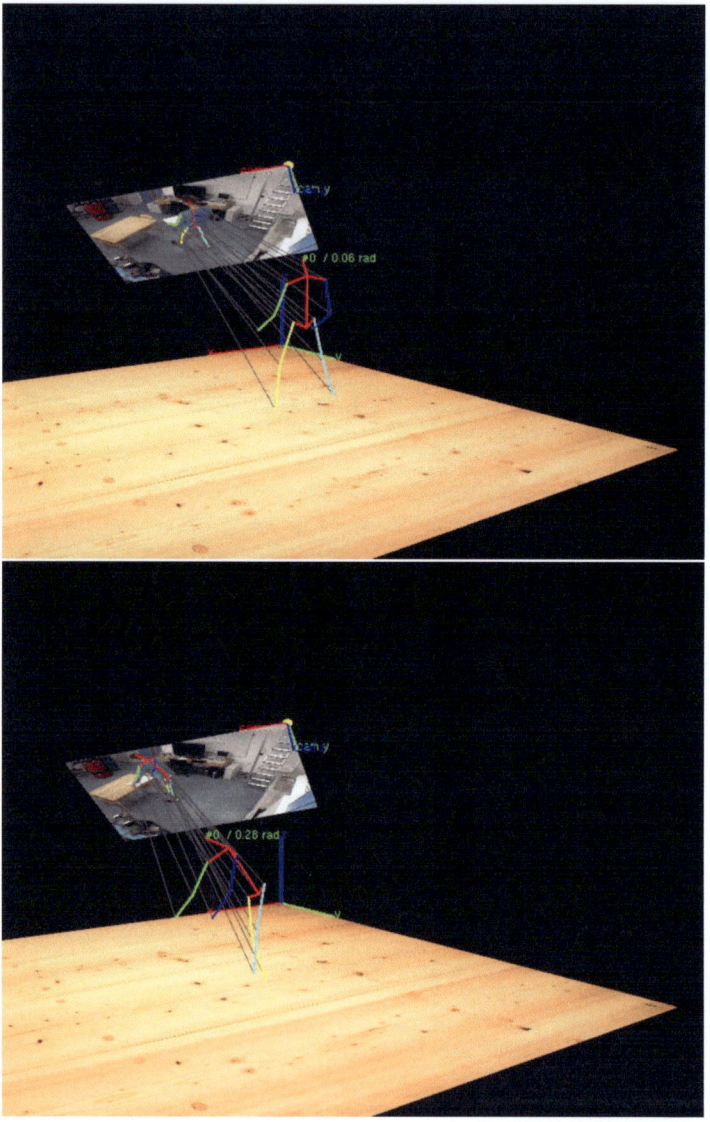

Figure 8.12.: Examples of reconstructed 3D pose estimates. Two further qualitative examples of reconstructed 3D poses.

8.3.5. Comparison with state-of-the-art

The method presented here needs as input a 2D pose estimate. For a fair comparison with other works we cannot use the 3D pose errors obtained for the ground-truth 2D input cases (I) or errors obtained for noisy 2D input poses (II), instead we have to use the results obtained for real estimated 2D poses (III).

	Evaluation here
dataset(s)	TUM kitchen + HumanEva
pose vector dimension	45
DATASET CHALLENGES	
1. cross evaluation	+
2. public	+
3. occlusions	−
4. non frontal poses	+
5. low resolution	−
6. background clutter	+
EXPERIMENTS CHALLENGES	
7. test persons new	+
8. test poses new	+
9. large pose variety	−
10. single images	+
11. small training sets	+
12. large evaluation	−
Overall difficulty	**8 of 12**
Error [cm]	**19.97cm**
Computation time [sec]	**4.9**

Table 8.4.: Assessment of the level of difficulty of our experiments. For a better comparison with state-of-the-art results, we assess the difficulty of our experiments conducted on the TUM kitchen and the HumanEva dataset.

For this case, we show the experiment settings in Table 8.4. The experiments were conducted not only on the TUM kitchen, but also the HumanEva dataset, where we included at least two cross evaluations (1) in experiments 9 and 10. Both datasets are publicly available (2), but do not contain occlusion scenarios (3). Many frames show non-frontal poses (4) at high resolution (5) with background clutter (6). There are experiments (exps. 5-6 and 9-10) where the train and test persons are different (7). Poses are always new (8), since the approach here does not make use of example poses: only knowledge about joint angle probabilities has to be provided. Poses are estimated on a per-frame basis (10), where the 15 landmark localization ISMs are trained on a single video each (11). Since there are only 2 different test persons, we cannot say that it is a large evaluation (12).

The error over both the HumanEva and the TUM kitchen sequences is 19.97cm. Table 3.2 shows that our experiments show a high level of difficulty compared to the evaluations conducted in related work. The 3D landmark localization error is similar to the 19-25cm reported by [Andriluka and Sigal, 2012], which uses a significantly smaller level of difficulty for their experiments (there: 4 of 12, here: 8 of 12).

Comparing the new fully automatic geometric reconstruction method for perspective projections with the extended, i.e., also fully automatic, geometric reconstruction method for scaled orthographic projections a reduction of 3D landmark localization error rates about 13% can be expected.

8.4. Conclusions

In this chapter we showed how to adopt the geometric reconstruction idea for 3D poses, originally presented in [Taylor, 2000] for scaled orthographic projections only, to perspective projections. The new method corresponds to a recursive 3D pose reconstruction algorithm where 3D pose candidates can be filtered already during reconstruction for joint limit violations. A final unique 3D pose estimate can be chosen based on the probability of the remaining pose candidates, which can be defined using the product of the joint state probabilities. We further proposed a new method to automatically determine the projection parameters (scale parameter s or focal length f) and the input parameter z_r (person to camera distance), based on the average probability of the set of reconstructed 3D poses for a given parameter choice. The same ideas can be used to extend the semi-automatic approach in [Taylor, 2000] to a fully automatic approach where the scale parameter s and an unique 3D pose estimate is determined automatically ("extended Taylor").

The experimental results show that the reconstructed 3D poses of the proposed method are better compared to the original method if there are strong perspective foreshortening effects. The geometric reconstruction approach is attractive, since in principle any 3D pose can be reconstructed without the need to have knowledge about 3D example poses as it is the case for the generative pose estimation approach presented in the previous chapter or, e.g., for learning based regression methods that need training images of poses (see also [Gong et al., 2011]). Further, the average landmark localization error of approx. 20cm obtained in the experiments here seems to indicate that the method performs similar as the generative 3D pose estimator presented in the previous chapter (at least for the HumanEva experiments).

Nevertheless, there are three drawbacks of the geometric reconstruction approach compared to the generative pose estimation approach presented in the previous chapter. First, it is currently not able to deal with occlusion cases since we need to observe all 2D limbs. Second, an unique 2D pose estimate is needed as input, but directly generating an unique 2D pose estimate from the landmark vote density maxima is dangerous, since the landmark vote density distributions are typically multi-modal. Third, the experimental results with noisy 2D input poses shows that the approach is sensitive to landmark localization errors, while the generative pose estimation approach from the previous chapter is not. The reason is that the working principle of the method here exploits the knowledge about measured 2D limb lengths. If the 2D landmark locations are wrong, the 2D limb lengths are wrong as well and for this, the displacement in the missing depth dimension will be estimated wrongly resulting in false 3D pose estimates.

For future work it is therefore essentially to incorporate some mechanism into the approach that allows the method to deal with occluded and wrongly estimated landmark locations. An interesting question is whether we can lift the uncertainty about the landmark locations represented by the vote distributions in some way up to the 3D world, e.g., by modeling the uncertainty about the limb displacements in the missing depth dimension.

9. Conclusions and outlook

9.1. Conclusions

In this thesis we showed how to use Implicit Shape Models (ISMs) for monocular HPE. The approach can directly be coupled with an ISM based person tracker. Local features associated with each person hypothesis can be reused to vote for landmark locations in a first step. Since the original ISM voting strategy produces rather unfocussed vote distributions for the task of landmark localization, we introduced a set of new voting strategies that can be used to generate more focused vote distributions, where more of the vote mass is casted near to the true landmark locations.

Although the new voting strategies help to improve landmark localization, the generated vote distributions are typically multi-modal, i.e., there are several possible locations for each landmark, mainly due to left-right body part ambiguities. Nevertheless, we showed how we can use such landmark vote distributions for estimating a 3D pose in such cases as well using a top-down 3D pose estimation approach. For this, 3D pose hypotheses are generated and projected to 2D in order to be compared directly with the vote distributions. The objective function used within a Particle Swarm Optimization framework to find a good pose / projection pair measures the vote density near to the projected landmark locations of a single 3D pose hypothesis. The pose hypotheses used are rotated, tilted, and scaled versions of example poses, retrieved from motion capture data, or generated from pose splines, a compact representation of motion sequences. Comparing projected 3D pose hypotheses in the voting space and not in the image space allows to test for millions of 3D pose candidates per second on a standard desktop PC, resulting in a fast 3D pose estimation approach.

We also presented an alternative bottom-up 3D pose estimation approach which starts with a 2D pose estimate and reconstructs corresponding 3D pose candidates using limb foreshortening information. We showed how to adopt this working principle for a perspective camera model, resulting in a recursive 3D landmark reconstruction algorithm. Further, we proposed to use the average probability of the reconstructed pose candidates to automatically estimate the person to camera distance and possibly missing camera calibration information as, e.g., the focal length. While this approach is attractive since it does not need knowledge about example 3D poses, it cannot deal with occlusions of landmarks in its current form since it is sensitive to noise and needs an unique 2D pose estimate as input.

To our knowledge, it is the first time, that the ISM model was used and extended for the task of anatomical landmark localization and that landmark vote distributions were used as input for a successive 3D pose estimation step. With this we have introduced a new framework for monocular human pose estimation from images using a standard object recognition framework, namely the ISM.

The idea to use the ISM for anatomical landmark localization was first published by the author of this thesis in [Müller and Arens, 2010]. In the meantime the idea was adopted to another sensor modality: depth cameras. Some of the members of the Kinect development team [Girshick et al., 2011] modified the original Kinect pose estimation algorithm by [Shotton et al., 2011] accordingly using our ideas presented in [Müller and Arens, 2010]. While in the original Kinect pose estimation algorithm each person pixel is classified to belong to a certain body part using a deep decision tree, in the modified version a Hough forest is used, where a set of votes is stored at each leaf to directly vote for the 3D location of the body part (joint). The evaluation results in [Girshick et al., 2011] show that the idea to vote for body part locations using local features helps to improve the pose estimation accuracy significantly, i.e., the idea of landmark localization using ISMs can also be adopted to the depth sensors domain. It is therefore a natural idea to try to adopt ideas such as the new voting strategies and the generative pose estimation method presented here to such sensor modalities in future as well.

9.2. Outlook

There are a lot of further ideas to continue the work presented in this thesis. Here we briefly describe the main issues we see to improve the landmark localization and pose estimation accuracy even further and integrate the modules into a complete system.

Semi-automatic generation of training data

For learning an ISM for each landmark we need training pairs in the form of (image, landmark ground truth location) pairs. For the quantitative evaluation experiments in this thesis, we could generate this training data automatically by projecting the 3D poses to 2D using the camera calibration information provided with the UMPM benchmark. But datasets that provide video synchronized with motion capture data and additionally camera calibration information are rare. Further, such datasets only show a limited number of poses recorded from specific camera viewpoints. For new poses and camera perspectives it is desirable to provide application specific training data. Unfortunately, labeling manually large amount of training data is time-consuming. One idea is therefore to let the user label only a limited number of example frames and to track the labeled landmarks for some frames before and after the ground truth labeled frame. If landmarks can be tracked reliable, e.g., to 50 frames before and 50 frames after the manually labeled frame – i.e., the user labels one frame and 100 frames are labeled automatically – this would result in a semi-automatic annotation procedure with a speed-up factor of approximately 100.

Fig. 9.1 shows an image from [Krah, 2013][1] where different ideas for semi-automatic landmark annotation were explored. The user labels some landmarks in a frame t. A dense optical flow (TV-L1) is computed for successive frames and the optical flow in some local area around a landmark is used for predicting the location of the landmark in previous frame t-1 and next frame t+1. Using the optical flow information and the predicted landmark locations from frame t-1, landmarks are then tracked to frame t-2, and using the landmark locations from frame t+1 tracked to frame t+2, etc. While optical flow is one possibility to predict landmark locations,

---

[1]Student thesis at Fraunhofer IOSB, supervised by the author of this thesis.

appearance model based methods that update an appearance model of the landmark on-the-fly while tracking (e.g., [Zhang et al., 2012]) are currently being explored for landmark tracking as well.

 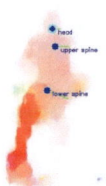

Figure 9.1.: Semi-automatic annotation of 2D poses. Optical flow (here: TV-L1) is used to track three landmarks, annotated for a sparse set of frames by a user. The green lines indicate the direction into which the landmarks move in the next frame based on the optical flow information.

Use multiple features as input

Currently only one type of local features (SURF, [Bay et al., 2006]) is used as input for the landmark localization step. For the task of pedestrian detection one of the best person detectors currently available – the Fastest Pedestrian Detector in the West (FPDW) [Dollár et al., 2009], [Dollár et al., 2010], [Dollár et al., 2011] – uses multiple feature types. The robustness and state-of-the-art performance of this detector can probably be traced back mainly to the fact that different features are used, as edge images, Gabor filter responses, gradient magnitude images, gradient histograms, threshold images, etc. This leads to the idea to improve the robustness of the landmark localization step by using multiple feature types as well. The integration of multiple features is straightforward. Instead of learning one ISM per landmark, we could learn one ISM per landmark and feature type and accumulate the votes for the landmark location from the different ISMs in one meta-voting map. It is highly interesting to see whether this helps to further focus the landmark vote densities near to the true landmark locations.

Pose graphs

For the generative 3D pose estimator presented in this thesis two different types of pose prior representations were tested: example poses and pose splines. The experimental results have shown that the usage of pose splines leads to similar 3D landmark localization errors as using example poses, while the number of 3D pose candidate evaluations needed till a final 3D pose estimate is found is significantly smaller. Nevertheless, pose splines have still one drawback. Each motion sequence is compressed to an isolated pose spline representation and the PSO based optimization is executed on each spline independently from all other splines. This means that for each new example motion sequence, a new spline has to be added to the set of all pose splines, i.e., the set of splines will grow linearly with the number of training sequences. An alternative idea is therefore to allow for connections between two poses from two different splines. The resulting pose prior representation would become a graph of 3D poses, where an edge between two 3D poses means that we can go from one pose (vertex 1) in the graph to another pose (vertex 2) by linear interpolation. The PSO based optimization has then to be initiated with a start population on all edges and vertices of such a graph and particles can move freely on the graph. For new motion sequences we could then traverse the contained 3D poses and check for each 3D pose whether it is already in the graph and add the 3D pose and new edges to other 3D poses on demand.

Exploit temporal dimension

Until now, the temporal dimension has not been exploited, i.e., both the geometric reconstruction and the generative pose estimation approach presented here do not make use of sequence information, but estimate poses on a per-frame basis. Using temporal information should help to solve for left/right ambiguities and compensate for erroneous landmark localization in individual frames. The generative pose estimation approach could be modified in a straightforward way to use temporal information by modifying the objective function to work with a short sequence of images and, e.g., to measure not only the vote density near to the projected landmark locations, but also to measure the continuity of the joint angle changes if we consider a certain pose hypothesis for the current frame.

Another idea is first to collect a set of pose candidates for each frame individually and then to search for a sequence of pose candidates through the candidate sets computed for each frame such that the joint angles change continuously (see [Brauer et al., 2011]).

Combined person tracking, pose estimation, and action recognition

In this thesis the two modules for landmark localization and pose estimation are examined independently from the person tracking and action recognition modules (see Fig. 1.2). For future work it is desirable not only to explore the whole image processing chain using all modules, but also to augment the modules by feedback channels, such that information does not flow only into one direction within the image processing chain. Currently one problem of person detectors and trackers is that vertical bar-like image structures as, e.g., lamp posts or tree trunks are often detected as persons. Within a complete image processing chain, where we try to localize anatomical landmarks and estimate a 3D pose for each person hypothesis provided by a person tracker, we could return some confidence measure about the landmark locations and the pose for each person hypothesis back to the person tracker. If the corresponding confidence values are smaller compared to the confidence values of real persons, this could help to eliminate such false positive person detections. Similar, the action recognition module could give feedback to the pose estimation module about its belief about the current action, which could be used by the pose estimator to further constrain the pose search space.

Appendix

A. Example training and test images

To give the reader a better impression of the training and test data used, we show one example video frame from each training and each test video used for each UMPM and HumanEva experiment in Chapter 7 with an odd experiment number. Note that the same train and test videos are used for all experiments i and $i+1$ where i is an odd number. For this we skip example frames from experiments with even experiment numbers.

Each example video frame shown here was drawn randomly between second 5 and second 45. We do not randomly extract frames before second 5, since at least for the UMPM dataset, the same pose is shown in the UMPM sequences in the first 5 seconds, since a start pose is needed by the landmark based motion capture system used for recording the UMPM dataset. The minimum length of a video is 45 seconds.

All UMPM[1] and HumanEva[2] video sequences used in this thesis can be downloaded and watched in their full length from the corresponding dataset websites.

---

[1]http://www.projects.science.uu.nl/umpm/
[2]http://vision.cs.brown.edu/humaneva/

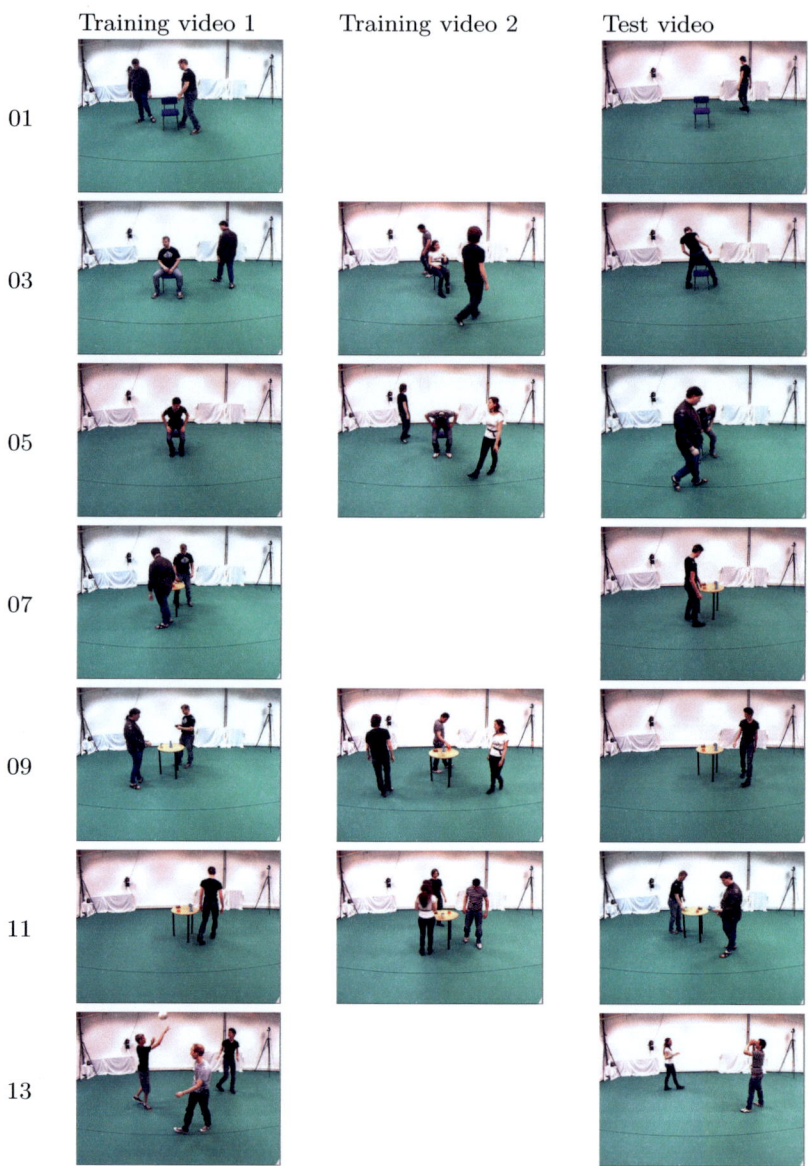

Table A.1.: Examples of training and test images, experiments 1-13

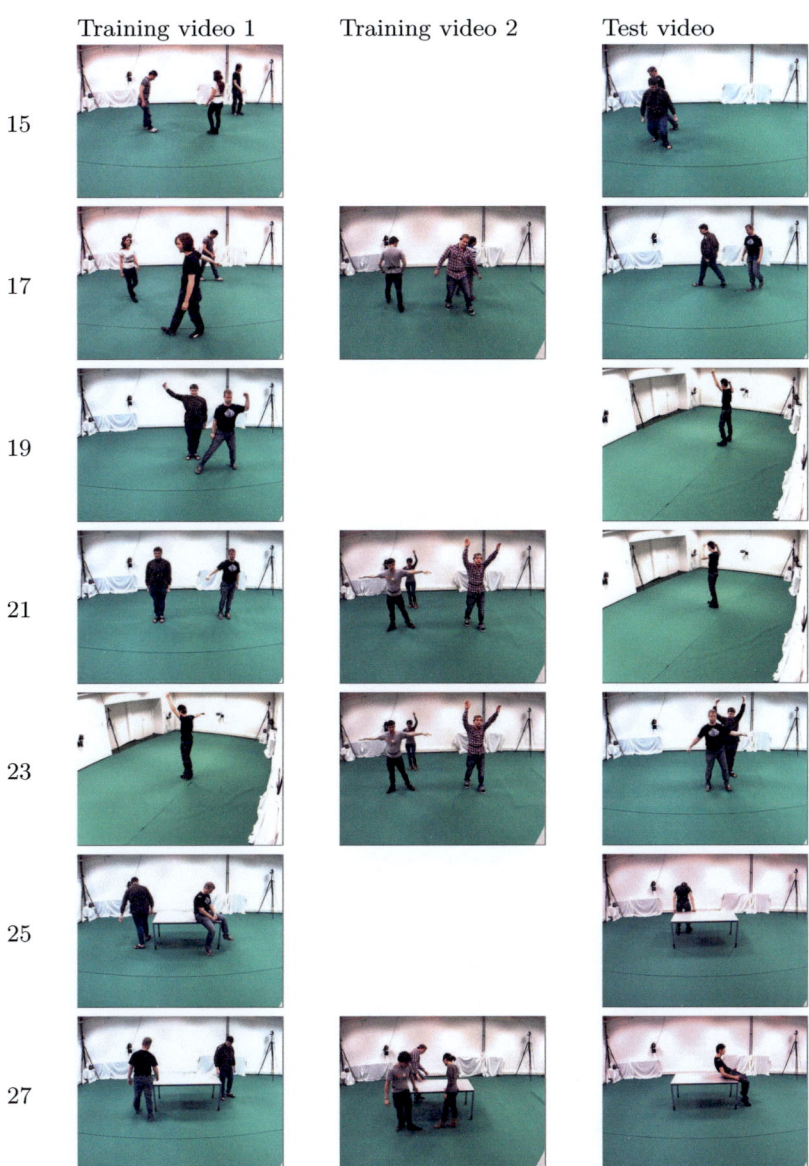

Table A.2.: Examples of training and test images, experiments 15-27

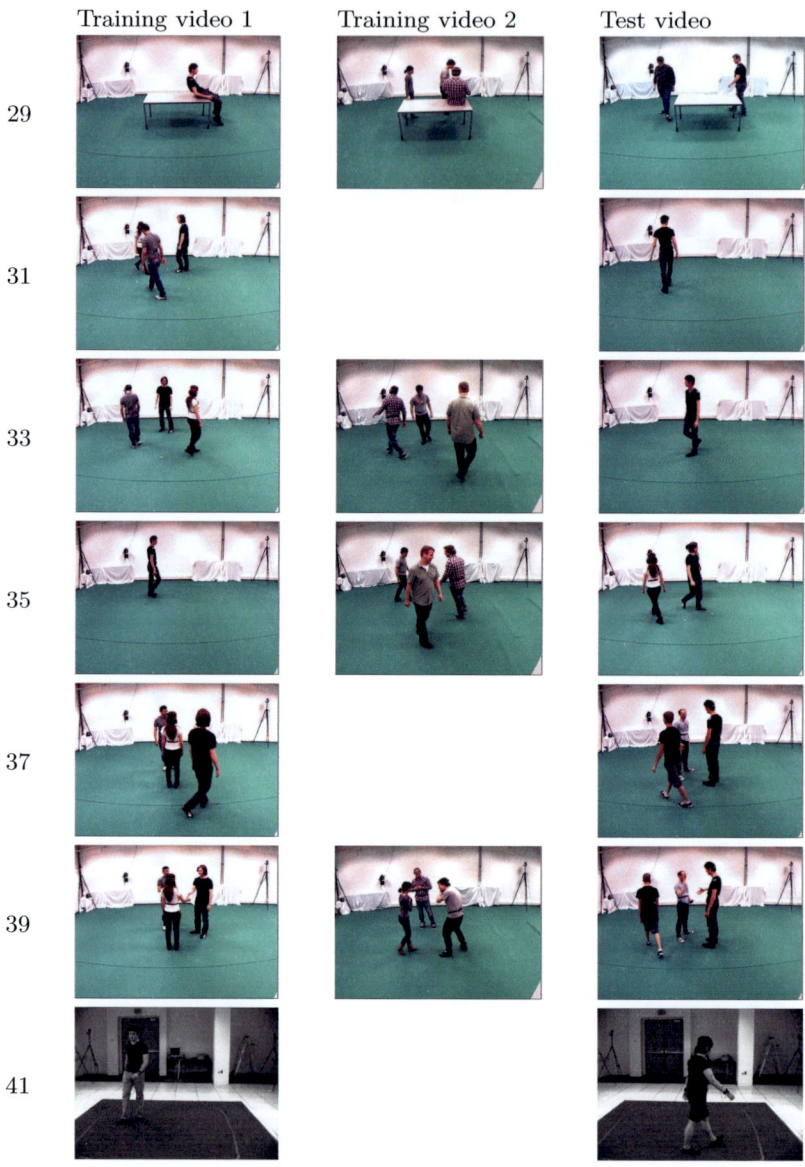

Table A.3.: Examples of training and test images, experiments 29-41

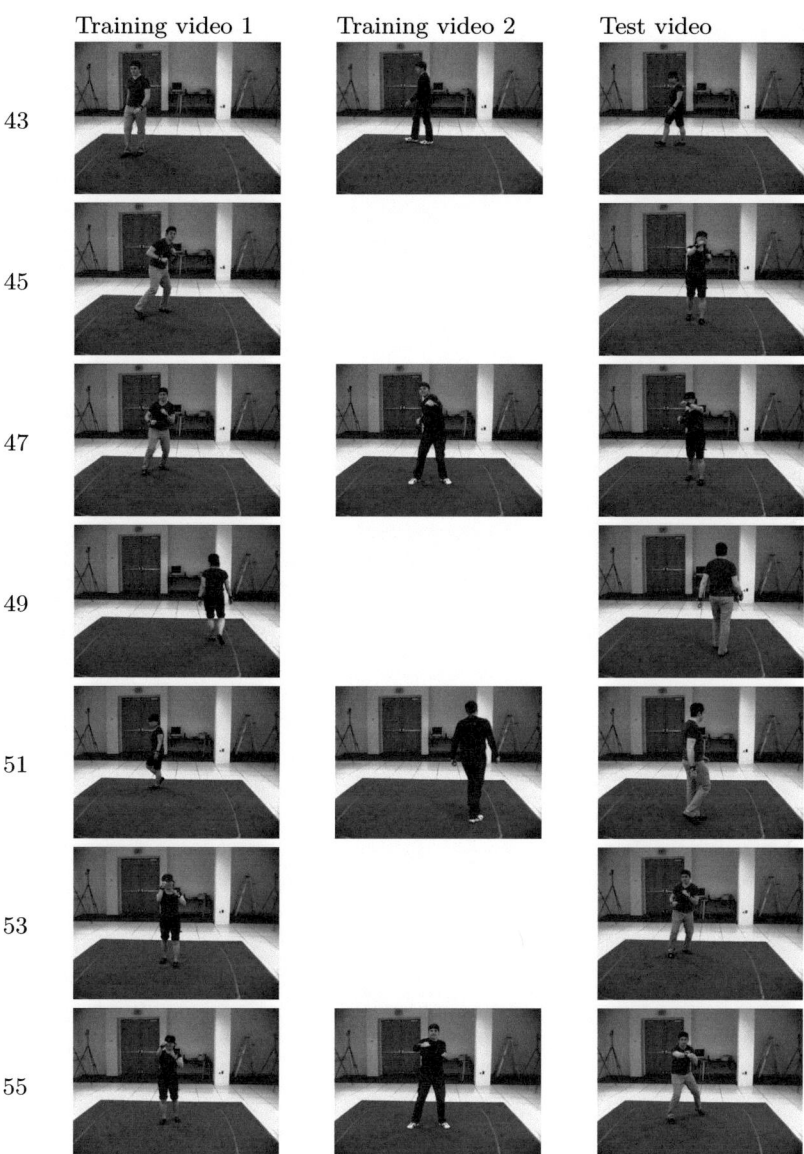

Table A.4.: Examples of training and test images, experiments 43-55

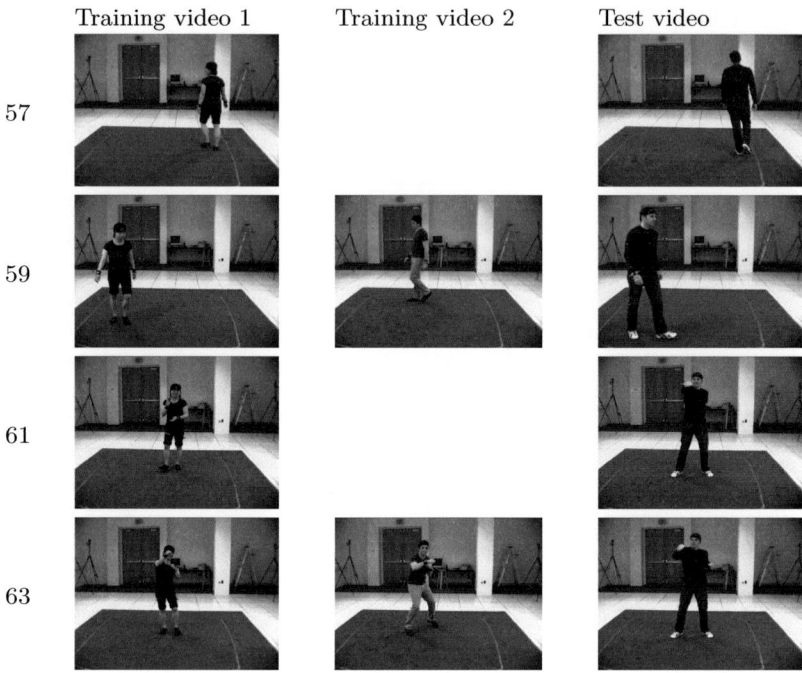

Table A.5.: Examples of training and test images, experiments 57-63

B. Example votemaps

Landmark ID	Landmark name
0	head
1	upper spine
2	lower spine
3	right shoulder
4	right elbow
5	right hand
6	left shoulder
7	left elbow
8	left hand
9	right hip
10	right knee
11	right foot
12	left hip
13	left knee
14	left foot

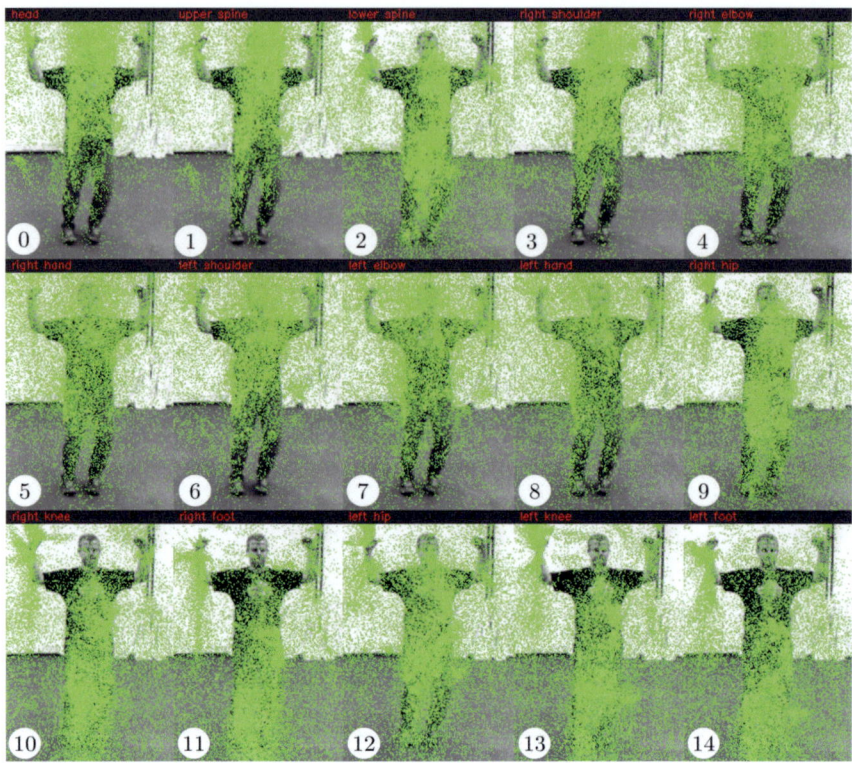

Figure B.1.: Vote locations generated by ORIG-VOT. Vote locations are indicated by green dots. Vote weights are not visualized. ORIG-VOT generates a lot of votes located at wrong image locations.

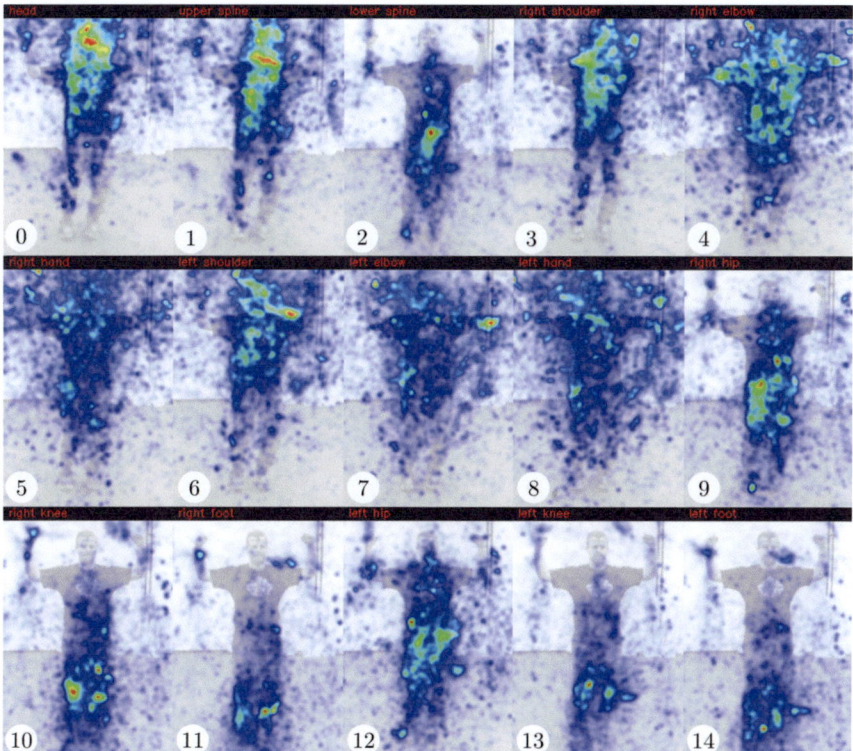

Figure B.2.: Vote density generated by ORIG-VOT. For each of the 15 anatomical landmarks the corresponding vote density is visualized by a heatmap (warm colors indicate high density). visualization, i.e., warm colors indicate high density.

Figure B.3.: Vote locations generated by COMBI-VOT. COMBI-VOT generates less votes than ORIG-VOT.

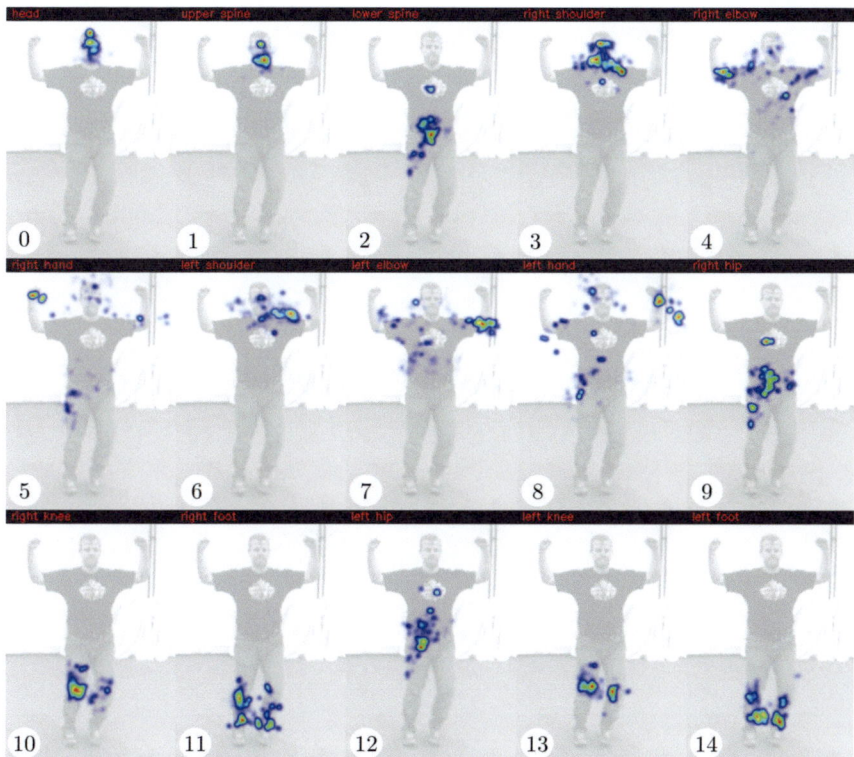

Figure B.4.: Vote density generated by COMBI-VOT. The vote density peaks for right elbow/foot, left hand/knee/foot are nearer located to the true landmark locations compared to the corresponding vote density peaks from ORIG-VOT shown in Fig. B.2. Only for the left hip the vote density peak is clearly wrong in this example here.

C. Joint angle statistics

The body model used in this thesis encodes the articulation of a person using both the 3D landmark coordinates and the joint angles representation. While mathematically each joint angle may take values in the range of $[-\pi, \pi]$, real human joints are constrained to sub-ranges. E.g., the elbows and knees can only take values from a range of a width less than π radians and not 2π radians. Further, some joint angles will occur more often than others.

Figs. C.1 - C.3 show the relative occurrence frequencies for some joint angles, computed based on the 2.779.646 CMU 3D poses.

Most joint angles are constrained to some sub-interval of the full $[-\pi, \pi]$ interval: e.g., the joint angle values for the 1 DOF knees and elbows are only within some limited range in $[0, \pi]$. Some joint angles are constrained even more, e.g., the head alpha and beta joint angles.

It can further be observed that the angular values are not uniformly distributed but that some angular values occur much more often than others. For some joint angles the angular values are distributed roughly according to a normal distribution.

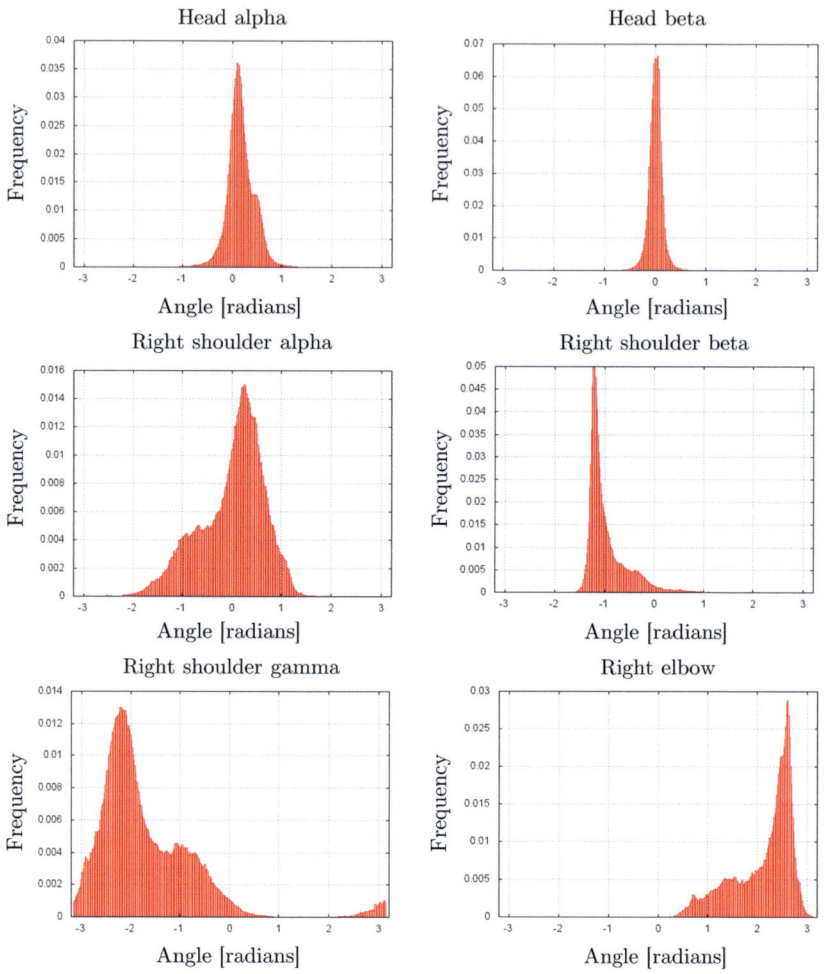

Figure C.1.: CMU database joint angle frequencies 1/3. Using the CMU motion capture database we can compute how often each angle value for each DOF of a joint occurs.

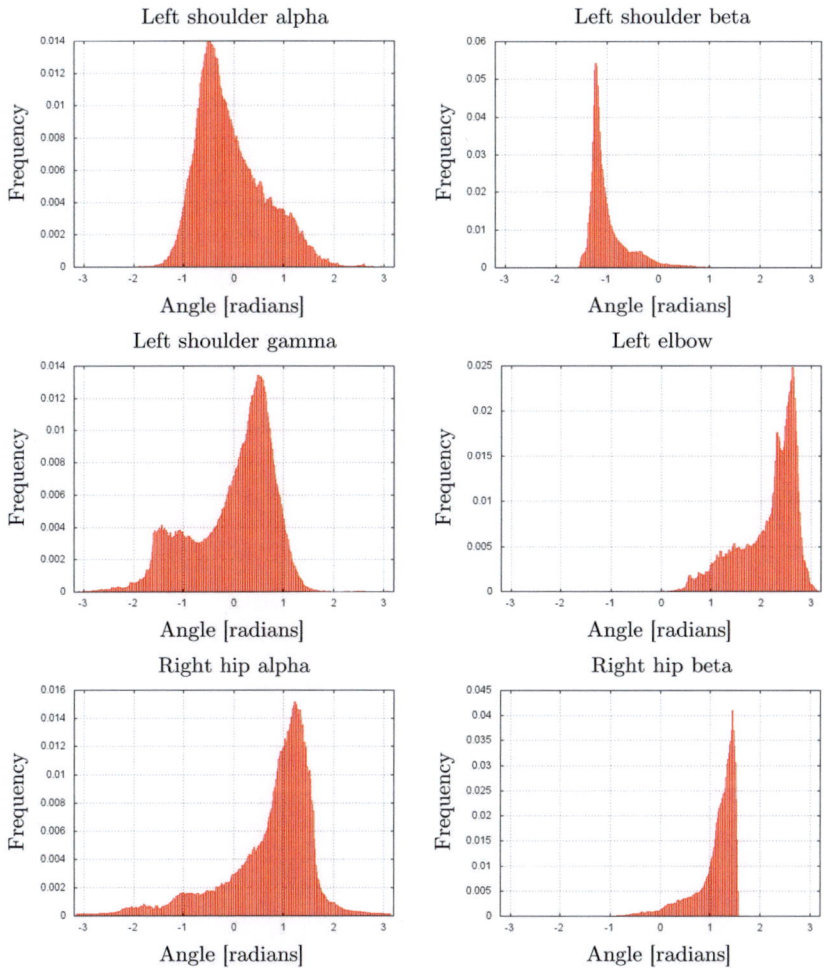

Figure C.2.: CMU database joint angle frequencies 2/3

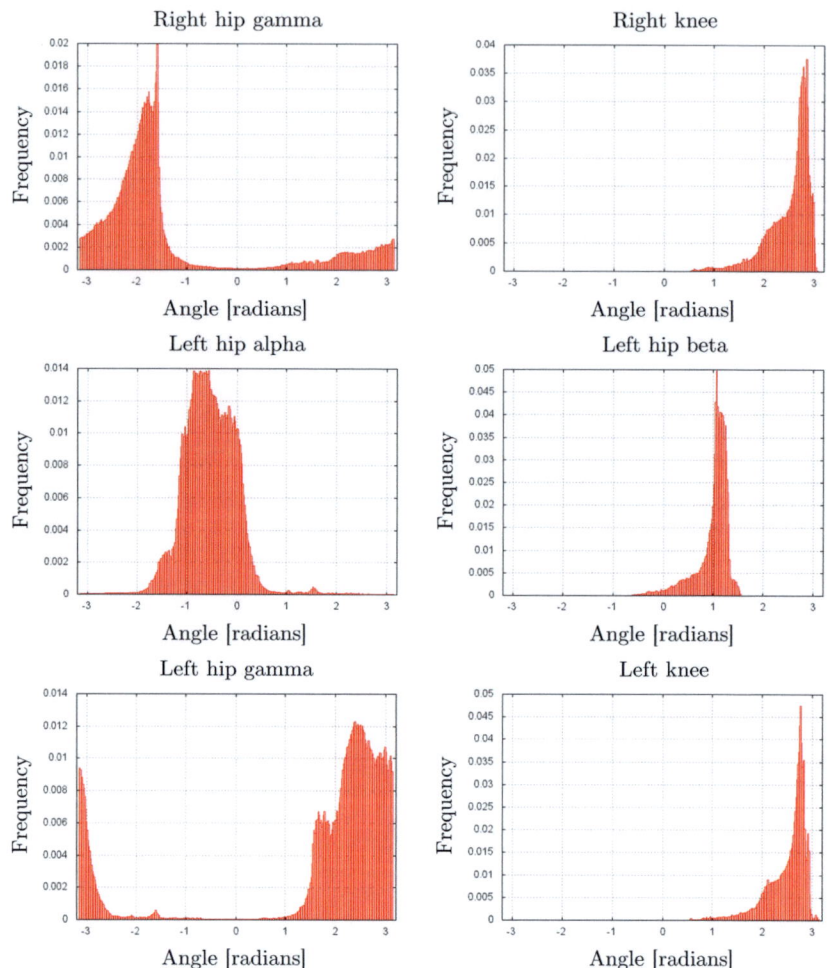

Figure C.3.: CMU database joint angle frequencies 3/3

List of Figures

List of Tables

List of thesis related publications by the author

Jürgen Brauer, Wolfgang Hübner, Michael Arens. Particle Swarm Optimization on Low Dimensional Pose Manifolds for Monocular Human Pose Estimation. In *Proc. of SPIE 2013, Optics and Photonics for Counter-terrorism, Crime Fighting and Defence IX, SPIE Security + Defence*, Dresden/Germany, **2013**.
▷ *related to Chapter 7*

Jürgen Brauer, Wolfgang Hübner, Michael Arens. Voting Strategies for Anatomical Landmark Localization using the Implicit Shape Model. In *Proc. of CAIP 2013, 15th Int. Conf. on Computer Analysis of Images and Patterns*. Springer Lecture Notes on Computer Science 8047, Part I, pp. 145-153, York/UK, **2013**.
▷ *related to Chapter 6*

Jürgen Brauer, Wolfgang Hübner, Michael Arens. Generative 2D and 3D Human Pose Estimation with Vote Distributions. In *Proc. of ISVC 2012, 8th Int. Symposium on Visual Computing*. Springer Lecture Notes on Computer Science 7431, Part I, pp. 470-481, Crete/Greece, **2012**.
▷ *related to Chapter 7*

Jürgen Brauer, Wenjuan Gong, Jordi Gonzàlez, Michael Arens. On the Effect of Temporal Information on Monocular 3D Human Pose Estimation. In *Proc. of ICCV 2011 Workshops, IEEE Int. Conf. on Computer Vision Workshops (ARTEMIS)*, pp. 906-913, Barcelona/Spain, **2011**.
▷ *related to Chapter 8*

Wenjuan Gong, **Jürgen Brauer**, Michael Arens, Jordi Gonzàlez. Modeling vs. Learning Approaches for Monocular 3D Human Pose Estimation. In *Proc. of ICCV 2011 Workshops, IEEE Int. Conf. on Computer Vision Workshops (PERHAPS)*, pp. 1287-1294, Barcelona/Spain, **2011**.
▷ *related to Chapter 8*

Jürgen Brauer, Michael Arens. Reconstructing The Missing Dimension: From 2D to 3D Human Pose Estimation. In *Proc. of REACTS 2011, REcognition and ACTion for Scene Understanding in conj. with CAIP 2011, 14th Int. Conf. on Computer Analysis of Images and Patterns*, pp. 25-39, Málaga / Spain, **2011**.
▷ *related to Chapter 8*

Jürgen Müller[1], Michael Arens. Human Pose Estimation with Implicit Shape Models (Best Paper Award). In *Proc. of ACM ARTEMIS 2010, Int. Workshop on Analysis and Retrieval of Tracked Events and Motion in Imagery Stream - in conj. with ACM Multimedia 2010 Conference*, Florence/Italy, **2010**.
▷ *related to Chapter 6*

---

[1]Due to a marriage the author of this thesis changed his last name in 2011: Müller → Brauer.

Bibliography

Aa, N.P. van der; Luo, X.; Giezeman, G.J.; Tan, R.T., and Veltkamp, R.C. Utrecht Multi-Person Motion (UMPM) Benchmark: a Multi-Person Dataset with Synchronized Video and Motion Capture Data for Evaluation of Articulated Human Motion and Interaction. In *HICV workshop - in conj. with ICCV 2011, Int. Conf. on Computer Vision*, 2011.

Agarwal, Ankur and Triggs, Bill. A Local Basis Representation For Estimating Human Pose From Cluttered Images. In *Proc. of ACCV 2006, Asian Conf. on Computer Vision*, pages 50–59, 2006a.

Agarwal, Ankur and Triggs, Bill. Recovering 3D Human Pose from Monocular Images. *IEEE Transactions on Pattern Analysis and Machine Intelligence*, 28:44–58, 2006b.

Andriluka, Mykhaylo and Sigal, Leonid. Human Context: Modeling Human-Human Interactions for Monocular 3D Pose Estimation. In *Proc. of AMDO 2012, Conf. on Articulated Motion and Deformable Objects*, Mallorca, Spain, July 2012.

Andriluka, Mykhaylo; Roth, Stefan, and Schiele, Bernt. Pictorial Structures Revisited: People Detection and Articulated Pose Estimation. In *Proc. of CVPR 2009, Int. Conf. on Computer Vision and Pattern Recognition*, pages 1014–1021, 2009.

Andriluka, Mykhaylo; Roth, Stefan, and Schiele, Bernt. Monocular 3D Pose Estimation and Tracking by Detection. In *Proc. of CVPR 2010, Int. Conf. on Computer Vision and Pattern Recognition*, USA, 2010.

Azad, Pedram. *Visual Perception for Manipulation and Imitation in Humanoid Robots*. PhD thesis, Karlsruhe Institute of Technology (KIT), 2008.

Ballard, Dana H. Generalizing the Hough Transform to Detect Arbitrary Shapes. *Pattern Recognition*, 13(2):111–122, 1981.

Bay, Herbert; Tuytelaars, Tinne, and Gool, Luc Van. SURF: Speeded Up Robust Features. In *Proc. of ECCV 2006, European Conf. on Computer Vision*, pages 404–417, 2006.

Belongie, Serge; Malik, Jitendra, and Puzicha, Jan. Shape Context: A New Descriptor for Shape Matching and Object Recognition. In *Neural Information Processing Systems Conf. (NIPS)*, pages 831–837, December 2000.

Bissacco, Alessandro; Yang, Ming-Hsuan, and Soatto, Stefano. Fast Human Pose Estimation using Appearance and Motion via Multi-Dimensional Boosting Regression. In *Proc. of CVPR 2007, Int. Conf. on Computer Vision and Pattern Recognition*, pages –1–1, 2007.

Bourdev, Lubomir and Malik, Jitendra. Poselets: Body Part Detectors Trained Using 3D Human Pose Annotations. In *Proc. of ICCV 2009, Int. Conf. on Computer Vision*, 2009.

Bratton, Daniel and Kennedy, James. Defining a Standard for Particle Swarm Optimization. In *Proc. of IEEE Swarm Intelligence Symposium 2007*, pages 120–127, 2007.

Brauer, Jürgen and Arens, Michael. Reconstructing the Missing Dimension: From 2D to 3D Human Pose Estimation. In *Proc. of REACTS 2011, REcognition and ACTion for Scene Understanding- in conj. with CAIP 2011, Int. Conf. on Computer Analysis of Images and Patterns*, pages 25–39, Spain, Málaga, 2011.

Brauer, Jürgen; Gong, Wenjuan; Gonzàlez, Jordi, and Arens, Michael. On the Effect of Temporal Information on Monocular 3D Human Pose Estimation. In *Proc. of ICCV 2011 Workshops, Int. Conf. on Computer Vision*, pages 906–913, November 2011.

Brauer, Jürgen; Hübner, Wolfgang, and Arens, Michael. Generative 2D and 3D Human Pose Estimation with Vote Distributions. In *Proc. of ISVC 2012, 8th Int. Symposium on Visual Computing, Springer Lecture Notes on Computer Science 7431, Part I*, page 470Ű481, Rethymnon, Crete, Greece, 2012. Springer-Verlag Berlin Heidelberg.

Brauer, Jürgen; Hübner, Wolfgang, and Arens, Michael. Voting Strategies for Anatomical Landmark Localization using the Implicit Shape Model. In *Proc. of CAIP, 15th Int. Conf. on Analysis of Images and Patterns, Springer Lecture Notes on Computer Science 8047, Part I*, volume Part I of *LNCS 8047*, pages 145–153, York, GB, 2013a.

Brauer, Jürgen; Hübner, Wolfgang, and Arens, Michael. Particle Swarm Optimization on Low Dimensional Pose Manifolds for Monocular Human Pose Estimation. In *Proc. of SPIE Volume 8901A, Optics and Photonics for Counterterrorism, Crime Fighting and Defence IX, SPIE Security + Defence 2013, Dresden / Germany*, September 2013b.

Bregler, Christoph and Malik, Jitendra. Tracking People with Twists and Exponential Maps. In *Proc. of CVPR 1998, Int. Conf. on Computer Vision and Pattern Recognition*, volume 0, page 8, Los Alamitos, CA, USA, 1998. IEEE Computer Society.

Charles, James and Everingham, Mark. Learning shape models for monocular human pose estimation from the Microsoft Xbox Kinect. In *Proc. of ICCV 2011 Workshops, Int. Conf. on Computer Vision*, pages 1202–1208. IEEE, 2011.

Cheng, Yizong. Mean Shift, Mode Seeking, and Clustering. *IEEE Transactions on Pattern Analysis and Machine Intelligence*, 17(8):790–799, 1995.

Cheung, Kong Man; Baker, Simon, and Kanade, Takeo. Shape-From-Silhouette of Articulated Objects and its Use for Human Body Kinematics Estimation and Motion Capture. In *Proc. of CVPR 2003, Int. Conf. on Computer Vision and Pattern Recognition*, June 2003.

Clerc, Maurice and Kennedy, James. The Particle Swarm - Explosion, Stability, and Convergence in a Multidimensional Complex Space. *IEEE Trans. Evolutionary Computation*, 6(1):58–73, 2002.

Comaniciu, Dorin; Ramesh, Visvanathan, and Meer, Peter. The Variable Bandwidth Mean Shift and Data-Driven Scale Selection. In *Proc. of ICCV 2001, Int. Conf. on Computer Vision*, pages 438–445, 2001.

Cortes, Corinna and Vapnik, Vladimir. Support-vector networks. *Machine Learning*, 20(3):273–297, 1995.

Craig, John J. *Introduction to Robotics: Mechanics and Control (3rd Edition)*. Prentice Hall, 3 edition, 2005.

Dalal, Navneet and Triggs, Bill. Histograms of Oriented Gradients for Human Detection. In *Proc. of CVPR 2005, Int. Conf. on Computer Vision and Pattern Recognition*, volume 1, pages 886–893, 2005.

Daubney, Ben; Gibson, David, and Campbell, Neill. Monocular 3D Human Pose Estimation using Sparse Motion Features. In *IEEE Workshop on Tracking Humans for Evaluation of their Motion in Image Sequences 2009 - in conj. with ICCV 2009, Int. Conf. on Computer Vision*, October 2009.

Delamarre, Quentin and Faugeras, Olivier. 3D Articulated Models and Multi-View Tracking with Silhouettes. In *Proc. of ICCV 1999, Int. Conf. on Computer Vision*, volume 2, page 716, Los Alamitos, CA, USA, 1999.

Dempster, A. P.; Laird, N. M., and Rubin, D. B. Maximum Likelihood from Incomplete Data via the EM Algorithm. *Journal of the Royal Statistical Society, Series B*, 39(1):1–38, 1977.

Dobler, Alexander. Modeling of Location Probabilities of Anatomic Markers for Feature based 2D Pose Estimation. Master's thesis, Karlsruhe Institute of Technology (KIT), 2012a.

Dobler, Alexander. Diploma Thesis Colloqiuum Talk: Modeling of Location Probabilities of Anatomic Markers for Feature based 2D Pose Estimation. Master's thesis, Karlsruhe Institute of Technology (KIT), 2012b.

Dollár, P.; Wojek, C.; Schiele, B., and Perona, P. Pedestrian Detection: An Evaluation of the State of the Art. *IEEE Transactions on Pattern Analysis and Machine Intelligence*, 99(PrePrints), 2011.

Dollár, Piotr; Tu, Zhuowen; Perona, Pietro, and Belongie, Serge. Integral Channel Features. In *Proc. of BMVC 2009, British Machine Vision Conf.*, 2009.

Dollár, Piotr; Belongie, Serge, and Perona, Pietro. The Fastest Pedestrian Detector In The West. In *Proc. of BMVC 2010, British Machine Vision Conf.*, Aberystwyth, UK, 2010.

Drummond, Tom and Cipolla, Roberto. Real-Time Tracking of Highly Articulated Structures in the Presence of Noisy Measurements. In *Proc. of ICCV 2001, Int. Conf. on Computer Vision*, pages 315–320, 2001.

Duda, Richard O. and Hart, Peter E. Use of the Hough Transformation to Detect Lines and Curves in Pictures. *Communications of the ACM*, 15(1):11–15, January 1972. ISSN 0001-0782.

Ek, Carl Henrik; Torr, Philip H. S., and Lawrence, Neil D. Gaussian Process Latent Variable Models for Human Pose Estimation. In *Proc. of MLMI 2007, 4th Int. Workshop on Machine Learning for Multimodal Interaction*, pages 132–143, 2007.

Ess, A.; Leibe, B.; Schindler, K.; , and van Gool, L. A Mobile Vision System for Robust Multi-Person Tracking. In *Proc. of CVPR 2008, Int. Conf. on Computer Vision and Pattern Recognition*. IEEE Press, June 2008.

Feldmann, Tobias. *Multikamerabasierte Poseschätzung von Menschen.* PhD thesis, Karlsruhe Institute of Technology (KIT), 2012.

Felzenszwalb, Pedro F. and Huttenlocher, Daniel P. Pictorial Structures for Object Recognition. *Int. Journal of Computer Vision*, 61(1):55–79, January 2005.

Fergus, R.; Perona, P., and Zisserman, A. Object Class Recognition by Unsupervised Scale-Invariant Learning. In *Proceedings of the IEEE Conference on Computer Vision and Pattern Recognition*, volume 2, pages 264–271, June 2003. URL http://www.robots.ox.ac.uk/~vgg.

Fernando De la Torre, Frade; Hodgins, Jessica K; Bargteil, Adam W; Martin Artal, Xavier; Macey, Justin C; Collado I Castells, Alexandre, and Beltran, Josep. Guide to the Carnegie Mellon University Multimodal Activity (CMU-MMAC) Database. Technical Report CMU-RI-TR-08-22, Robotics Institute, Pittsburgh, PA, April 2008.

Ferrari, V.; Marín-Jiménez, M.J., and Zisserman, A. 2D Human Pose Estimation in TV Shows. In et al., D. Cremers, editor, *Proc. of Statistical and Geometrical Approaches to Visual Motion Analysis*, LNCS, pages 128–147. Springer, 2009.

Fischler, M. A. and Elschlager, R. A. The Representation and Matching of Pictorial Structures. *IEEE Transactions on Computers*, 22(1):67–92, January 1973.

Fukunaga, K. and Hostetler, L. The Estimation of the Gradient of a Density Function, with Applications in Pattern Recognition. *IEEE Transactions on Information Theory*, 21(1):32–40, January 1975.

Gall, Jürgen and Lempitsky, Victor. Class-Specific Hough Forests for Object Detection. In *Proc. of CVPR 2009, Int. Conf. on Computer Vision and Pattern Recognition*, pages 1022–1029, Miami, Florida, 2009. IEEE. ISBN 978-1-4244-3992-8.

Girshick, Ross; Shotton, Jamie; Kohli, Pushmeet; Criminisi, Antonio, and Fitzgibbon, Andrew. Efficient Regression of General-Activity Human Poses from Depth Images. In *Proc. of ICCV 2011, Int. Conf. on Computer Vision*, 2011.

Gong, Wenjuan; Brauer, Jürgen; Arens, Michael, and Gonzàlez, Jordi. Modeling vs. Learning Approaches for Monocular 3D Human Pose Estimation. In *Proc. of ICCV 2011 Workshops, Int. Conf. on Computer Vision*, pages 1287–1294, November 2011.

Grauman, Kristen and Leibe, Bastian. *Visual Object Recognition*. Synthesis Lectures on Artificial Intelligence and Machine Learning. Morgan & Claypool Publishers, 2011.

Gupta, Abhinav; Chen, Francine; Kimber, Don, and Davis, Larry S. Context and Observation Driven Latent Variable Model for Human Pose Estimation. In *Proc. of CVPR 2008, Int. Conf. on Computer Vision and Pattern Recognition (CVPR)*, 2008.

Hen, Yap Wooi and Paramesran, R. Single Camera 3D Human Pose Estimation: A Review of Current Techniques. In *Proc. of Int. Conf. for Technical Postgraduate (TECHPOS)*, pages 1–8, Kuala Lumpur, 2009.

Hofmann, M. and Gavrila, D. M. Multi-view 3D Human Pose Estimation in Complex Environment. *International Journal of Computer Vision*, 96(1):103–124, 2012.

Hough, Paul. Method and Means for Recognizing Complex Patterns. U.S. Patent 3.069.654, December 1962.

Ivekovič, Špela; Trucco, Emanuele, and Petillot, Yvan R. Human Body Pose Estimation with Particle Swarm Optimisation. *Evolutionary Computation*, 16(4):509–528, December 2008.

Ji, Xiaofei and Liu, Honghai. Advances in View-Invariant Human Motion Analysis: A Review. *IEEE Transactions on Systems, Man, and Cybernetics, Part C*, 40(1):13–24, 2010.

Jiang, Hao. 3D Human Pose Reconstruction Using Millions of Exemplars. In *Proc. of ICPR 2010, 20th Int. Conf. on Pattern Recognition*, pages 1674–1677, 2010.

Jüngling, K. *Ein generisches System zur automatischen Detektion, Verfolgung und Wiedererkennung von Personen in Videodaten*. PhD thesis, Karlsruhe Institute of Technology (KIT), 2011.

Jüngling, K. and Arens, M. Detection and Tracking of Objects with Direct Integration of Perception and Expectation. In *Proc. of ICCV 2009 Workshops, Int. Conf. on Computer Vision*, pages 1129–1136, 2009.

John, Vijay; Trucco, Emanuele, and Ivekovic, Spela. Markerless Human Articulated Tracking using Hierarchical Particle Swarm Optimisation. *Image and Vision Computing*, 28(11):1530–1547, November 2010.

Kennedy, James. Population Structure and Particle Swarm Performance. In *Proc. of CEC 2002, Congress on Evolutionary Computation*, pages 1671–1676. IEEE Press, 2002.

Kennedy, James and Eberhart, Russell C. Particle Swarm Optimization. In *Proc. of ICNN 1995, Int. Conf. on Neural Networks*, pages 1942–1948, 1995.

Krah, Sebastian. Entwicklung und Vergleich von Verfahren zur semiautomatischen 2D Posen Annotation. Student thesis at Karlsruhe Institute of Technology (KIT), September 2013.

Kuehne, Hildegard; Gehrig, Dirk; Schultz, Tanja, and Stiefelhagen, Rainer. On-line Action Recognition from Sparse Feature Flow. In *Proc. of VISAPP 2012, Int. Conf. on Computer Vision Theory and Applications*, pages 634–639, 2012.

Lampert, Christoph H.; Blaschko, Matthew B., and Hofmann, Thomas. Beyond Sliding Windows: Object Localization by Efficient Subwindow Search. In *Proc. of CVPR 2008, Int. Conf. on Computer Vision and Pattern Recognition*, 2008.

Lawrence, Neil and Hyvärinen, Aapo. Probabilistic Non-Linear Principal Component Analysis with Gaussian Process Latent Variable Models. *Journal of Machine Learning Research*, 6:1783–1816, 2005.

Lehmann, Alain; Leibe, Bastian, and Gool, Luc van. PRISM: PRincipled Implicit Shape Model. In *Proc. of BMVC 2009, British Machine Vision Conf.*, pages 64.1–64.11, 2009.

Lehmann, Alain; Leibe, Bastian, and Gool, Luc J. Van. Fast PRISM: Branch and Bound Hough Transform for Object Class Detection. *Int. Journal of Computer Vision*, 94(2):175–197, 2011.

Leibe, Bastian and Schiele, Bernt. Interleaved Object Categorization and Segmentation. In *Proc. of BMVC 2003, British Machine Vision Conference*, page 759–768, 2003.

Leibe, Bastian; Ettlin, Alan, and Schiele, Bernt. Learning Semantic Object Parts for Object Categorization. *Journal of Image and Vision Computing*, 26(1):15–26, 2008a.

Leibe, Bastian; Leonardis, Aleš, and Schiele, Bernt. Robust Object Detection with Interleaved Categorization and Segmentation. *Int. Journal of Computer Vision*, 77:259–289, May 2008b.

Levine, Sergey; Wang, Jack M.; Haraux, Alexis; Popović, Zoran, and Koltun, Vladlen. Continuous Character Control with Low-Dimensional Embeddings. *ACM Transactions on Graphics*, 31(4):28, 2012.

Li, Meng; Yang, Tao; Xi, Runping, and Lin, Zenggang. Silhouette-Based 2D Human Pose Estimation. In *Proc. of ICIG 2009, 5th Int. Conf. on Image and Graphics*, ICIG '09, pages 143–148, Washington, DC, USA, 2009. IEEE Computer Society.

Lowe, David G. Distinctive Image Features from Scale-Invariant Keypoints. *Int. Journal of Computer Vision*, 60(2):91–110, November 2004.

Müller, Jürgen and Arens, Michael. Human Pose Estimation with Implicit Shape Models. In *Proc. of ACM ARTEMIS 2010, Int. Workshop on Analysis and Retrieval of Tracked Events and Motion in Imagery Stream - in conj. with ACM Multimedia 2010 Conf.*, ARTEMIS '10, pages 9–14, New York, NY, USA, 2010. ACM. ISBN 978-1-4503-0163-3.

Moeslund, Thomas B. and Granum, Erik. A Survey of Computer Vision-Based Human Motion Capture. *Computer Vision and Image Understanding*, 81(3):231–268, March 2001.

Moeslund, Thomas B.; Hilton, Adrian, and Krüger, Volker. A Survey of Advances in Vision-Based Human Motion Capture and Analysis. *Computer Vision and Image Understanding*, 104(2):90–126, November 2006.

Mordatch, Igor; Coleman, Patrick; Singh, Karan, and Balakrishnan, Ravin. Spatial Pose Trees: Creating and Editing Motions Using a Hierarchy of Low Dimensional Control Spaces. In *Proc. of Eurographics/ ACM SIGGRAPH Symposium on Computer Animation*, pages 1–9, 2006.

Mori, Greg and Malik, Jitendra. Recovering 3D Human Body Configurations Using Shape Contexts. *IEEE Transactions on Pattern Analysis and Machine Intelligence*, 28(7):1052–1062, 2006.

Parameswaran, V. and Chellappa, R. View Independent Human Body Pose Estimation from a Single Perspective Image. In *Proc. of CVPR 2004, Int. Conf. on Computer Vision and Pattern Recognition*, volume 2, pages II–16 – II–22 Vol.2, june-2 july 2004.

Poli, R.; Kennedy, J., and Blackwell, T. Particle Swarm Optimisation: An Overview. *Swarm Intelligence Journal*, 1:33–57, 2007.

Pons-Moll, Gerard; Baak, Andreas; Gall, Juergen; Leal-Taixe, Laura; Mueller, Meinard; Seidel, Hans-Peter, and Rosenhahn, Bodo. Outdoor Human Motion Capture using Inverse Kinematics and von Mises-Fisher Sampling. In *Proc. of ICCV 2011, Int. Conf. on Computer Vision*, November 2011.

Poppe, Ronald. Vision-Based Human Motion Analysis: An Overview. *Computer Vision and Image Understanding*, 108(1-2):4–18, 2007.

Quinonero-Candela, Joaquin; Rasmussen, Carl Edward, and Herbrich, Ralf. A Unifying View of Sparse Approximate Gaussian process Regression. *Journal of Machine Learning Research*, 6:2005, 2005.

Ramanan, Deva. Learning to Parse Images of Articulated Bodies. In Schölkopf, B.; Platt, J., and Hoffman, T., editors, *Advances in Neural Information Processing Systems*, volume 19, pages 1129–1136. MIT Press, Cambridge, MA, 2007.

Ramirez, Camillo. Time Invariant Action Recognition with 3D Pose Information based on the Generalized Hough Transformation. Master's thesis, TU Braunschweig, 2013.

Rasmussen, Carl Edward and Williams, Christopher K. I. *Gaussian Processes for Machine Learning*. The MIT Press, 2005. ISBN 026218253X.

Roth, Stefan; Sigal, Leonid, and Black, Michael J. Gibbs Likelihoods for Bayesian Tracking. In *Proc. of CVPR 2004, Int. Conf. on Computer Vision and Pattern Recognition*, pages 886–893, 2004.

Safonova, Alla; Hodgins, Jessica K., and Pollard, Nancy S. Synthesizing Physically Realistic Human Motion in Low-Dimensional, Behavior-Specific Spaces. In *Proc. of ACM SIGGRAPH 2004*, SIGGRAPH '04, pages 514–521, New York, NY, USA, 2004. ACM.

Sedai, Suman; Bennamoun, Mohammed, and Huynh, Du Q. Context-Based Appearance Descriptor for 3D Human Pose Estimation from Monocular Images. In *Proc. of DICTA 2009, Digital Image Computing: Techniques and Applications*, pages 484–491, 2009.

Seemann, Edgar; Leibe, Bastian, and Schiele, Bernt. Multi-Aspect Detection of Articulated Objects. In *Proc. of CVPR 2006, Int. Conf. on Computer Vision and Pattern Recognition*, pages 1582–1588, 2006.

Seemann, Edgar; Fritz, Mario, and Schiele, Bernt. Towards Robust Pedestrian Detection in Crowded Image Sequences. In *Proc. of CVPR 2007, Int. Conf. on Computer Vision and Pattern Recognition*, 2007.

Shin, Hyun Joon and Lee, Jehee. Motion Synthesis and Editing in Low-Dimensional Spaces. *Computer Animation and Virtual Worlds 2006*, 17: 219–Ű227, 2006.

Shotton, Jamie; Fitzgibbon, Andrew W.; Cook, Mat; Sharp, Toby; Finocchio, Mark; Moore, Richard; Kipman, Alex, and Blake, Andrew. Real-Time Human Pose Recognition in Parts from Single Depth Images. In *Proc. of CVPR 2011, Int. Conf. on Computer Vision and Pattern Recognition*, pages 1297–1304, 2011.

Sidenbladh, Hedvig; Black, Michael J., and Sigal, Leonid. Implicit Probabilistic Models of Human Motion for Synthesis and Tracking. In *Proc. of ECCV 2002, European Conf. on Computer Vision*, pages 784–800, 2002.

Sigal, Leonid and Black, Michael J. Predicting 3D People from 2D Pictures. In *Proc. of AMDO 2006, 4th Int. Conf. on Articulated Motion and Deformable Objects*, pages 185–195, 2006a.

Sigal, Leonid and Black, Michael J. HumanEva: Synchronized Video and Motion Capture Dataset for Evaluation of Articulated Human Motion. Technical report, Brown University, 2006b.

Sigal, Leonid; Balan, Alexandru O., and Black, Michael J. Combined discriminative and generative articulated pose and non-rigid shape estimation. In *Proc. of NIPS 2007, Neural Information Processing Systems*, 2007.

Sigal, Leonid; Balan, Alexandru, and Black, Michael. HumanEva: Synchronized Video and Motion Capture Dataset and Baseline Algorithm for Evaluation of Articulated Human Motion. *Int. Journal of Computer Vision*, 87(1):4–27, March 2010.

Singh, Vivek Kumar; Muhammad, Furqan Khan, and Nevatia, Ram. Multiple Pose Context Trees for estimating Human Pose in Object Context. In *Proc. of CVPR 2010, Int. Conf. on Computer Vision and Pattern Recognition*, 2010.

Sminchisescu, C. *3D human Motion Reconstruction in Monocular Video. Techniques and Challenges*, volume 36 of *Human Motion Understanding, Modeling, Capture and Animation*. Springer, October 2007.

Sminchisescu, Cristian and Telea, Alexandru. Human Pose Estimation from Silhouettes. A Consistent Approach Using Distance Level Sets. In *Proc. of WSCG 2002, Int. Conf. on Computer Graphics, Visualization and Computer Vision*, 2002.

Sminchisescu, Cristian and Triggs, Bill. Kinematic Jump Processes for Monocular 3D Human Tracking. *Proc. of CVPR 2003, Int. Conf. on Computer Vision and Pattern Recognition*, 1:69, 2003.

Sudowe, Patrick and Leibe, Bastian. Efficient Use of Geometric Constraints for Sliding-Window Object Detection in Video. In *Proc. of ICVS, 8th Int. Conf. on Computer Vision Systems*, pages 11–20, 2011.

Tangkuampien, T. and Suter, D. Real-Time Human Pose Inference using Kernel Principal Component Pre-Image Approximations. In *Proc. of BMVC 2006, British Machine Vision Conf.*, 2006.

Taylor, Camillo J. Reconstruction of Articulated Objects from Point Correspondences in a Single Uncalibrated Image. *Computer Vision and Image Understanding*, 80:349–363, 2000.

Tenorth, Moritz; Bandouch, Jan, and Beetz, Michael. The TUM Kitchen Data Set of Everyday Manipulation Activities for Motion Tracking and Action Recognition. In *Proc. of ICCV 2009 Workshops, IEEE Int. Workshop on Tracking Humans for the Evaluation of their Motion in Image Sequences (THEMIS) - in conj. with ICCV 2009*, 2009.

Thomas, Alexander; Ferrari, Vittorio; Leibe, Bastian; Tuytelaars, Tinne, and Gool, Luc J. Van. Using Recognition to Guide a Robot's Attention. In Brock, Oliver; Trinkle, Jeff, and Ramos, Fabio, editors, *Robotics: Science and Systems*. The MIT Press, 2008.

Tian, Yan; Sigal, Leonid; Badino, Hernan; De la Torre Frade, Fernando, and liu, Yong. Latent gaussian mixture regression for human pose estimation. In *Asian Conference on Computer Vision (ACCV)*, November 2010.

Urtasun, Raquel; Fleet, David J.; Hertzmann, Aaron, and Fua, Pascal. Priors for People Tracking from Small Training Sets. In *Proc. of ICCV 2005, Int. Conf. on Computer Vision*, volume 1, pages 403–410, 2005.

Viola, Paul A. and Jones, Michael J. Rapid Object Detection using a Boosted Cascade of Simple Features. In *Proc. of CVPR 2001 (1), Int. Conf. on Computer Vision and Pattern Recognition*, pages 511–518, 2001.

Wang, Heng; Ullah, Muhammad Muneeb; Kläser, Alexander; Laptev, Ivan, and Schmid, Cordelia. Evaluation of local spatio-temporal features for action recognition. In *Proc. of BMVC 2009, British Machine Vision Conf.*, 2009.

Wang, Jack M.; Fleet, David J., and Hertzmann, Aaron. Gaussian Process Dynamical Models. In *Proc. of NIPS 2005, Neural Information Processing Systems*, pages 1441–1448. MIT Press, 2005.

Wei, Xiaolin K. and Chai, Jinxiang. Modeling 3D Human Poses from Uncalibrated Monocular Images. In *Proc. of ICCV 2009, Int. Conf. on Computer Vision*, pages 1873 –1880, October 2009.

Wiley, Douglas J. and Hahn, James K. Interpolation Synthesis of Articulated Figure Motion. *IEEE Computer Graphics and Applications*, 17(6): 39–45, November 1997.

Yang, Yi and Ramanan, Deva. Articulated Pose Estimation with Flexible Mixtures-of-Parts. In *Proc. of CVPR 2011, Int. Conf. on Computer Vision and Pattern Recognition*, pages 1385–1392, 2011.

Yao, A.; Gall, J., and van Gool, L. Coupled Action Recognition and Pose Estimation from Multiple Views. *Int. Journal of Computer Vision*, 100 (1):16–37, October 2012.

Yao, Bangpeng and Fei-Fei, Li. Modeling Mutual Context of Object and Human Pose in Human-Object Interaction Activities. In *Proc. of CVPR 2010, Int. Conf. Computer Vision and Pattern Recognition*, San Francisco, USA, June 2010a.

Yao, Bangpeng and Fei-Fei, Li. Grouplet: A Structured Image Representation for Recognizing Human and Object Interactions. In *Proc. of CVPR 2010, Int. Conf. Computer Vision and Pattern Recognition*, San Francisco, USA, June 2010b.

Yu, T.H.; Kim, T-K., and R., Cipolla. Unconstrained Monocular 3D Human Pose Estimation by Action Detection and Cross-modality Regression Forest. In *Proc. of CVPR 2013, Int. Conf. Computer Vision and Pattern Recognition*, 2013.

Zhang, Kaihua; Zhang, Lei, and Yang, Ming-Hsuan. Real-time compressive tracking. In *Proc. of ECCV 2012, 12th European Conference on Computer Vision, Volume Part III*, ECCV'12, pages 864–877, Berlin, Heidelberg, 2012. Springer-Verlag. ISBN 978-3-642-33711-6. doi: 10.1007/978-3-642-33712-3_62.

Zhang, Zheng; Seah, Hock Soon, and Quah, Chee Kwang. *Particle Swarm Optimization for Markerless Full Body Motion Capture*, pages 201–220. Berlin: Springer, 2011. ISBN 978-3-642-17389-9.

Zivkovic, Zoran. Improved Adaptive Gaussian Mixture Model for Background Subtraction. In *Proc. of ICPR 2004, Int. Conf. on Pattern Recognition*, volume 2 of *ICPR '04*, pages 28–31, Washington, DC, USA, 2004. IEEE Computer Society. ISBN 0-7695-2128-2.

Zuffi, S.; Freifeld, O., and Black, M. J. From Pictorial Structures to Deformable Structures. In *Proc. of CVPR 2012, Int. Conf. Computer Vision and Pattern Recognition*, pages 3546–3553. IEEE, June 2012.

SCHRIFTENREIHE AUTOMATISCHE SICHTPRÜFUNG UND BILDVERARBEITUNG
(ISSN 1866-5934)

Herausgeber: Prof. Dr.-Ing. Jürgen Beyerer

Band 1   JONATHAN BALZER
          Regularisierung des Deflektometrieproblems Grundlagen und Anwendung. 2008
          ISBN 978-3-86644-230-6

Band 2   IOANA GHETA
          Fusion multivariater Bildserien am Beispiel eines Kamera-Arrays. 2011
          ISBN 978-3-86644-684-7

Band 3   STEFAN BRUNO WERLING
          Deflektometrie zur automatischen Sichtprüfung
          und Rekonstruktion spiegelnder Oberflächen. 2011
          ISBN 978-3-86644-687-8

Band 4   JAN WASSENBERG
          Efficient Algorithms for Large-Scale Image Analysis. 2012
          ISBN 978-3-86644-786-8

Band 5   MARTIN GRAFMÜLLER
          Verfahrensfortschritte in der robusten Echtzeiterkennung von Schriftzeichen. 2013
          ISBN 978-3-86644-979-4

Band 6   JÜRGEN BRAUER
          Human Pose Estimation with Implicit Shape Models. 2014
          ISBN 978-3-7315-0184-8